The Hurlers

Kevin Kerrane

A
REDEFINITION
BOOK

PITCHING POWER AND PRECISION

The Hurlers

No other place on the field commands as much attention as the pitcher's mound. A batter shares his box with dozens of others each game, but if a pitcher is right, the mound is his all day.

A Great Day
on the Mound

I t will be one of the best pitching matchups in a long time," said Houston manager Hal Lanier. "Like Sandy Koufax against Juan Marichal." Lanier was right. The 1986 National League Championship Series opened with a confrontation that brought back memories of other classic showdowns in baseball history: Philadelphia's Robin Roberts and Brooklyn's Don Newcombe on the last day of the 1950 season, Detroit's Denny McLain and St. Louis' Bob Gibson in the 1968 World Series. This one pitted Dwight Gooden of the Mets against Mike Scott of the Astros: power against power, a young phenom against a rejuvenated veteran.

Each pitcher was the ace of his staff, and the two staffs were the best in baseball. The entire championship series tested those staffs to the fullest over six dramatic games, the last two in extra innings. Game 1 was an appropriate beginning: every pitch mattered.

It was a duel of Cy Young Award winners. A year earlier, Dwight Gooden had been the National League's prize pitcher, a 20-year-old sophomore with a record of 24–4 and a 1.53 ERA. In 1986 Gooden dropped down a notch (it would have been almost impossible not to) but finished strong, with a 17–6 record, winning his last three decisions.

The new NL Cy Young candidate was Mike Scott—a sure thing after leading the league in ERA, innings pitched and strikeouts. In 32 of his 36 starts, Scott allowed three runs or less. In the Astros' pennant clincher he hurled a no-hitter against the Giants.

Scott had once been a New York Met, but was traded to the Astros in

Met first baseman Keith Hernandez fanned three times against Astro starter Mike Scott in Game 1 of the 1986 NLCS, then turned his frustration on umpire Doug Harvey.

Mike Scott's split-finger fastball kept the Mets—the NL's top run-scoring team—off balance and off the bases in Game 1. Eight of his fourteen strikeouts came against the heart of the Mets' lineup—Keith Hernandez, Gary Carter and Darryl Strawberry.

Tale of the Tape

October 8, 1986

Dwight Gooden		Mike Scott
21	Age	31
6'2"	Height	6'2"
198 lbs.	Weight	210 lbs.
Right	Throws	Right
94 mph	Fastball	92 mph
Curve	2nd Pitch	Split-finger Fastball

1986 Regular Season

Dwight Gooden		Mike Scott
17–6	Won–Lost	18–10
2.84	ERA	2.22*
250	Innings	275⅓*
197	Hits	182
12	Complete Games	7
2	Shutouts	5*
200	Strikeouts	306*
80	Walks	72

*Denotes League Leader

1982 after several mediocre seasons. As late as 1984, Scott's career won-lost record was 29–44; he was a career loser with a bleak future. Then Scott spent ten days with Houston's former pitching coach Roger Craig, the guru of the split-finger fastball. Scott made the pitch his own, and turned his career around. In 1985 he went 18–8; in 1986 he went 18–10 and suddenly, at age 31, became a dominating strikeout pitcher.

Some opposing hitters offered another explanation for the sharp swerves of his pitches. In 1985 Leon Durham of the Cubs claimed to have found a small piece of sandpaper on the mound after one of Scott's games. Scott was widely suspected of scuffing the ball, roughening one side in order to make his pitches sail and dip like a Wiffle Ball. He denied the charge, but added, "If they're worried about what the ball's doing, that's another pitch I have, even if I don't have it." Just before the league championships began, Gary Carter of the Mets revived the issue by telling the press, "It is the consensus around the league that Mike Scott cheats."

When Carter stood in against Scott in the top of the first inning, with two out and a man on first, a chorus of boos filled the Astrodome. Standing expressionless on the mound, Scott rocked and fired. The ball veered down as Carter swung and missed. The second pitch, a fastball, jumped so quickly past his bat that Carter asked plate umpire Doug Harvey to check the ball. Harvey did, amid another torrent of boos, then flipped it back to Scott. The next pitch was a fastball up and in, and Carter flailed at it for strike three. Scott's confident walk off the mound seemed to say, "Top that." In the bottom of the first, Gooden set the Astros down in order on three fly balls to left.

The last time Gooden and Scott shared the mound had been on July 19 in Houston, but neither went the distance. Gooden was knocked out in the

Except for Glenn Davis' second-inning home run, Dwight Gooden was tough when he needed to be in the NLCS opener. He allowed five Houston runners to reach third base, but only Davis scored. "Give Doc some credit," Hernandez said. "He pitched his butt off."

Met catcher Gary Carter got pounded at the plate all night long in Game 1. He struck out three times against Scott, and in the bottom of the fifth he was bowled over by Houston's Billy Hatcher (above) trying to score from third on a ground ball. Carter held on to the ball and kept the Astros from increasing their 1–0 lead.

sixth and left trailing, 4–0. Scott took a shutout into the ninth, gave up three big hits, and left leading, 4–2. Houston reliever Dave Smith gave up a game-tying homer, then became the winning pitcher when Houston scored in the bottom of the ninth.

This time the first inning set the tone for the entire game. This was to be a pitcher's duel in a pitcher's ballpark. According to one statistical study, run production in the Astrodome is about 17 percent below the league average. Hitters generally agree on the reasons. "You're indoors," Gary Carter says, "so there's never a breeze to push a ball out, or annoy an outfielder. And then there's the air itself, heavy somehow under that dome, as if they'd squeezed more air in than belonged. A long ball seems to die in there."

As a team of pitching, defense and speed, the Astros were tailored to their stadium. They were much less explosive than the Mets; during the regular season they scored 129 fewer runs. Aside from power hitter Glenn Davis at first base, they were mostly short-ball hitters and aggressive baserunners. Against Dwight Gooden their main challenge would be to get men on base.

Davis, 1 for 11 lifetime against Gooden, led off the Houston second. None of Davis' 31 regular-season homers had come against the Mets. Gooden started him with a fastball up and in for ball one. A second fastball was also supposed to be out of the strike zone. "I was trying to throw outside," Gooden said later, "but it ran back over the plate." Carter described it as "Doc's only bad pitch of the night." Davis turned on the ball and drove a rising liner to left center that kept on sailing. It cleared the fence as the Dome erupted.

Suddenly behind 1–0, Gooden struggled to reestablish his rhythm. He loaded the bases, then pitched his way out of the jam. The key was his

strikeout of challenger Mike Scott. Gooden reached back, nothing fancy, and simply did what he had become famous for doing: blowing a hitter away. At the plate Scott was embarrassed all night. He came to bat with a total of seven men on base and stranded them all, striking out twice and bouncing into a double play.

But on the mound Scott took sweet revenge. Big and sleepy-looking, he unwound slowly and unleashed fastballs that jumped in menacingly toward right-handed hitters. And then there were the mystery pitches that seemed to vanish at home plate. Umpire Doug Harvey could find no evidence of scuffing; he said every ball he checked was "as smooth as a baby's bottom." Harvey described Scott's split-finger as the ultimate weapon: a pitch with "the velocity of a Sandy Koufax fastball and the movement of a Koufax curve. It's like a fastball with a bomb attached to it."

Scott ran into trouble in the top of the sixth. After leadoff man Lenny Dykstra walked, Wally Backman drove a fastball over the head of Houston left fielder Jose Cruz. "I figured it was off the wall and a tie game," Backman said. But Cruz stayed with the ball and, with his back to the infield, made a sensational catch at the warning track.

Scott went to work on Keith Hernandez. On a 3–2 count, as Dykstra stole second, Hernandez took a split-finger for strike three. It was a "back-door" pitch—in this case, a right-hander's breaking ball nicking the outside corner on a left-handed hitter. Hernandez swore the pitch was a ball, and he argued at length but in vain. Then Scott ended the inning by whiffing Carter for his ninth strikeout.

Gooden kept it a 1–0 game by pitching out of more trouble in the fourth and fifth innings. In midgame he found his groove and began getting ahead

Wednesday, October 8, 1986
Astros 1, Mets 0

New York	ab	r	h	rbi	Houston	ab	r	h	rbi
Dykstra,cf	3	0	1	0	Hatcher,cf	3	0	0	0
Bckmn,2b	4	0	0	0	Doran,2b	4	0	0	0
Hrndz,1b	4	0	1	0	Walling,3b	4	0	0	0
Carter,c	4	0	0	0	Davis,1b	4	1	1	1
Strwbry,rf	4	0	1	0	Bass,rf	4	0	2	0
M.Wlsn,lf	4	0	0	0	Cruz,lf	4	0	1	0
Knight,3b	4	0	0	0	Ashby,c	1	0	1	0
Santana,ss	2	0	1	0	Rynlds,ss	3	0	2	0
Mazzilli,ph	1	0	0	0	Thon,ss	0	0	0	0
Orosco,p	0	0	0	0	Scott,p	3	0	0	0
Gooden,p	2	0	0	0					
Heep,ph	1	0	1	0					
Elster,ss	0	0	0	0					
Totals	33	0	5	0	Totals	30	1	7	1

New York			000	000	000	–	0
Houston			010	000	00x	–	1

GWRBI – Davis. E – Reynolds. DP – New York 1. LOB – New York 7, Houston 8. 2b – Bass. HR – Davis (1). SB – Hatcher (1), Dykstra (1), Bass (1), Strawberry (1).

New York	IP	H	R	ER	BB	SO
Gooden,L 0-1	7	7	1	1	3	5
Orosco	1	0	0	0	0	1
Houston						
Scott,W 1-0	9	5	0	0	1	14

Umpires – HP, Harvey; 1B, Weyer; 2B, Pulli; 3B, Rennert; Left, West; Right, Brocklander. T – 3:00. A – 44,131.

Gary Carter's frustration grew with each strikeout. When he had tired of arguing with umpire Doug Harvey (above, left), Carter (above, right) angrily asked Astro catcher Alan Ashby, "How would you like to be hitting that stuff?" "No thanks, I'll stick to catching it," Ashby replied.

in the count. By the Houston sixth, Gooden looked like his "old" self, the flowing 20-year-old of the year before. He struck out two in the sixth, and two more in the seventh as the duel intensified with every pitch. The seventh was a 1-2-3 inning for both pitchers.

But Met manager Davey Johnson needed offense, and he had a bullpen full of other good arms. With one out in the eighth he decided to pull Gooden for pinch-hitter Danny Heep, the left-handed outfielder Houston traded to the Mets for Mike Scott in 1982.

Heep singled, and then Dykstra singled to put the tying run at second. Facing Backman, Scott cranked up the fastball and went for the strikeout. "His heat appears faster," Backman said, "because he sets you up so well with that split-finger." Strike three was an overpowering pitch on the outside corner. With two out Scott faced Hernandez again. "The idea with Keith," Scott said, "is to try to keep the ball up and in. He's most dangerous when he can get the ball out in front of the plate." On another 3–2 count Scott blistered the fastball inside, letter-high, and Hernandez swung and missed to end the threat.

The Mets threatened again in the ninth. With one out and Darryl Strawberry on second, Mookie Wilson drove a hard grounder toward right field. First baseman Glenn Davis made a beautiful diving stop, and on his knees threw to Scott covering first. As Scott narrowly won the race with Wilson, Strawberry advanced to third, the first Met all night to get that far. The tying run was 90 feet away. With two outs the hitter was Ray Knight, already 0 for 3 with a strikeout. Scott went back to the fastball and Knight fouled it off. After taking another fastball for strike two, Knight protested that the pitch was several inches outside. Then he ended the game by waving at a pitch in exactly the same spot.

As the Gooden-Scott contest shows, an all-out pitching duel may lack explosive offense, but it continues to excite spectators and to stretch players' abilities to the limit, at the plate and in the field. Unlike an all-out slugfest, a pitching duel can provide a different kind of power—the style, craft and will of two matadors in the arena.

Scott not only won a duel. He set the tone for the whole playoff series. He had held the league's most potent offense to five singles, and he made good hitters look bad. Gary Carter said that Scott "haunted" the Mets, especially after he beat them again in Game 4, yielding only three more singles in a 3–1 victory over Sid Fernandez. In that game some New York players were collecting scuffed game balls, hoping to find evidence of sandpapering. Houston manager Hal Lanier said, "If they have balls they're saving over there, they ought to bring 'em over and he'll sign 'em." "He already has," said Davey Johnson of the Mets.

When Dwight Gooden was asked if he ever threw a scuffball or a spitball, he grinned and shook his head. "Maybe down the road a little," he said. With the playoffs tied at two games each, Gooden came back in Game 5 against the Astros' Nolan Ryan, 17 years his senior. It was another pitching gem: 1–1 into the 12th, when, with both starters gone, Gary Carter singled to win it for the Mets.

The end of the series was all the beginning had promised. Game 6 went to 16 seesaw innings before the Mets won, 7–6. A loss would have forced them to meet Mike Scott in Game 7. "We didn't want to face him again," Johnson said of the series MVP. "That's why we played this game like it was the last. I feel as if we've been paroled and pardoned."◗

Hernandez had trouble with Harvey, and both had trouble with Scott's split-finger. But manager Davey Johnson refused to make Harvey the scapegoat. "The umpiring didn't beat us tonight," he said. "Glenn Davis and Mike Scott did."

A Dream At-Bat

To illustrate the confrontation between pitcher and hitter, Miami Herald *sportswriter Peter Richmond devised a fictional at-bat pitting Cy Young Award winner Dwight Gooden of the Mets against three-time NL batting champion Tony Gwynn of the Padres. Richmond interviewed both players during spring training in 1988, and the article appeared on March 18.*

What goes through their heads when the best meet the best? With the pennant on the line?

We devised a dream at-bat: Dwight Gooden of the Mets on the mound, Tony Gwynn of the Padres at the plate, bases loaded, two out, bottom of the ninth, pennant at stake.

"Sounds good to me," Gwynn said from Yuma, Ariz., "Let's do it."

First, each offers some observations about the other.

Gooden, speaking at Mets camp in Port St. Lucie on Gwynn: "He gets his hits off me. But I've done well against him. You have to pitch him the opposite of everyone else because he anticipates what you're doing so well.

"I won't throw him any changeups or off-speed curves because his reactions are too good. Also, he has some power, so I have to be extra careful. Every now and then he'll straighten up a little at the plate and then I'll know he's going to try to hit for power."

Gwynn on Gooden: "I've seen every pitch he throws. He's one heck of a competitor. He knows how to attack a hitter. When I go up against him I realize he's got a game plan. He's not going to just be throwing the ball.

"Against Gooden I just want to get my bat on the ball. I don't want him to strike me out. His fastball is an overpowering fastball, and very rarely will I catch up with it. I might foul off a few down the left-field line. I know from experience he won't throw me off-speed stuff."

All right. Gwynn steps to the plate.

Gooden: "I'd start him off with a high fastball inside. Letter-high.

Gwynn: "I'm going to take it."

It's inside. The count is 1–0.

Gooden: "Same pitch again."

Gwynn: "Yeah–that makes plenty of sense to me. On the first pitch, I'm taking, and if it's a ball he knows I'm taking again. So he comes right back for a fastball."

This one slices the black on the rear inside corner of the plate: 1–1.

Gooden: "I throw him a hard curve. Hard breaking stuff."

Gwynn: "Taking it back to previous at-bats, I bet he comes back with a hard, snapping breaking ball. Not the slow overhand hook, but one that's got some snap."

Gwynn fouls it off: 1–2.

Gooden: "I'll paint him a fastball away. A half-inch off the plate. Hopefully, he goes for it."

Gwynn: "You betcha! That makes plenty of sense. With two strikes as a hitter I'm trying to protect the plate."

For the sake of drama, the pitch sails a foot outside. Gwynn holds off: 2–2.

Gooden: "Then I come back with the fastball up and in."

Gwynn: "Yep, I'm going to be looking for that."

But it's high. The count is loaded. The runners are going. The season is on the line.

Gooden: "I throw him the hard hook."

Gwynn: "There it is. Yes, sir. I was going to say it before you said it. He's going to come back with the hard overhand curveball. There have been times he's thrown me fastballs—three, four in a row, and after the first two you say to yourself, 'Sooner or later he's going to come with the hard overhand curve,' but you can't look for it. You have to look for the fastball."

Gwynn fouls it off. Still 3–2.

Gooden: "Then I just hump it up and reach for the extra fastball. The best fastball I can throw."

Gwynn: "Let's do it."

For the sake of fairness, let's leave it right there. The Gooden fastball is sailing in. The runners are going. Gwynn sets. He explodes out of his crouch. . . .

When the Mets' Dwight Gooden (left) and the Padres' Tony Gwynn (below) square off, it's strength against strength. Gooden has averaged 8.2 strikeouts a game in his five years in the majors, while Gwynn, a three-time NL batting champ, has struck out just once every $4^1/_2$ games in his career.

Who Owns Home Plate?

Early Wynn used to say, "The pitcher's mound is my office, a place where I conduct my business." And every time Tom Seaver walked to the mound and began smoothing the dirt, he called it "setting up shop." The mound is the center of the diamond, the starting point for all the game's action. And it is the highest spot on the field, "the hill" where every hurler tries to be the king. The pitcher is always trying to extend his domain beyond the mound. He wants air rights over home plate—ownership of the strike zone.

The strike zone—mid-torso to knees over the plate—is not a sharply defined box; it's more like a balloon—a changing space under constant revision during any single game. It can be expanded or compressed by all sorts of variables, most obviously the size and stance of the hitter.

Sometimes a strike zone is simply as big as a batter—or umpire— makes it. And sometimes the pitcher is able to "sell" a pitch to both of them by putting the ball securely in the zone in the early innings, and gradually pushing it beyond the fringe. Scott McGregor says, "Once a pitcher has proved to the umpire and the hitter that he can throw strikes, he can start expanding the strike zone a little because they're used to seeing strikes."

Tug McGraw used to talk as if the pitcher could move the zone forward or backward by changing speeds. "If I start a hitter off with a fastball, and he's late on it, then I'll give him a harder fastball inside and make him say, 'Geez, I really gotta be quicker here.' Now the ball's deep in the strike zone. It's farther over the plate before he's making contact. As soon as I get the

The 1959 World Series was a contest of relievers. In Game 4 (opposite), 92,650 fans at Memorial Coliseum saw LA's Gil Hodges beat Chicago's Gerry Staley with an eighth-inning homer.

After the Yankees' Ed Lopat (right) faced Brooklyn's Preacher Roe in a duel of junkballers in the 1952 World Series, Yankee manager Casey Stengel said, "You pay all that money to great big fellas with a lot of muscles who go up there and start swinging. And those two give 'em a little of this and a little of that and swindle 'em."

Tug McGraw's ability to keep hitters off balance by changing speeds helped the Phillies win their first world championship in 1980. McGraw won one game and saved two in the World Series against Kansas City, twice ending games by striking hitters out with the bases loaded.

hitter thinking, 'I gotta quicken up,' now I take something off with a screwball or a curve or a change. I got him going quick and the ball's not there yet. He's out in front of it, and I'm pulling the strike zone out to me. By the same token, if a hitter gets around on my fastball and pulls it foul, I'll throw him a slow pitch and make him quick again, and get him thinking: 'I gotta wait, I gotta wait.' And when I think he's waiting, now I bust him hard inside again and push the strike zone back."

Traditionally, the most direct way to assert ownership of the plate has been to move hitters back with high inside fastballs. But pitchers can manipulate space in other ways. Three Finger Brown, who pitched for St. Louis, Chicago and Cincinnati from 1903 to 1916, believed in getting a hitter out by working against his batting stance. "If a batter had a straight-up stance, close to the plate, I'd pitch inside to him. If he crouched, I'd try to keep the pitch a little high, and a fellow who stood away from the plate was fed outside pitches. The main objective is to take the power away from the hitter—keep him from putting much wood against the ball."

Allie Reynolds used the space of the ballpark itself as an element of pitching strategy. At home in Yankee Stadium, with the center field wall 461 feet away, he liked to work against right-handed power hitters by starting at two balls and no strikes. Then Reynolds would put a fastball on the outside corner. "They would be ready and anxious on the 2-0 count. But they'd try to pull that outside pitch and would hit a fly ball to center field. I was lucky to have good outfielders with the Yankees, so even if they hit it deep it was just an out. I don't know how many times one of them would say to me, 'You lucky so-and-so, I just missed getting that one.' They didn't have any idea what had happened."

Cincinnati's Pete Rose (above, right) had never faced Luis Tiant, Boston's master pitching craftsman, before the 1975 World Series, and it took him a while to adjust. After going 1 for 7 against him in Games 1 and 4, Rose finally got two hits off Tiant in Game 6.

Pitchers battle hitters in time as well as space. In effect, changing the speed of a pitch changes the speed of the bat, and a variation of only .01 second in a hitter's swing can be the difference between a pop-up to third base and a home run to center field. The wisdom of Warren Spahn remains as true as ever: "Hitting is timing. Pitching is upsetting timing."

The change of pace is regarded as the best pitch by many because it affects the hitter's mind as well as his bat. Unless he guesses the pitch correctly, a change makes the hitter stop and then restart the surge of his body into the ball, making that ball seem inert: "a dead fish," in baseball slang. "It's like trying to hit a water balloon," catcher Rick Dempsey says. Oakland batting coach Bob Watson, who hit in the majors for 19 years, found change-up artist Scott McGregor a more formidable opponent than speed demon Goose Gossage. "McGregor doesn't get you out, he lets you get yourself out."

The pitcher also controls time by establishing a particular rhythm, a pattern of pauses that feels right to him or wrong to the hitter. Eddie Plank was one of the most effective dawdlers of all time. His teammate Eddie Collins said: "Plank would fuss and fuddle with the ball, with his shoes, and then try to talk with the umpire. Then he would attempt to pick off the baserunners, which he frequently did. Then, suddenly, Plank would turn his attention to the fretting batter again, who would in all probability pop up in disgust."

Lew Burdette's fidgety style made hitters fidgety—his own manager, Fred Haney, said, "Burdette would make coffee nervous." But it also affected his teammates. Slow rhythm can in fact work against the rest of the team. Bob Gibson once observed, "If a pitcher takes a lot of time, or if he throws a lot of pitches that are taken for balls, his infielders start to relax. Maybe they're playing back on their heels instead of on their toes. By working

6'2" 185 lbs. b 6/7/33
BL TL

HERB SCORE
Left-Handed Pitcher

Herb Score's first two years in the majors were as impressive as anyone's. Score was offered contracts by 14 of the 16 major league clubs. He signed with Cleveland for a $60,000 bonus, then was named 1955 Rookie of the Year after going 16–10 with a 2.85 ERA. His 245 strikeouts not only led the league, but are still an AL rookie record.

Score went 20–9 in 1956, lowered his ERA to 2.53, and led the American League in strikeouts with 263 and shutouts with five. Score had a blazing fastball, often compared with that of teammate Bob Feller, a better than average curve, and tremendous competitive instincts. He allowed an average of just 6.04 hits per nine innings in his first two seasons.

But all that promise came to an end on May 7, 1957. A line drive off the bat of New York's Gil McDougald struck Score flush on the right eye—physicists figured the ball was traveling 130 mph—breaking his nose and shattering his future.

Score made an attempt at a comeback, pitching five more years in the majors, but never came close to his former level of greatness. His name still evokes some of baseball's great unanswered questions. What if Score had been able to duck McDougald's line drive? Would there be a plaque in Cooperstown bearing his name, and when fans argued who was the best left-hander of all time, would Herb Score be mentioned?

Griffith Stadium

From 1892 to 1961, with a few short breaks, major league baseball was played at the corner of 7th Street and Florida Avenue, N.W., in Washington, DC. Sometimes it didn't look much like major league baseball, especially to the hometown fans, who endured 50 losing seasons in 68 years.

Baseball came to the nation's capital in 1892, thanks to George and Jacob Earle Wagner, who built the 6,500-seat National Park, acquired a National League franchise, and named the team the Senators. Washington lost its franchise in 1900 when the National League cut the number of its teams from twelve to eight. In 1901 the District of Columbia got an American League franchise, and after two seasons at a stadium in northeast Washington, the team switched over to National Park.

On April 14, 1910, William Howard Taft inaugurated the tradition of having the President of the United States open each baseball season by throwing out the first ball at the Senators' Opening Day game. The tradition continued on and off in Washington until the Senators moved after the 1971 season. More dependable on Opening Day than the president was Senators' ace Walter Johnson. In 1910 Johnson pitched the first of his 14 openers. He was 9–5 with seven shutouts on Opening Day.

A fire all but destroyed the stadium in the spring of 1911, but it was rebuilt quickly, and in 1912—under new manager Clark Griffith—the Senators had their first winning season. By 1920 Griffith had become team president, and the stadium got a new name—his. The Senators won pennants in 1924, 1925 and 1933, but the ensuing years produced many more losses than wins. Still, Griffith Stadium remained a showcase for some of baseball's most powerful sluggers.

Perhaps the stadium's most unusual attribute was the zig and zag the center field wall took to dodge five houses and a large tree that were there first. Also in center field was a small box known as the "dog house," which was used to store the flag. The box was in play. One day in the early 1900s, a Senators' line drive found its way into the dog house. Philadelphia outfielder Socks Seybold tried to go in after the ball but got stuck, and by the time he and the ball were freed the fortunate hitter had circled the bases.

For the most part, Griffith Stadium was a pitcher's park—very deep to left and center fields, less so to right field. It featured a 31-foot-high wall in center field that only three men—Clint Johnson, Babe Ruth and Mickey Mantle—ever hit balls over. Mantle also was one of only two players to clear the wall behind the left field bleachers.

The other man to clear the left field bleacher wall was negro league star Josh Gibson, who did it twice while playing for the Homestead Grays. By the late 1930s, the Senators had dropped in the standings and Griffith was having trouble covering his expenses, so he arranged for the Pittsburgh-based Grays to use his stadium as their second home field. The Grays played half their home games in Washington from 1937 to 1948. Attendance for negro league baseball was booming, and fans flocked to Griffith Stadium to see the Grays' home run tandem of Buck Leonard and Gibson. Leonard and Gibson led the Grays to back-to-back negro league world championships in 1943 and 1944.

The third Senators' franchise moved from Griffith Stadium in 1962 to DC Stadium, now known as Robert F. Kennedy Memorial Stadium. Griffith Stadium was demolished in 1965.

Long to left, short to right, and downhill from home to first, Griffith Stadium (above) had a little something for everyone. For the 1924 World Series, temporary seats (left) were installed in front of the left field bleachers to accomodate overflow crowds. Clark Griffith (right) went from pitcher's mound to dugout to office of the president with the Senators. In 1961, Griffith's nephew, Calvin Griffith, moved the team to Minnesota.

Griffith Stadium

7th Street and
  Florida Avenue, NW
Washington, DC

Built 1892

Demolished 1965

Washington Senators, AL
  1911–1961

Seating Capacity 27,410

Style
Grass surface, asymmetrical

Height of Outfield Fences
Left field foul pole to center
  field: 12 feet
Dead center field: 31 feet
Right center field: 41 feet
Right field foul pole: 30 feet

Dugouts
Home: 1st base
Visitors: 3rd base

Bullpens
Recessed: foul territory
Home: right field corner
Visitors: left field corner

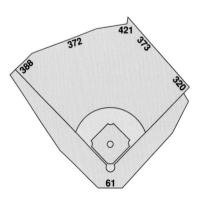

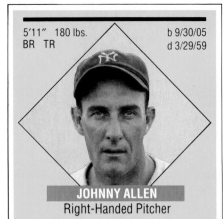

5'11" 180 lbs. b 9/30/05
BR TR d 3/29/59

JOHNNY ALLEN
Right-Handed Pitcher

"I believe you'd throw at your own mother," one opponent said to Johnny Allen. "Oh, no, I wouldn't throw at her," Allen replied. "But I might brush her back a little."

Raised in a North Carolina orphanage, Allen was nicknamed "The Tarheel Typhoon." Temperamental and moody, he carried on running battles with teammates, managers, sportswriters and especially umpires. He called the men in blue "fatheads," and in 1943 he punched and choked umpire George Barr for calling a balk. Allen was fined $1,000 and suspended for 30 days.

The Typhoon blew into the major leagues in 1932 with a 17–4 season for the Yankees. With the Indians in 1937, Allen carried a 15–0 record into the final day, and then pitched on two days rest, trying to match the AL record for most consecutive wins in one season, held by Walter Johnson, Smoky Joe Wood, Lefty Grove and Schoolboy Rowe. Allen lost 1–0 to Detroit southpaw Whistling Jake Wade, who pitched a one-hitter.

Allen was especially tough on right-handed batters. Sportswriter Dan Daniel said, "His sidearm fastball, especially when it comes out of a white-shirted bleacher background, sneaks up on the hitter with malign effect."

Allen developed arm trouble in the late 1930s, then struggled through the World War II seasons before retiring with a record of 142–75. But in 1948, Allen returned to baseball, in the Class B Carolina League. As an umpire.

Grover Cleveland Alexander wasted no time on the mound, even in the World Series. His four complete game efforts in the Series—with the Phils in 1915 and the Cardinals in 1926 and 1928—averaged one hour, 58 minutes.

quickly, I think I make my fielders more alert." Working fast may also help the pitcher's own fielding. Gibson and Jim Kaat, two of modern baseball's fastest workers, were also two of its greatest glovemen. Both were also very aggressive—between them they hit 224 batsmen—and their pitching pace was a statement in itself about whose ballgame it was. The message was the same as Grover Cleveland Alexander's. When Alexander was asked why he worked so fast, he replied, "What do you want me to do? Let them sons of bitches stand up there and think on my time?"

Beyond space and time, the struggle for home plate is also a battle of wits. Dave Winfield gives the perspective from the batter's box: "Good hitters don't just go up and swing. They always have a plan. Call it an educated deduction. You visualize. You're like a good negotiator. You know what you have, you know what he has, then you try to *work it out*."

From the pitcher's perspective, the main issue remains non-negotiable—prevent runs. To do that, the pitcher can alternately tease and challenge, challenge and tease. "You would be amazed," Whitey Ford said, "how many important outs you can get by working the count to where the hitter is sure you're going to throw to his weakness and then you throw to his power instead." The point is not necessarily to make the hitter guess wrong; it may be simply to make him start guessing. Tug McGraw says, "If you can get a hitter guessing, and then he guesses right, he'll usually swing at it even if it's out of the strike zone—because he guessed right. So you start the ball off in the strike zone, and he chases it no matter what it does." The simplest kind of teasing is "showcasing" a pitch: letting the hitter know you have it, but keeping it outside the strike zone, or at least outside *his* zone.

The brushback pitch establishes territorial rights. Designed to move hitters away from the plate, it often moves them off their feet as well—as here against Jack Clark.

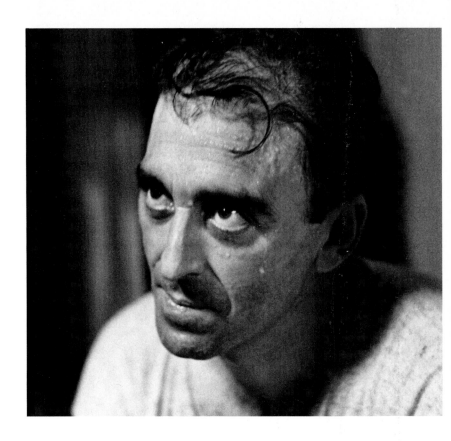

Even though Wrigley Field is among the best hitters' parks, when Ferguson Jenkins was on the mound the plate belonged to him. Jenkins won 20 or more games six straight seasons for the Cubs, 1967 to 1972.

A great fastball hitter, for example, might see one delicious fastball in every at-bat . . . always six tantalizing inches off the outside corner.

Ed Lopat took the concept of showcasing one step further, using his teaser pitches as probes of the batter's responses. "The reflexes of a batter tell you what he's looking for. I watch his reactions, watch the hands on the bat. If I threw a fastball, did he show me that he was a little late?" The problem with a great hitter like Ted Williams, Lopat said, was that he could *fake* a response to decoy the pitcher. "And you say to yourself, 'You dirty so-and-so, you're thinking the same way I am.' And if that first pitch you threw him was a ball, now you have to make the next pitch a strike and try to hit a spot where he won't lose it. . . . It was a battle of wits. That's why I enjoyed it so."

Bob Feller says that he didn't learn how to pitch to Joe DiMaggio until just before DiMaggio retired. "I started throwing him fastballs in tight, around his fists and his belt, crowding him, pushing him back. If I'd have done that earlier, I would have been all right. But I didn't do that. I was afraid I'd hit him."

Whitlow Wyatt had no such fear. Pitching for the Dodgers in the fifth game of the 1941 World Series, he watched DiMaggio dig in at the plate. "Wyatt didn't like that," said Dodger outfielder Pistol Pete Reiser. "First pitch, Joe goes down. He didn't say anything. He gets up, digs in again. Second pitch—whiz!—down he goes again." Years later DiMaggio told Reiser that Wyatt was "the meanest guy I ever saw in my life." Wyatt might have taken that as a compliment. He once said, "You ought to play it mean. They ought to hate you on the field."

Wyatt, who lasted 16 major league seasons, was an intimidator, and he

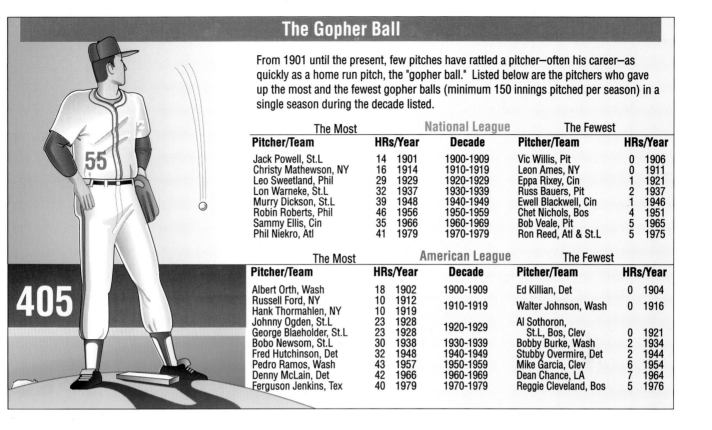

The Gopher Ball

From 1901 until the present, few pitches have rattled a pitcher—often his career—as quickly as a home run pitch, the "gopher ball." Listed below are the pitchers who gave up the most and the fewest gopher balls (minimum 150 innings pitched per season) in a single season during the decade listed.

The Most			National League	The Fewest		
Pitcher/Team	HRs/Year		Decade	Pitcher/Team	HRs/Year	
Jack Powell, St.L	14	1901	1900-1909	Vic Willis, Pit	0	1906
Christy Mathewson, NY	16	1914	1910-1919	Leon Ames, NY	0	1911
Leo Sweetland, Phil	29	1929	1920-1929	Eppa Rixey, Cin	1	1921
Lon Warneke, St.L	32	1937	1930-1939	Russ Bauers, Pit	2	1937
Murry Dickson, St.L	39	1948	1940-1949	Ewell Blackwell, Cin	1	1946
Robin Roberts, Phil	46	1956	1950-1959	Chet Nichols, Bos	4	1951
Sammy Ellis, Cin	35	1966	1960-1969	Bob Veale, Pit	5	1965
Phil Niekro, Atl	41	1979	1970-1979	Ron Reed, Atl & St.L	5	1975

The Most			American League	The Fewest		
Pitcher/Team	HRs/Year		Decade	Pitcher/Team	HRs/Year	
Albert Orth, Wash	18	1902	1900-1909	Ed Killian, Det	0	1904
Russell Ford, NY	10	1912	1910-1919	Walter Johnson, Wash	0	1916
Hank Thormahlen, NY	10	1919				
Johnny Ogden, St.L	23	1928	1920-1929	Al Sothoron,		
George Blaeholder, St.L	23	1928		St.L, Bos, Clev	0	1921
Bobo Newsom, St.L	30	1938	1930-1939	Bobby Burke, Wash	2	1934
Fred Hutchinson, Det	32	1948	1940-1949	Stubby Overmire, Det	2	1944
Pedro Ramos, Wash	43	1957	1950-1959	Mike Garcia, Clev	6	1954
Denny McLain, Det	42	1966	1960-1969	Dean Chance, LA	7	1964
Ferguson Jenkins, Tex	40	1979	1970-1979	Reggie Cleveland, Bos	5	1976

typifies a whole group of pitchers who flourished from about 1920 to 1970. The intimidators were psychological warriors. The number of batters they actually hit was less important than the implied threat that they *could* hit anyone at any time with no remorse. On the mound, in their domain, they often projected distinct dramatic personalities. Burleigh Grimes, known as "Ol' Stubblebeard" and "Burleigh the Belligerent," never smiled—except when he had just forced a batter to hit the deck. Vic Raschi perfected a threatening stare that was almost a brushback in itself. Bob Gibson's own catchers were afraid of him. "Bob wasn't unfriendly when he pitched," Joe Torre recalls. "I'd say it was more like hateful."

Some intimidators stayed in character off the mound, at least in their comments to the press. Early Wynn was fond of pronouncements like "I've got a right to knock down anybody holding a bat," or "You'll never be a big winner until you start hating the hitter." In fact, Wynn hit only 65 batters in 4,564 career innings, a lower average than Bob Feller's. He specialized in the brushback, not the beanball, and he used it strategically as an extra pitch. He made believers out of hitters—Mickey Mantle said that Wynn was mean enough to throw into the opposing dugout—but he didn't want blood. He wanted home plate.

Another scheming meanie was Sal Maglie, who avoided getting to know hitters personally. "I might like them," he said, "and then I might not want to throw at them." Maglie earned his nickname—"The Barber"—by giving batters close shaves; his control was so fine that he could scare them without hitting them. Like Whitlow Wyatt, he made special targets out of opponents foolish enough to dig in. "He was the only man I've ever seen pitch a shutout on a day when he had absolutely nothing," Alvin Dark said. "Maglie got by on meanness."

Vic Power (right) was a brushback pitcher's dream. The journeyman first baseman's crouch invaded the strike zone and made him a tempting target. But Power, a lifetime .284 hitter, could come out of his crouch with authority, and hit ten or more homers eight times in his 12-year career.

Lefty Grove, who pitched for the Athletics and Red Sox from 1925 to the 1940s, was too fast to risk shaving batters. "I've thrown at guys, but never at their heads," he said. Grove aimed for the rear pocket. His special targets were batters who hit balls back through the mound—his mound. His territorial instincts were so keen that he even threw at teammates. "When he was just pitching batting practice," said his Philadelphia teammate Doc Cramer, "you hit one through the box and you'd go down on the next pitch. In batting practice. On the last swing we'd try to hit one back through him, just to rile him up."

Relief pitching raises the stakes in the battle between pitcher and hitter. And it creates a different kind of cat-and-mouse game. For example, who were the toughest hitters that Tug McGraw ever faced?

"All the guys who didn't strike out much," McGraw says, "because I was coming in with men on base. Tim Foli, a .240 hitter—if you're a starter, he's no threat. But if you're a reliever, you might come in against him with a man on third and one out, and you know he struck out ten times in 600 at-bats last year, and all he has to do to beat you is hit a ground ball or a fly ball.

"Designing the outs was a key part of being a relief pitcher. Say you need a strikeout—that's your primary objective—and your second objective is a pop-up, so you pitch accordingly. Or you need a double play, so you try to set the hitter up to hit a ground ball. I used to like to set guys up for screwballs and then throw a slider inside to get a soft ground ball. And when I did pull it off, it was the greatest thrill. I walked a lot of guys and got the bases loaded and stuff—all by trying to design outs. I wanted to get a hitter out in a certain way, and if I couldn't, sometimes it was worth putting him on and pitching to the next guy. There was a method to my madness." ◗

The Cardinals' Bob Gibson (opposite) said, "A brushback is not to scare a hitter or to hit him. It is to make him think," but despite his educational intentions, Gibson remained the most feared pitcher of his era.

WALTER JOHNSON NUMBER

Walter Johnson

A talent as big as Walter Johnson's couldn't remain hidden for long, even in the wilds of the northern Rockies. But at the turn of the century, Weiser, Idaho, was far enough removed that it took the persistence of a traveling liquor salesman to bring Johnson—a confirmed teetotaler—and his priceless fastball to the major leagues.

The salesman wrote to then-New York Highlanders' manager Clark Griffith and Washington Nationals' manager Joe Cantillon. His letters spoke of a young man with an amazing fastball and the control to go with it. "He knows where he's throwing, because if he didn't there would be dead bodies strewn all over Idaho." But the Highlanders, a solid club then, weren't interested.

Cantillon, on the other hand, had inherited a Washington team that lost 95 games in 1906, so in the spring of 1907 he sent injured catcher Cliff Blankenship on a western swing to scout Kansas outfielder Clyde "Deerfoot" Milan and Johnson. Blankenship signed Milan, who later became one of the game's best base-stealers, then headed north to find the 19-year-old Johnson. "What I found when I got to Weiser was a boy—a big, husky boy and a green one, too," Blankenship said. "He knew nothing of the fine points of baseball but he could put more smoke on that old baseball than I ever dreamed possible."

Johnson, who had never allowed more than five hits in any game in two years of semi-pro ball in Weiser, signed with Washington for a $100 bonus, $350 per month, and guaranteed return transportation if his major league career didn't work out.

Johnson's pitching was sensational from the start; it was the performance of his teammates that didn't quite work out. In 1907 Johnson had a 1.87 ERA, fourth best in the American League, but went 5–9. The Nationals finished last, losing 102 games. Johnson improved to 14–14 and 1.64 in 1908, including three shutouts in four days, but Washington went in the other direction. The next year the team dropped 108 games.

Johnson was a gentle man, and his vast reservoir of patience was severely tested in 1909 when his Washington teammates failed to score in ten of his 25 losses, still an American League record for shutout losses in a season. Johnson's 65 career shutout losses are also a major league record. His most amazing statistic may be his 65 complete 1–0 games; he won 38, lost 27. No one else has hurled even half that many. For almost two decades it was a standing joke in the American League that Johnson should sue his team for non-support.

But in 1910 Johnson's talent exploded, and not even Washington's lackluster offense could keep him from his first winning record, 25–17, the first of ten straight 20-win seasons. Even more impressive were his 313 strikeouts, almost twice as many as his previous high and at the time second only to Rube Waddell's 349 in 1904.

Though the Nationals continued to hover near the bottom of the standings, Johnson's sidearm fastball remained the most potent pitch in the league. In 1912 Clark Griffith became Washington's manager. Johnson responded with 32 wins—including a record 16 in a row—a 1.39 ERA and 303 strikeouts, and the team finished a surprising second. In 1913 he did even better, turning in one of the game's greatest single-season performances. The numbers are still astounding: 36–7, 1.09 ERA, 11 shutouts, a record string of $55^{2}/_{3}$ scoreless in-

At age 36, Johnson pitched out of four jams in four innings in Game 7 of the 1924 World Series to secure Washington's only world championship. "When future generations are told about this game," wrote sportswriter Bill Corum, "the boy with his first glove and ball crowding up to his father's knee, will beg: 'Tell me about Walter Johnson.'"

WALTER JOHNSON

Right-Handed Pitcher
Washington Senators 1907–1927
Hall of Fame 1936

GAMES	**802**
INNINGS	
Career	5,923⅔
Season High	373
WINS	
Career *(2nd all time)*	416
Season High *(4th all time)*	36
LOSSES	
Career *(3rd all time)*	279
Season High	25
WINNING PERCENTAGE	
Career	.599
Season High	.837
ERA	
Career *(7th all time)*	2.17
Season Low *(3rd all time)*	1.09
GAMES STARTED	
Career *(8th all time)*	666
Season High	42
COMPLETE GAMES	
Career *(5th all time)*	531
Season High	38
SHUTOUTS	
Career *(1st all time)*	110
Season High *(6th all time)*	11
STRIKEOUTS	
Career *(6th all time)*	3,508
Season High	313
WALKS	
Career	1,405
Season High	132
NO-HITTERS	**1920**
WORLD SERIES	**1924,1925**
MOST VALUABLE PLAYER	
Chalmers	1913
League	1924

nings, and just 38 walks in 346 innings, less than one per game. Johnson was named the league's MVP, and again Washington finished second.

Johnson averaged 24 wins over the next six years, and ran his string of AL strikeout titles to eight, but the Senators were still without a pennant. Johnson's excellence became expected, and he rarely disappointed his fans. In 1916 he pitched 371 innings, and hit more home runs—one—than he gave up. In 1918 he matched zeroes with Chicago's Lefty Williams for 18 innings until Washington scored a run on a wild pitch. In 1920 arm trouble struck the 32-year-old sidearmer, though on July 1 he pitched his only career no-hitter, a 1–0 win over Boston in which he struck out ten and walked none. Only an error by Washington second baseman Bucky Harris kept it from being a perfect game.

By 1924, Johnson was, by most accounts, way past his prime. He even threw a curve on occasion. But the Senators, now managed by Harris and fea-

During spring training in 1926, Johnson (above) was surrounded by admirers in Daytona Beach. He then came north and pitched his seventh and last Opening Day shutout, beating Philadelphia 1–0 in 15 innings.

turing stars like Goose Goslin and Sam Rice, were in the pennant chase, and Johnson reached back to find one more great season. He went 23–7, led the league in strikeouts and shutouts, and for once had some help from other Washington pitchers like Firpo Marberry, Tom Zachary and George Mogridge.

The Senators fought off the Yankees in the stretch drive, then turned their attention to the NL champion New York Giants. Johnson, the fans' hero, finally got a chance at a World Series. In Game 1 he lost a 4–3 heartbreaker in 12 innings. He lost again in Game 5, which gave the Giants a 3–2 lead, and newspapers bemoaned the tragic fate of the beloved pitcher. But in fairy tale fashion Johnson got one last chance, this time as a relief pitcher in the ninth inning of Game 7 with the score tied, 3–3. He held John McGraw's Giants scoreless for four innings, and in the bottom of the 12th the fates conspired to give Johnson and Washington a bizarre run. With one out, Giants' catcher Hank

Gowdy tripped over his mask and dropped a foul pop by Muddy Ruel. Given new life, Ruel doubled. Johnson reached first on an error, and when leadoff batter Earl McNeely's grounder hit a pebble and bounced over third baseman Freddie Lindstrom's head, the world championship run scored.

Jack Bentley, the losing pitcher in Game 7, claimed the pebble was placed there by a higher power. "Walter Johnson was such a lovable character that the good Lord didn't want to see him get beat again," he said.

Johnson won 20 games in 1925 as the Senators repeated as AL champs, and at 37, Johnson roared into the World Series, allowing just one run and 11 hits in complete game wins over Pittsburgh in Games 1 and 4. But The Big Train injured his leg on the bases in Game 4, and was battered for 15 hits and took the loss in a cold, rain-soaked Game 7. "With mud shackling his ankles and water running down his neck, the grand old man of baseball suc-

Johnson (above) hit .433 in 1925, his last 20-win season. Johnson and Tiger center fielder Ty Cobb (right) battled each other for 21 seasons.

cumbed to weariness, a sore leg, wretched support and the most miserable weather conditions that ever confronted a pitcher," wrote sportswriter James Harrison.

Johnson retired in 1927 after spending 21 consecutive seasons with the same team, still a record for pitchers. He returned in 1929 to manage the Senators for four seasons and the Indians for three.

Johnson's achievements are enriched by how well most have stood the test of time. Although he pitched in an age of contact hitters, his 3,508 career strikeouts are still an AL record. His major league records include 12 league strikeout titles, 18 years with 100 or more strikeouts, and 110 career shutouts. He was an outstanding control pitcher as well, averaging just over two walks per nine innings in his career.

But he was more than just one of the game's greatest pitchers. He was a model of gentility during the roughest days of baseball. Although he hit 206 batters in his career, he never intentionally threw at anyone; he was too afraid of hurting someone with his blazing fastball. Ty Cobb took advantage of Johnson's good nature by crowding the plate, forcing Johnson to throw outside the strike zone, then to come in with slow stuff that the Detroit star would be waiting for.

Johnson also never complained about the lack of offensive support that plagued his career. The closest things he had to vices were his affinities for hunting dogs and fast cars. One of his nicknames, "Barney," came from race driver Barney Oldfield. The other, "Big Train," referred to the speed of his fastball. Maybe the fact that the great Cobb had to resort to chicanery to get hits off Johnson is the best measure of Johnson's talent. Cobb described him this way: "Just speed, raw speed, blinding speed, too much speed."

Good Stuff

"In the village grammar school the star hurler has speed, some semblance of control, and nothing else. Gradually he develops a curve. Then perchance he acquires a smattering of the slowball. If he enters the minors he may experiment with the spitball. These four types comprise the entire range of pitching possibilities so far evolved."

—*Baseball Magazine, 1913*

For most pitchers, whatever else they master, the fastball does come first. It's the most natural pitch, the easiest to control, and probably the least injurious to the arm. Even an "ordinary" major league fastball is hard to hit. Even a great hitter gears up for it and adjusts for everything else. "The toughest pitchers for me over the years have been fastball guys," Mike Schmidt says. "Any pitcher is trouble if he has enough of a fastball that I can't adapt to it when I'm looking for the breaking ball."

For Tom Seaver, who threw the fastball about two pitches out of three, it was the "cornerstone" of his art, because it set up all other pitches. "The inside fastball," he said, "is the pitch that will establish the outside corner for you." Seaver thought of every pitch as having "three dimensions": velocity, movement, and location. The fastball offers an especially clear illustration of Seaver's insight.

The average major league fastball travels about 86 miles an hour, or 126 feet a second. From release point, three or four feet in front of the rubber, to the heart of home plate, it takes less than half a second.

In the early 1900s when the great Walter Johnson was in his prime, a fastball was called a "swift," and Johnson's was the swiftest. Bob Feller reasoned that Johnson must have been the fastest ever "for the simple reason that he didn't have a curveball and he struck out so many hitters." Johnson, like a mythic warrior, grew ever more committed to a single overpowering

The Dodgers' Orel Hershiser (opposite) dominated NL hitters in 1988. He threw a record 59 straight shutout innings and won two World Series games.

Detroit southpaw Mickey Lolich (right) was an overweight fastball pitcher with staying power. In 1978 he became one of just two men since 1917 to pitch more than 375 innings in a season. The other to do it was knuckle ball specialist Wilbur Wood in 1972.

Smokey Joe Williams (above) was an overwhelming fastball pitcher in negro league baseball from 1897 to 1932. In exhibition games against major league teams, Williams went 20–7 and once struck out 20 in a no-hitter against the 1917 NL champion New York Giants.

weapon. "I used to pitch one wiggly to about four or five fast ones," he said, "but I could never seem to get very much on my curves, and so I have come to depend almost solely on speed."

The second pitching dimension is movement. Thrown with a whippy sidearm delivery, Johnson's fastball jumped up and in toward right-handed batters. Feller's fastball had a similarly wicked hop. But a fastball can do more than just rise. Los Angeles Dodger Orel Hershiser is a master of the "heavy" fastball, or the sinker. In the hands of Hershiser, Bob Lemon and Ferguson Jenkins, this pitch can showcase a special kind of pitching skill—the designing of ground-ball outs. Hershiser, an expert designer, says that "hand discipline" is the key. "It's not just the arm that throws the ball. My whole game is really working around my hand, because my arm coming through is the same every time. The positioning of my fingers creates the spin that makes the ball change direction."

The third dimension, location, means more than just control. Working a pitch within the corners of the strike zone is what every pitcher has to do. But as Tom Seaver says, a fastball is often most effective outside the strike zone, either as a temptation or a threat. The pitcher who moves the ball around can move the hitter too, and "in and out" is usually more strategic than "up and down."

Of modern fastballs, not just the fastest, but the most three-dimensional belonged to Sandy Koufax—after he learned control in mid-career. He rarely hit batters, yet he was confident enough to pitch inside. "Pitching is the art of instilling fear by making a man flinch," Koufax said. In the early 1960s Koufax's fastball made him the baseball hero of a Texas schoolboy named Nolan Ryan. "He was the king," Ryan says. "I liked him because he was a fastball pitcher and so was I. Speed always attracts."

What was once called the slow ball is now a "change-up," but its purpose is the same—to disrupt the hitter's timing. Before the curve became popular, pitchers teased hitters with subtle variations in speed. Later hurlers adopted the "change of pace" as a third pitch, complementing the fastball and curve.

To throw a good change-up, the pitcher takes something off the ball while bringing his arm through at normal speed. One version is the palm ball, held deep in the hand so the fingertips cannot impart snap or speed; then there's the slip pitch, released with thumb and fingers to the sides of the ball like a slider; and the fadeaway, an early version of the screwball, thrown with an inward turn of the wrist that subtracts velocity.

With the change-up—as with the screwball—many of the very best practitioners have been left-handers: Eppa Rixey, Herb Pennock, Warren Spahn, Eddie Lopat, Johnny Podres, John Tudor, Scott McGregor. In the early 1980s McGregor added a new dimension to the slow ball's element of surprise. Ray Miller, then McGregor's pitching coach at Baltimore, said, "Hitters around the league know about his change-up now, and Scotty has that great ability to know what they're expecting. He'll throw them the change-up anyway . . . only slower."

The 1877 *Spalding Guide* observed that "the perfection of curved pitching" was the most important trend of the decade. "Any professor can in his study prove from the books that the thing is impossible," the *Guide* said, "and many ballplayers can show him in the field that it is not only possible but common."

Physicists now say that the ball does curve, but that its arc is continuous,

A Dixie Cup lid was an appropriate place for a portrait of Preacher Roe, who was born in Ashflat, Arkansas. After going 4–15 with a 5.25 ERA with Pittsburgh in 1947, Roe was traded to Brooklyn. In 1948 he added the spitball to his array of off-speed pitches and improved his record to 12–8 and 2.62.

6' 180 lbs.
BR TR
b 1/23/40

LUIS TIANT
Right-Handed Pitcher

Luis Tiant's career took almost as many twists and turns as did his vast array of pitches and motions. One of the most colorful and successful pitchers of the 1960s and 1970s, Tiant won 229 games pitching for six teams in his 19-year career.

In his windup, Tiant would literally turn his back to hitters and hide the ball until the last second before unleashing his assortment of pitches and speeds. He could deliver the ball from a straight overhand, three-quarters or sidearm position. Tiant's stretch position was unique, as his hands dipped and swerved dozens of times on their way to his belt.

The son of a famed Cuban pitcher known as "El Tiante," Tiant reached the majors with Cleveland in 1964 and pitched a three-hit shutout in his first major league start. In 1968 he had his finest season, going 21–9 with a league-leading 1.60 ERA and nine shutouts. Opposing batters hit .168 against Tiant, the lowest single season average in history.

Arm trouble hampered Tiant until 1972, when he won 15 games for Boston, including four straight shutouts. He won 20 or more games in three of the next four seasons for the Red Sox, including two World Series wins against Cincinnati in 1975. Tiant was 3-0 lifetime in postseason play, and the man Boston manager Darrell Johnson wanted when he needed a win. "If a man put a gun to my head and said, 'I'm going to pull the trigger if you lose this game,' I'd want Luis Tiant to pitch," Johnson said.

In the 1960s the best NL curveball belonged to Sandy Koufax. The AL's best hook belonged to Camilo Pascual (above), who led the league in strikeouts from 1961 to 1963 for the Minnesota Twins.

only *appearing* to break more sharply as it nears the plate. Whereas a fastball acquires backspin from the middle finger at the instant of release, a curve acquires topspin as it rolls across the index finger. With this topspin, the raised seams of the baseball pull a thin layer of air more rapidly underneath the ball, reducing air pressure and causing an "out drop." The more rapid the topspin rotation, the more the ball seems to the hitter to "fall off the table."

Of the many claimants to the curveball's discovery, the man most often credited is Hall of Famer William Arthur "Candy" Cummings, who said that he broke off the first bender in 1867 pitching for the Excelsior Club of Brooklyn in a game against Harvard. Cummings claimed that the curveball existed in his mind long before it existed in reality.

In 1863, at age 15, he and some friends were throwing clam shells, experimenting with ways they could be sailed. Cummings figured that he ought to be able to sail a baseball too, and for four years he tried every imaginable way to do it. "I had not one single word of enouragement in all that time," Cummings said, "while my attempts were a standing joke among my friends." But after his breakthrough in the Harvard game, "the baseball came to have a new meaning for me; it almost seemed to have life."

A wrist-break in the pitcher's delivery became legal in 1872, the year Cummings began his professional career. Over the next six seasons he won 145 games in the National Association and the National League. He threw underhand, of course, wearing a kid glove on his pitching hand to prevent blisters, imparting sidespin with a final finger snap.

With legalization of overhand pitching in 1884, the curve could be thrown faster and be made to break downward as well as away. After 1893 pitchers had a full 60' 6" in which to make it happen. The honor roll of

great curveballers begins with Mordecai "Three Finger" Brown, whose mangled hand created arcs of unique beauty. Also on the list, though it hardly seems fair, are two all-time fastballers: Feller and Koufax. Jim Palmer, a modern curveball master, threw the pitch so hard that his wrist snap was audible.

In the 1980s, Palmer says, the curve has become a little less popular but no less effective. "It has become harder to get over because of the shrinking strike zone. It's a good pitch to use after you establish the fastball. You try to get the hitter to chase one down and away. Even if he hits it, he'll lose power."

Tug McGraw has heard two theories about how the screwball got its name. "The first is that you throw it with a screwing motion, like screwing in a lightbulb. The second theory is that it screws up the hitters." Lightbulbs and screws are tightened in a clockwise direction, so the comparison holds true only for left-handers. Since the pitcher rotates his hand and wrist to the inside, the ball rarely has the velocity of a normal curve, and it may baffle hitters more by its "stalling" effect than by its reverse break to the side.

The pitch gained early popularity with southpaw pitchers against right-handed hitters, for a "reverse curve" that breaks away from the hitters' power. A clear majority of screwball pitchers have been lefties, among them Carl Hubbell, Harry Brecheen, Warren Spahn, Mike Cuellar, Fernando Valenzuela . . . and Tug McGraw.

Rube Foster, the father of Negro League baseball, was a right-handed screwball pitcher—and a magnificent one—at the turn of the century. Another righty, New York Giant Christy Mathewson, did more than anyone

Carl Hubbell

They called him "King Carl" and "The Meal Ticket." His career included some of the most brilliant pitching performances and seasons of all time, yet some bad advice from one of baseball's greatest hitters almost ended Carl Hubbell's career before it got started.

In 1926 Hubbell was invited to spring training with the Detroit Tigers after having won 17 games for Oklahoma City the year before. With Tiger player-manager Ty Cobb looking on, Hubbell uncorked his bread-and-butter pitch—the screwball—which essentially is a backwards curve, and for left-handed pitchers breaks down and away from right-handed hitters. Cobb didn't like what he saw. "Forget those freak pitches, kid. All you'll do is hurt your arm."

Hubbell, then just 23, did as he was told. "What could I do?" he recalled. "I was just a naive country boy. He was Ty Cobb. I forgot about it. I never threw that pitch again as long as I was in Detroit."

Without the screwball, Hubbell moved from Toronto to Beaumont, Texas, but nowhere near the majors until 1928, when his contract was bought by the New York Giants. This time, Hubbell decided to stick with his best pitch. Giant manager John McGraw liked what he saw, and Hubbell went 10–6 with a 2.83 ERA that year.

Hubbell averaged 17 wins from 1929 to 1932, and in 1929 pitched a no-hitter against Pittsburgh. Hubbell's 1933 season included a then-NL record 46 straight scoreless innings and league bests with 23 wins, a 1.66 ERA and ten shutouts. On July 2 Hubbell and St. Louis' Tex Carleton locked up in a duel that was still scoreless when Carleton left for a pinch-hitter in the 16th. In the bottom of the 18th Hughie Critz's single scored Jo-Jo Moore to give the Giants a 1–0 win and Hubbell a tie for the record for baseball's longest shutout.

In the 1933 World Series against the Washington Senators, Hubbell established his reputation as a big-game pitcher. He beat the Senators in Games 1 and 4, allowing no earned runs in 20 innings. He was named the NL's Most Valuable Player.

Hubbell went 21–12 in 1934 with a league-leading 2.30 ERA and eight saves. His brightest moment came in the All-Star Game against a quintet of the game's greatest hitters, all of whom later made the Hall of Fame, but none of whom—as became vividly apparent—had ever seen anything like Hubbell's screwball. Hubbell gave up a single and a walk to start the game, bringing Cub catcher Gabby Hartnett to the mound. "Come on, Hub, throw that thing," Hartnett said. "Hell, I can't hit it and they can't either."

Hubbell struck out Babe Ruth on three low screwballs. The Babe never took his bat off his shoulder. Lou Gehrig struck out only 31 times all season, but couldn't solve Hubbell's knee-high screwballs, and struck out swinging. Boston's Jimmie Foxx managed a foul tip before going down swinging to end the inning. Hubbell had fanned Ruth, Gehrig and Foxx on 12 pitches. He spun Chicago's Al Simmons into a knot to open the second, then faced Joe Cronin, who fanned just 28 times that season. But Cronin went down swinging, and Hubbell set a record that was not matched until 52 years later—by another screwball pitcher, Dodger Fernando Valenzuela.

The violent wrist break necessary to throw an effective screwball began to give Hubbell arm problems in 1934, so in 1935 he worked to improve his curve, and won 23 games. By 1936 he could throw the screwball again, and with his new repertoire Hubbell won 26 games, including 16 straight from July 17 until the end of the season. The Giants won the pennant; King Carl won his second MVP.

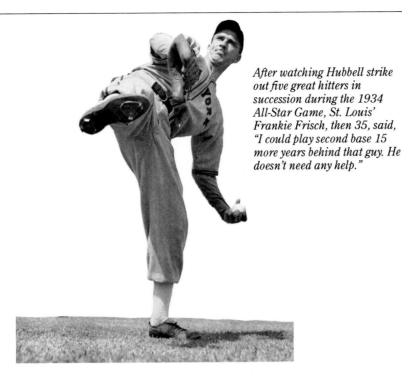

After watching Hubbell strike out five great hitters in succession during the 1934 All-Star Game, St. Louis' Frankie Frisch, then 35, said, "I could play second base 15 more years behind that guy. He doesn't need any help."

CARL
HUBBELL

Left-Handed Pitcher
New York Giants 1928–1943
Hall of Fame 1947

GAMES	**535**
INNINGS	
Career	3,589⅓
Season High	313
WINS	
Career	253
Season High	26
LOSSES	
Career	154
Season High	12
WINNING PERCENTAGE	
Career	.622
Season High	.813
ERA	
Career	2.97
Season Low	1.66
GAMES STARTED	
Career	432
Season High	35
COMPLETE GAMES	
Career	258
Season High	25
SHUTOUTS	
Career	36
Season High	10
STRIKEOUTS	
Career	1,678
Season High	159
WALKS	
Career	724
Season High	67
NO-HITTERS	1929
WORLD SERIES	1933,1936
	1937
MOST VALUABLE PLAYER	
	1933,1936

In the 1936 World Series against the Yankees, Hubbell tossed a seven-hitter in Game 1 and had his screwball dipping so fiercely that the Giants did not record one putout on a fly ball in the entire game. But the King's magic left him in a 5–2 loss in Game 4, and the Yankees won the Series in six games. In 1937 Hubbell went 22–8 with a league-leading 159 strikeouts. The Giants again won the pennant, but again lost to the Yankees in the World Series. Hubbell picked up the only Giant win in the Series with a six-hitter in Game 4.

By 1938 the snap was gone from Hubbell's screwball. He went 13–10 that year but had an operation to remove bone chips from his elbow, and won just 11 games in each of the next four seasons. After going 4–4 in 1943, Hubbell retired and became director of the Giants' farm system, a job he held until 1979. He died in 1988.

Among left-handers, Hubbell is the greatest control pitcher in history. He averaged 1.8 walks per nine innings. Cub second baseman Billy Herman said his team's bench emptied when Hubbell was on the mound, as players stood on the dugout steps to watch Hubbell at work, mixing his screwball, curve, change-up and fastball. "He didn't have overpowering stuff, but he was a marvel to watch," Herman said.

6′ 190 lbs. b 7/26/23
BR TR

HOYT WILHELM
Right-Handed Pitcher

By the time he threw his first major league pitch, Hoyt Wilhelm was already 28 years old and had spent ten years in the minors. By the time he threw his last—five days short of his 49th birthday—he had pitched in more major league games than anyone else before or since.

Wilhelm, who learned to throw a knuckleball from an article he read about knuckleballer Dutch Leonard, used the fluttering pitch to register a record 123 relief wins. In 1985 he became the first reliever to be elected to the Hall of Fame. For 21 years and 1,070 games, Wilhelm's knuckleball baffled hitters—and his own catchers. He held opposing batters to a .215 average, the third lowest of any pitcher.

Wilhelm wasted no time once he finally made the majors. With the New York Giants in 1952, he went 15–3 with 11 saves and a 2.43 ERA in 71 appearances. He was a starter for three of his four years with Baltimore, and in 1958 pitched a no-hitter against the soon-to-be-world-champion Yankees.

At an age when almost all players have long since retired, Wilhelm had some of his best years. After the age of 40, he went 52–41, had 115 saves and a 2.11 ERA in 459 games. When he retired in 1972, Wilhelm had finished 651 games—for the Giants, Cardinals, Indians, Orioles, White Sox, Angels, Braves, Cubs and Dodgers. And he was already old enough to receive benefits under baseball's pension plan.

Negro league star Andrew "Rube" Foster earned his nickname when he beat the great Rube Waddell in a 1902 exhibition game. Foster, who relied on the screwball as his "out" pitch, won 51 games that year for the Cuban X Giants.

to bring the screwball to prominence in the dead-ball era. Mathewson's pitch was called the "fadeaway" or "fallaway," because it seemed to float up to the plate and then simply die. Modern screwballs often act the same way. Mathewson thought his best pitch was a regular curve, and he used the fadeaway sparingly. "Pitching it ten or 12 times a game kills my arm, so I save it for the pinches." By contrast, Carl Hubbell estimated that he threw the screwball 50 percent of the time—in almost 3,600 innings from 1928 to 1943. By midcareer his left arm was permanently twisted inward, and the loss of flexibility affected his other pitches. But he remained a supreme artist, playing the screwball off against curve and fastball with a brilliance—and superb control—that fascinated even his opponents. "When Hub was wild," Johnny Vander Meer said, "he threw the ball over the heart of home plate."

Baseball historians trace the knuckle ball back to 1905, when Ed Cicotte and Nap Rucker were minor league teammates in Augusta, Georgia. Experimenting with various grips and releases, Cicotte and Rucker discovered that startling effects could be produced by minimizing rotation of the ball on its way to home plate. The scientific explanation is that the ball's raised stitches disrupt airflow, so that small changes in pressure create sudden swerves.

Every knuckle ball artist seems to throw the pitch a little differently, but they all grip the ball tightly with the fingertips—not the knuckles. Hoyt Wilhelm, who toured the majors as a reliever from 1952 to 1972, released the ball with a loose wrist. For Phil Niekro the knuckler required a stiff wrist, stiff elbow and stiff shoulder. But after three decades, Niekro said, "I still don't know why the ball does what it does."

A hard-luck pitcher in Houston, Mike Cuellar turned his screwball into a winning pitch when he joined the talented Baltimore staff. From 1969 to 1974 Cuellar averaged 21 wins a season for the Orioles and played on five division championship teams.

Six Pitches

FASTBALL

The pitch that sets up all the others, a fastball gets backspin and movement by rolling off the index and middle fingers.

CURVEBALL

A wrist snap to the outside sends a righty's curve breaking to the left and down; a lefty's will break right and down.

SCREWBALL

Thrown with an inside wrist snap, the screwball breaks down and in the opposite direction of a curveball.

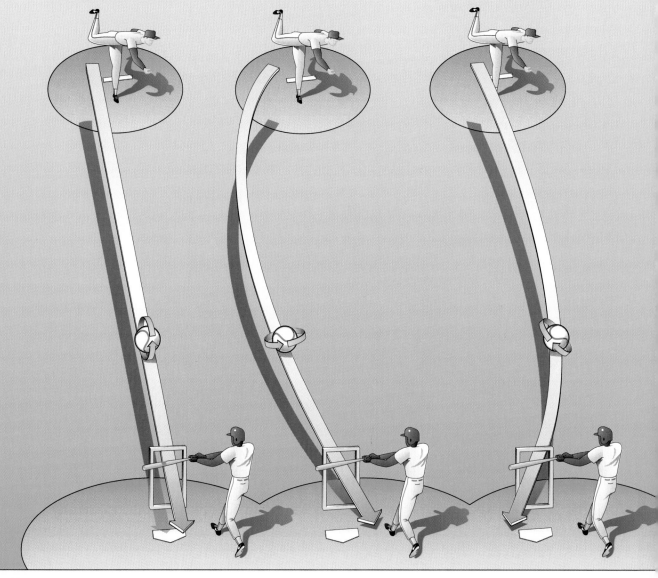

Pictured and described here are the grip, rotation and movement of six of baseball's most widely used pitches, as thrown by a right-handed pitcher to a left-handed batter. When thrown by a left-hander, the curve, screwball and slider will both rotate and break in the opposite direction.

KNUCKLEBALL

A knuckler is released with hardly any spin, and air currents can make it jump unpredictably on its way to the plate.

SLIDER

A cross between a fastball and a curve, a good slider is only 5 mph slower than a fastball and has a late, lateral break.

SPLIT-FINGER

Tough to throw and tougher to hit, the split-finger looks like a fastball, but spins slowly with a late, sharp, downward break.

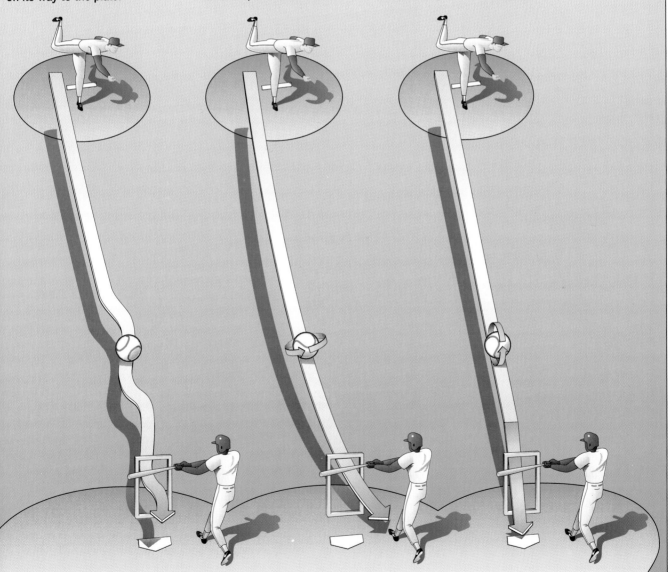

Throwing the knuckle ball puts hardly any strain on a pitcher's arm. Phil Niekro (right) threw the knuckler almost exclusively for 24 years, and won 114 games after the age of 40, more than anyone else.

Baltimore's Gus Triandos, who was charged with four passed balls in one inning trying to catch Hoyt Wilhelm's knuckle ball, got help from a larger, more flexible mitt (above).

For Charlie Hough, tutored by Wilhelm, the secret was relaxation. "Instead of bearing down, I had to throw softer." A knuckle ball usually floats in at 50 or 55 mph. The ball takes so long to get to the plate and is so hard to catch, baserunners can have a field day. Hough's solution was to work on pick-offs. "Wilhelm never taught me a move to first, because his was awful. So I watched Phil Niekro. Now I use a quicker motion off the stretch that makes me tough to run on. One year I picked off 11 runners."

In 1945 the Washington Senators almost won the pennant with a staff that had four knuckle ball pitchers: Dutch Leonard, Roger Wolff, Johnny Niggeling and Mickey Haefner. The catcher was Rick Ferrell, exempt from service in World War II at age 39. Some said that Ferrell would have been safer in the Army. The Senators' catchers allowed 40 passed balls that year. Ferrell caught from a half-standing position instead of a crouch, making it easier to spring or dive for errant butterflies.

"How in hell is a man going to hit a ball that the catcher can't even catch?" Billy Goodman once asked. Goodman, who batted .300 in a 16-year career, is only one of many hitters demoralized by the knuckler. On the other hand, Dick Allen claimed that the pitch was no problem for him. "I never worry about it," he said. "I just take my three swings and go sit on the bench. I'm afraid if I even think about hitting it, I'll mess up my swing for life."

The same principle that governs the aerodynamics of knucklers applies to spitballs and scuffballs. The spitball pitcher minimizes the ball's rotation—not with his grip but by applying saliva or grease to the fingertips and then squeezing the ball out the way one would squeeze a watermelon seed.

The scuffer alters the airflow around the ball by creating some irregularity on the surface: a cut, a rough spot, or a glob of mud rubbed into a seam. Whenever one side of the ball is rougher than the other, the pitcher creates a "whiffle" effect simply by holding the rough side away from the direction he wants the ball to break. If the ball is scuffed on the right, for example, an overhand fastball will veer to the left.

In the dead-ball era, pitchers were allowed to wet the ball with the residue of anything chewable: tobacco, slippery elm, licorice, or even coffee beans. The ball quickly became discolored and hard to see, and it might not be replaced for several innings. It might also be doctored illegally—roughened by a file, an emery cloth, or a bottle cap. Righty Ed Cicotte of the 1919 White Sox, co-discoverer of the knuckle ball, is also credited with inventing the shine ball. This pitch worked by making one side of the ball *smoother.* Cicotte hid paraffin or talcum powder in his uniform, catcher Bob O'Farrell said. "Every chance he got he'd rub the ball there. That would make the ball slide off his fingers and put a real break on it. Acted something like a spitter. A catcher's life wasn't easy."

The first spitter may have been thrown by Baltimore's Bobby Mathews, who had three straight 30-victory seasons in the 1880s. The man who did most for the spitball, and vice versa, was Ed Walsh, handsome hero of the turn-of-the-century White Sox. Walsh threw the pitch two ways: as a sudden sinker when he came straight overhand, and as a shooting curve when he came sidearm. The overhand version was hardest to hit, according to Detroit Tigers' Sam Crawford. "I think that ball disintegrated on the way to the plate and the catcher put it back together again. I swear, when it went past the plate it was just the spit went by." For six years, 1907 through 1912, Walsh aver-

In 1944 the Washington Senators obtained Rick Ferrell (second from right), an outstanding defensive catcher, to handle a pitching staff that included four knuckle ball specialists. From left to right, three of the four were Roger Wolff, Dutch Leonard and Mickey Haefner. The other was Johnny Niggeling.

When Jim Bouton came up with the Yankees in 1962, he had an overpowering fastball—and an unorthodox delivery that often left his cap in the dirt.

Top Ten Intimidators

In 1920, Cleveland's Ray Chapman was struck in the head and killed by a pitch thrown by New York's submarine-ball pitcher Carl Mays. Whether or not it is done intentionally, hitting a batter with a pitched ball is the pitcher's ultimate form of intimidation. Below are the top ten all-time leaders in hit batsmen.

Pitcher/Years	Hit Batsmen	Innings Pitched	Hit Batsmen per 9 Innings Pitched
Chick Fraser, 1896-1909	215	3,356	0.6
Walter Johnson, 1907-1927	206	5,924	0.3
Eddie Plank, 1901-1917	188	4,505	0.4
Joe McGinnity, 1899-1908	184	3,441	0.5
Jim Bunning, 1955-1971	160	3,759	0.4
Don Drysdale, 1956-1969	154	3,432	0.4
Howard Ehmke, 1915-1930	137	2,821	0.4
Hooks Dauss, 1912-1926	121	3,391	0.3
Jack Warhop, 1908-1915	114	1,424	0.7
George Uhle, 1919-1936	113	3,120	0.3

aged almost 375 innings a season. Then he hurt his arm and could only throw the sidearm spitter, but he lasted five more seasons on courage and guile.

When doctored deliveries were banned after the 1919 season, a grandfather clause allowed 17 established spitball pitchers to continue throwing it. For three of them—Stan Coveleski, Urban "Red" Faber and Burleigh Grimes—the spitter became a ticket to the Hall of Fame. But it's likely that the Hall will soon enshrine at least one illegal spitballer: Gaylord Perry.

Perry began throwing the spitter in 1964, at age 25, when his career with the Giants was in danger. In 1966 Perry won 21 games. He later became the first pitcher since Cy Young to record a 20-win season in each league, but in 1968 he had to alter his tactics because of a new rule forbidding pitchers to bring their hands to their mouths. "Anyone who had money in petroleum jelly stocks must have made some quick profits," Perry said. He rarely walked to the mound without globs behind the ears and on the back of the neck, or without a tube in the hip pocket of his uniform. He joked about his tricks but was careful to maintain what is now called "deniability." In 1971, when Perry's daughter Alison was five, a reporter asked if her daddy threw a greaseball. "It's a hard slider," she said.

The modern slider is generally credited to George Blaeholder, an otherwise undistinguished hurler with the 1930s St. Louis Browns. Its ancestors were the old "sailing fastball" or "nickel curve" of deadball days. A slider is usually five to seven mph slower than the same pitcher's fastball, and it breaks much less than the curve. Instead of "falling off the table," the pitch appears to veer or "slide" a few inches sideways and down as it reaches the plate. It is thrown somewhat like a football pass, with the

Gaylord Perry was a master at doctoring a baseball from 1962 to 1983. He was even better at not getting caught. Perry won more than 300 games for eight teams before he was caught and fined in 1980 for applying a foreign substance to the ball.

5'10" 175 lbs.
BB TR

b 10/19/1876
d 2/14/48

THREE FINGER BROWN
Right-Handed Pitcher

At the age of 7, Mordecai Peter Centennial Brown lost his index finger when he got his right hand caught in a feed cutter. With the hand still in a cast, Brown broke two fingers while trying to catch a hog, leaving what remained of his right hand twisted and misshapen.

Nineteen years later, major league hitters discovered that Brown's twisted hand could spin a curve with a very nasty break. Ty Cobb called it "the most devastating pitch I ever faced."

After a mediocre rookie season with St. Louis in 1903, Brown—now known as Three Finger Brown—was traded to the Cubs and for the next nine years was one of the most dominant pitchers in baseball, averaging 21 wins per season. Six times Brown posted ERAs of under 2.00, including a 1.04 mark—the second best of all time—in 1906. He doubled as the Cubs' bullpen ace, and led the NL in saves from 1908 to 1911.

Brown was especially effective in big games, and from July 12, 1905 to October 8, 1908, he beat friend and rival Christy Mathewson—the greatest pitcher of the era—nine straight times. The last win in Brown's streak came in the game that decided the 1908 pennant. He went on to post two wins and 11 scoreless innings in the Cubs' World Series win over Detroit.

Brown's career totals include 239 wins, a 2.06 ERA—third best of all time—57 shutouts, and five World Series wins.

Burleigh Grimes, who was one of just 17 pitchers allowed to throw spitballs after the pitch was banned in 1919, covered his mouth with his glove before every pitch. Grimes won 270 games from 1916 to 1934 while hitters guessed whether the ball was wet or not.

thumb and fingers at the sides of the ball and the wrist held stiff. The difference between this delivery and the pronounced wrist snap on a good curve explains why very few hurlers have been able to master both. Southpaw Steve Carlton was one of them.

Trying to hit Carlton, Willie Stargell said, was "like drinking coffee with a fork." His slider broke down so sharply that it was usually out of the strike zone, but to hitters it looked like a good fastball until the last instant.

The slider came into its own in the 1940s. Spud Chandler learned it in 1941 and, "it turned everything around for me." Johnny Sain used the slider to pitch his way to the majors in 1942. After World War II the pitch was popularized by Mel Parnell, Bob Lemon and Sal Maglie. Ted Williams said that the slider actually altered his hitting strategy because it gave pitchers an alternative to the fastball on a 3–1 count.

Sain taught the slider to both Whitey Ford and Denny McLain. "Ford learned it in one day and used it immediately," Sain said. Other recent practitioners have included Sparky Lyle, Ron Guidry and Dennis Eckersley. The pitch is here to stay. But Tom Seaver issued one other warning. "A poorly thrown slider, the infamous 'hanging slider,' can be tagged a long way," Seaver says. "Proportionately, more home runs are hit on bad sliders than any other pitch." The reason, according to Seaver, is that a flat slider lacks velocity, movement and location. It's a *no*-dimensional pitch.

The newest weapon in the pitcher's arsenal, the split-finger fastball, is a retooled version of the forkball. As both names suggest, the pitch is thrown with the ball scissored between the index and middle fingers, so hurlers with big hands have an advantage.

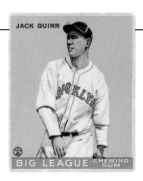

JACK QUINN

BIG LEAGUE CHEWING GUM

John Picus Quinn

In 1920 John Picus "Jack" Quinn was one of 17 pitchers designated by the major leagues as legal spitballers licensed to throw the pitch until the end of their careers. Quinn was 37 at the time, and rumored to be even older. No one could have imagined that his career still had 13 seasons to run—some of them stellar—or that he would outlast all of the other legal spitballers except for Burleigh Grimes. Sportswriters eventually dubbed Quinn "the Methuselah of the mound."

Quinn's age is only one of the mysterious details of his background. His family was either Welsh, Polish or Greek. He was born John Quinn Picus, or Paykos, in either Jeansville or Hazleton, Pennsylvania. The reported year of his birth, 1883, is also suspect.

By his own account, Quinn never attended school; he was a child laborer in the coal mines. At some point in the late 1890s, after barely escaping a mine fire, he left home and hopped freight trains across the country. "I had to fight to make my way," he said. "I got help from no one. I started out with only a dirty, ragged, unmatched suit of clothes, a tattered cap, a strong pair of soles on my shoes, and my two fists."

Quinn broke into professional baseball in 1903 in the Pennsylvania State League. As a fastball and curveball pitcher he made good progress, but when he added the spitball in 1908 he went 14–0 at Richmond and then was sold to the Yankees. Unlike most of the other early spitballers, Quinn found tobacco juice and slippery elm unnecessary. "I stick to chewing gum," he said. "People think spitballs are messy things. Mine aren't. I just touch my first two fingers to my lips ever so slightly. I always make that motion. Sometimes there's enough

perspiration on my hand to suffice."

This relatively dry spitter broke down sharply but usually stayed in the strike zone. Quinn remained a control artist throughout his career, with a lifetime average of less than two walks per game. Faking the spitball on every delivery was especially effective because of Quinn's other weapons, which included a no-name pitch—described as a "cousin to the knuckler"—thrown without using the index finger. In later years, as a crafty veteran in the era of the lively ball, Quinn developed a paralyzing change-up and was still stingy with home runs.

Quinn's travels in baseball were even more varied than in his freight-hopping youth. He jumped to the Federal League in 1914. Then, as part of the major league peace agreements he was banished for a season to the Pacific Coast League. After a second stint with the Yankees, and three years with the Red Sox, he joined the 1926 rotation of Lefty Grove, Rube Walberg and Ed Rommel for Connie Mack's Philadelphia Athletics. In 1928, at age 45, Quinn posted a record of 18–7. Two years later Mack decided that Quinn was finally finished. He was wrong.

In 1931 and 1932 Quinn was the relief ace of the Brooklyn Dodgers, appearing in a total of 81 games and leading the NL in saves both years. By pitching until he was 48, Quinn became the oldest pitcher ever to win a major league game, a record he still holds. After retiring with a career record of 247–217 and a 3.27 ERA, he continued to pitch in the minors. Not until 1935, when he was 51 years old, and in his 32nd season as a professional pitcher, did John Picus Quinn throw baseball's last legal spitter.

Before his days as baseball's most successful pitching coach, Roger Craig (above, right) was one of baseball's least successful pitchers. Only a ninth-inning grand slam by New York Mets teammate Jim Hickman (above, left) on Aug. 9, 1963, kept Craig from losing his 19th straight decision.

"Tiny" Bonham, one of the first successful forkballers, was 6'2" and 215 pounds—with hands to match. He used the pitch to win 103 games in the 1940s with the Yankees and Pirates. Two postwar forkball pitchers, Murry Dickson and Roy Face, were small by major league standards but had unusually large and strong hands. The hands of Bruce Sutter, who led the NL in saves for six straight years, 1979 to 1984, are a full joint longer than normal.

The traditional forkball works as a change-up: the pitcher brings his arm forward at normal speed but releases the ball as a kind of slip pitch. If he adds topspin, by pushing with his thumb or by snapping his wrist, he can make the ball drop dramatically. And if he throws with enough velocity, the forkball becomes a split-finger fastball—the closest thing yet to a dry spitter.

Roger Craig learned the forkball as a Dodger hurler in the 1950s. As a manager and coach in the 1980s, Craig taught it to whole staffs of pitchers in Detroit, San Diego and San Francisco. He also did free-lance tutoring for clients like Mike Scott. "You don't need huge hands like Scott's," Craig says. "You can adapt the pitch, maybe just using it as a straight change-up. And a young pitcher can throw it with maximum arm speed without hurting himself."

Craig called the forkball/split-finger "the pitch of the 1980s." Will there be a pitch of the 1990s, or a new weapon for the new millenium? The answer may depend on the future of the strike zone, or on changes in equipment, playing surfaces, and ballpark architecture. But two points seem beyond dispute. First, the fastball will remain supreme. Second, the catalog of pitches in this book will someday seem as limited and quaint as the 1913 survey in *Baseball Magazine.* ◗

Bruce Hurst did something very few southpaws have ever done—post a winning record at hitter-friendly Fenway Park. In eight years with Boston, he won 55, lost 33 at Fenway. Of pitchers with more than 50 wins there, only Mel Parnell and Lefty Grove had better winning percentages.

The No-Hitter

From 1900 to 1988, there were 87 no-hitters thrown in the National League and 92 in the American League—almost exactly one per year. The no-hitter's only serious rival in terms of baseball rarity is the triple play. In terms of dramatic tension, it has no rival, except the perfect game.

To pitch a no-hitter, a pitcher must have three things: his best stuff, a solid defense behind him, and a reasonable amount of good luck. To pitch a perfect game—in which no runners reach base—a pitcher must add pinpoint control, be supported by flawless defense, and quadruple his luck.

The list of 14 pitchers who have thrown perfect games includes a few all-time greats like Cy Young, Addie Joss, Sandy Koufax and Catfish Hunter. But it also includes such forgettable names as Charlie Robertson, whose lifetime record is 49–80, and Len Barker, whose lifetime ERA is 4.35.

The most famous perfect game ever pitched was the work of a hurler who lost more often than he won. Although Don Larsen was coming off a strong 11–5 season for the Yankees when he took the mound in Game 5 of the 1956 World Series against the Brooklyn Dodgers, no one has ever pitched a more unlikely perfect game. Just two years earlier he had endured a dismal 3–21 season with Baltimore; in his only start in the 1955 Series he was pounded by these same Dodgers; and just three days before he had been knocked out of the box in the second inning of Game 2. But Larsen threw just 97 pitches in Game 5, and went to a 3 and 2 count only once, in the first inning against shortstop Pee Wee Reese, before striking him out.

In the ninth, Larsen retired Carl Furillo on a fly to right and Roy Campanella on a grounder to second. In what was his final at-bat in the major leagues, pinch-hitter Dale Mitchell—who had struck out just 119 times in almost 4,000 career at-bats—took a called third strike to stamp Larsen's name in baseball's book of great performances.

Larsen's feat was magnified because it came in a World Series game. Harvey Haddix is a familiar name because he was perfect longer than anyone else. Haddix had won 20 games for St. Louis in 1953 but by 1959 was a .500 pitcher, toiling for the Pittsburgh Pirates, his fourth team in four years. But on May 26, Haddix had his best stuff, which was too good even for the Milwaukee Braves, whose potent lineup included Eddie Mathews, Hank Aaron and Joe Adcock. Milwaukee's Lew Burdette kept the Pirates scoreless too, and Haddix pushed on into extra perfect innings. Through 12 innings the Braves put no one on base, but in the unlucky 13th a throwing error put the perfect game to rest, and a home run by Adcock made a loser out of Haddix.

With his 11-strikeout no-hitter against Los Angeles on September 26, 1981, Nolan Ryan set himself apart as the only pitcher ever to throw five no-hitters. Ryan threw his first four no-hitters in just three seasons to tie Sandy Koufax for most career no-hitters, then had to wait six years for number five. Koufax threw one no-hitter each season from 1962 to 1965, the last a 14-strikeout perfect game.

There's an extremely fine line between the sparkle of a no-hitter and the fizzle of a one-hitter. Cleveland great Bob Feller threw three no-hitters, but he had four times as many one-hitters. Even more ill-fated were the no-hit efforts of Hall of Famer Grover Cleveland Alexander and Cooperstown prospects Steve Carlton and Don Sutton. Alexander won 373 games but never pitched a no-hitter. He threw a record four one-hitters in 1915,

Before Don Larsen (above) went out to pitch in the ninth inning of Game 5 of the 1956 World Series, second baseman Billy Martin (above, left) gave Yankee infielders an order: "Nothing gets through." Two outs later, Larsen fanned Dale Mitchell to complete the perfect game, then made a good catch on Yogi Berra (right).

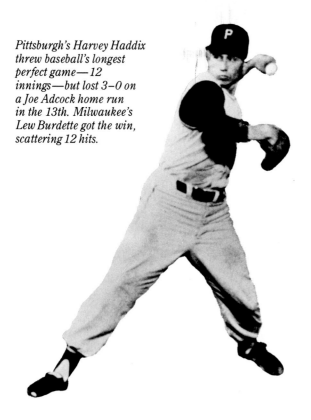

Pittsburgh's Harvey Haddix threw baseball's longest perfect game—12 innings—but lost 3–0 on a Joe Adcock home run in the 13th. Milwaukee's Lew Burdette got the win, scattering 12 hits.

Perfection

There have been only 14 perfect games in major league history. The pitchers, dates and scores of these milestone achievements, in which not a single batter reached base in nine innings, are listed below.

Pitcher & Club	Date	Score
Lee Richmond, Wor, NL	6/12/1880	1-0
Monte Ward, Prov, NL	6/17/1880	5-0
Cy Young, Bos, AL	5/5/1904	3-0
Addie Joss, Clev, AL	10/2/1908	1-0
Ernie Shore, Bos, AL	6/23/1917	4-0
Charlie Robertson, Chi, AL	4/30/1922	2-0
Don Larsen, NY, AL	10/8/1956	2-0 *
Harvey Haddix, Pitt, NL	5/26/1959	0-3 * *
Jim Bunning, Phil, NL	6/21/1964	6-0
Sandy Koufax, LA, NL	9/9/1965	1-0
Catfish Hunter, Oak, AL	5/8/1968	4-0
Len Barker, Clev, AL	5/15/1981	3-0
Mike Witt, Cal, AL	9/30/1984	1-0
Tom Browning, Cin, NL	9/16/1988	1-0

* World Series
* * 12 innings

and once threw eight innings of hitless ball before a scratch single by St. Louis' Arthur Butler broke it up. Carlton threw six near no-hitters, while Sutton gave opponents just one hit on five separate occasions; neither ever recorded a no-hitter.

No-hitters tend to occur in spurts. The 1960s were high times for National League pitchers, as 23 no-hitters—more than in any other decade—were thrown. The American League high came in the dead-ball decade of 1910–1919. Some years are just snake-bit when it comes to no-hitters, like 1988, when eight pitchers lost no-hitters in the ninth inning. Toronto's Dave Stieb was a victim of extreme cruelty, as he lost no-hitters with two outs in the ninth on two consecutive starts. Though Stieb is an outstanding pitcher, those two ninth-inning hits kept him from sharing the spotlight that shines on the only man ever to pitch back-to-back no-hitters—Johnny Vander Meer in 1938.

Like most pitchers who flirted with no-hitters from time to time, Vander Meer had a blazing fastball. In just his second year with the Cincinnati

Reds, Vander Meer's first no-hitter came on June 11 against Casey Stengel's Boston Bees. "Vandy" had his sinker working, and allowed just five fly balls in the game, while walking three and striking out four. Four days later the Reds were in Brooklyn and things weren't quite so easy. Vander Meer walked eight batters, including three in the ninth to load the bases with one out. A grounder to third by Brooklyn's Ernie Koy forced the runner out at home, bringing up Dodger player-manager Leo Durocher. With the count 1 and 2, Durocher cracked a liner to center that Harry Craft made a shoestring catch on, preserving Vander Meer's place in history. The Cincinnati left-hander, who wound up with a career won-lost mark of 119–121, added three more no-hit innings in his next start before the string was broken.

The tension that builds during a no-hitter is heightened by baseball's unwritten law that forces the pitcher into isolation, and the dugout into silence, between innings. Even a casual mention that a no-hitter is in progress is considered a jinx. Lar-

BROOKLYN, WEDNESDAY, JUNE 15, 1938   Ptd. in U.S.A. ©NCI

VanderMeer Pitches 2 No Hitters

Brooklyn, 1938.—A crowd of 40,-000 came to see the first night baseball game in Ebbets Field. But Johnny VanderMeer, Cincinnati southpaw stole the show. Last Saturday afternoon, he had pitched a no-hit, no-run game.

Until the seventh inning, not one Dodger reached second base. In that inning VanderMeer walked Lavagetto and Dolf Camilli; when he easily pitched out of the hole. The Brooklyn crowd was cheering for him to come through.

In the eighth inning, Johnny put out the Dodgers in one, two, three order. He started the ninth easily enough by making Buddy Hassett ground out. Suddenly, VanderMeer seemed to have lost control of his fast ball. He walked Phelps, Lavagetto and Camilli to load the bases.

The crowd sat tense as Vandy pitched to Ernie Koy. The ball was hit on the ground and Phelps was forced at the plate. Leo Durocher, a good pinch hitter, was up. He hit a short fly which Harry Croft easily caught. It was all over—Cincinnati won 6 to 0, and VanderMeer had set a record—2 no-hit, no-run games in succession.

Cincinnati has been a hotbed of no-hitters and perfect games over the years. In 1988 Tom Browning (left) threw the NL's first perfect game in 23 years. Johnny Vander Meer (above) was immortalized for his two consecutive no-hitters for the 1938 Reds, but in 1947 Cincinnati's Ewell Blackwell came within two outs of duplicating Vander Meer's feat. Jim Maloney also threw three career no-hitters with the Reds, including two in 1965.

sen, a notoriously carefree personality, shocked the Yankee dugout when he came in after the seventh inning, punched Mickey Mantle playfully on the arm and asked, "Do you think I'll make it?" The superstitious silence reigned in the broadcast booth as well, as announcer Mel Allen never told listeners that Larsen was pitching a perfect game until it was over. And the Yankee right-hander himself admitted later that his playfulness was just an act: "I was so weak in the knees out there I thought I was going to faint."

Pressure can also overtake the team that's on the short end of a no-hitter. It's the ultimate humiliation, realizing that you've gone nine full innings and not even managed one lousy hit. And if it takes good luck to pitch a no-hitter, it takes bad luck to find yourself the opposing pitcher, for no matter what you do, it isn't enough. With Minnesota and Detroit, Jim Perry had to endure this fate three times—once each against California's Nolan Ryan, Oakland's Vida Blue, and Kansas City's Steve Busby.

And for every Don Larsen there is a Bill Bevens. In the 1947 World Series, Bevens, another fireballer, came within one out of pitching the first no-hitter in World Series history. Bevens won seven, lost 13 for a Yankee team that won 97 games. He had walked six men through eight innings in Game 4, and led 2–1 going into the ninth. With two out and one on, Al Gionfriddo stole second, causing Yankee manager Bucky Harris to walk Pete Reiser intentionally, even though it meant putting the winning run on base. Cookie Lavagetto came up to pinch-hit for Eddie Stanky, and on a 0–1 pitch he lined a double off the right field wall, ending both Bevens' bid for a no-hitter and the game. It was Lavagetto's last big league hit.

Rhythms and Forms

After facing an overhand or three-quarters delivery for seven or eight innings, hitters got an entirely different look from 1980s Kansas City relief ace Dan Quisenberry. And with Quisenberry's control, it was usually a short look. He walked one batter every 13 innings in 1983.

Bob Feller's blazing fastball didn't burn out in the late innings or late season. He built up his endurance on his father's Iowa farm, where as a child he'd throw every day, inside the barn during the winter. Feller (right) went on to lead the AL five times in innings pitched for Cleveland, and his 36 complete games in 1946 have not been matched since.

At 6'6" and 250 pounds, Lee Smith is the personification of power. A relief specialist who blows his 99-mph fastball by hitters for just one or two innings at a time, Smith has been successful even though he has pitched most of his games in two great hitters' parks—Wrigley Field and Fenway Park.

To throw a ball ninety miles an hour, the hand behind it must be moving the same speed. Think about it: the arm and the hand holding the ball—a yard of human bone, sinew and muscle— go from zero to ninety miles an hour in less than a tenth of a second. The hand stops; the ball flies. In sports like javelin throwing and cricket, the hurler develops speed by running toward the target. The baseball pitcher works from a standing start, giving the ball momentum out of the force of his own body movement, the energy of swivel and whip.

Throwing a ball is not just in the arm and hand. The pitching motion is a coordinated launch maneuver, from legs to hips to trunk to arm to forearm to hand to fingertips. As each body segment moves, the next picks up the speed of the one driving it and adds more speed until the ball is released.

Pitching motions are almost as individual as fingerprints. The motions of any two pitchers differ far more than the motions either one uses to throw his various pitches. Most variations occur in the stretch or first movement of a windup which sets the thrower's inner timing. Tests show that pitchers working from a stretch position can throw just as fast as from a full windup. With that in mind, most pitching coaches encourage simplicity. Gone are the days of the windmill windup. Jack Bentley, a southpaw with John McGraw's Giants of the 1920s, used to swing his arms through a series of pretzel con- volutions, succeeding mainly in tiring himself out. "When it gets to the seventh inning," Bentley admitted, "I feel the effects." Even the full arm pump, so recognizable in a pitcher like Bob Gibson, is now out of fashion. The no- windup style, introduced by Don Larsen in the 1950s and popularized by Jim Kaat in the 1970s, has become commonplace.

Today almost all pitchers start the delivery by bringing their hands to-

gether in front of the body. That simple beginning still leaves room for idiosyncratic gestures and postures. Veteran pitcher Doyle Alexander, for example, rounds his shoulders as if collapsing into himself, then pivots, raising his hands and front knee very slightly. Most pitchers bring the knee toward the upper body, but Alexander brings the upper body toward the knee—and then rocks through with a stiff—but effective—release. The Cubs' Rick Sutcliffe swings his front foot back and around until the sole faces center field, drops his right hand with the ball hooked in toward the forearm, and then uses his height to thrust down off the mound onto a front leg that remains stiff until the instant of release.

Left-handers, as usual, are unorthodox in special ways. Many, like Tommy John or John Smiley, seem to come around the front leg instead of stepping straight toward home plate. Others, like John Tudor and Sid Fernandez, still have the arm down, ball pointing at the ground, when the front foot hits, so that in the last interval before launch they have to snake the arm both up and forward. Ricky Horton does not drop his arm at all—he brings it straight back and throws like a catcher—and at the top of the delivery he actually hesitates for a split second. These herky-jerky hurlers, lefty and righty, carry on a great pitching tradition: preventing the hitter from getting an early visual lock on the ball, and disrupting his timing by creating an alternate tempo.

Ted Williams once said, "Sometimes a pitcher with bad mechanics can interfere with *my* mechanics." Williams had particular trouble with Yankee left-hander Ed Lopat, whose little tics, dips and fakes could distract the most disciplined hitter. Of course, a jerky style can also lead to sore arms or control problems. "Once one of those herks and jerks gets out of sync," Tug

An effective motion is the key to effective pitching. At right, Vida Blue, Oakland's ace left-hander in the 1970s, shows the three phases of a pitching motion: **cocking, launching** and **follow-through**. The **cocking phase** lasts the longest, about 1.5 seconds, and has the effect of winding a spring. The pitcher must avoid "opening his hips" too soon, cutting the energy of the body's swivel action. In the **launching phase**, the pitcher's compressed muscles uncoil to full extension, as the hand achieves the speed of the pitch itself, perhaps 90 mph or more. During the **follow-through**, muscles compress again, braking the violent acceleration of the arm and stabilizing the pitcher's body.

Cocking *begins when the forward leg—the left leg of a right-handed pitcher—shifts back to take the body's weight. At this point, some pitchers bring their arms above their heads, though increasingly the fashion is to rest both hands at belt-level. As the leg moves forward, hips, trunk and shoulders rotate a full 90 degrees; the front leg lifts and swings across the body. As the knee reaches its highest point, the throwing hand comes out of the glove, the throwing arm arcs backward and down and then up again before the front foot lands. The hips rotate forward, turning the trunk from hips to shoulders. The lower body—hips and legs—"opens" or turns toward the batter.*

McGraw says, "it can be hell putting the motion back together." McGraw cites three pitchers—Steve Blass, Kevin Saucier and Joe Cowley—who had to retire from baseball when, suddenly and mysteriously, they could no longer throw strikes. "They may have had psychological problems, but the fact is that none of those three guys had fluid deliveries to begin with. When a pitcher has a lot of little twitches, he has more things that can go wrong."

But there are exceptions. Relief ace Gene Garber's "little twitches" enhanced a full repertoire of off-speed stuff. Garber swiveled his pitches from a low sidearm angle, tilting his upper body down to maintain that groove. Garber was sometimes compared to the Red Sox' Luis Tiant, who used several different arm angles and a whirling style that became even more twitchy when he pitched from the stretch. It was said of Tiant that no matter where you sat in the ballpark, there was a point in his delivery when he could look you in the eye.

At the other extreme are smoothies. One of the most memorable was Oriole Jim Palmer, whose motion was so fluid and loose-jointed that it created its own distractions for hitters. Palmer's grace came from full extension of his long arms and legs, and from a symmetry that brought the glove hand far forward to balance the throwing hand reaching back. Hypnotized batters said of Palmer that "his arms and legs come at you."

Orel Hershiser is a contemporary smoothie, especially in the consistency of his arm motion. Even before the delivery, Hershiser performs a selection of little mannerisms—sweeping his right foot in front of the rubber, adjusting the bill of his cap, or wiggling an arm above his head—then takes

The launch is explosive. Once the front foot is planted and the hips open, the upper torso lets go. Hand and ball stall for an instant, then fly. The arm extends into nearly a straight line from the far shoulder, across the back, right to the fingertips. The elbow straightens, maximizing speed by extending the arm almost fully. The wrist does not actually snap as the ball is released, but the forearm has already begun to "pronate"—to turn rapidly as the fingers give spin to the ball.

In the follow-through, this pronation helps to slow the speed of hand and arm, finally braking the arm movement entirely. Upper and lower body muscles help by catching up with the arm, especially as the back leg comes forward for balance and extension. Most pitching injuries occur as a result of failure to follow-through completely. A full follow-through helps to absorb and distribute the shock of deceleration, and also puts the pitcher in a good fielding position.

the sign by standing motionless, hands to his sides, almost at attention. Hershiser completes a high knee lift by swinging the left foot back across the body—a more supple version of Rick Sutcliffe's leg motion—and as he rotates toward home that front foot becomes a trigger, springing the hips open as it hits the ground.

Smoothies are usually long and lean. And because a longer arm is a more efficient lever, they are often power pitchers. The best example is Walter Johnson, who had a whipcord body, 6′1″ and 190 pounds, with a remarkable arm span of $78\frac{1}{2}$ inches. Johnson could sit erect in a chair with his elbows resting on his lap. In 1913, as part of *Baseball Magazine's* special study of speed pitching, he was tested and measured in detail. The study concluded that "Johnson has the ideal pitcher's arm, long, sinuous, with a wiry strength which in no wise impairs its celerity of movement."

Johnson had such an easy motion, Detroit's Sam Crawford said, that he looked as if he were just playing catch. "That's what threw you off. He threw so nice and easy—and then *swoosh*, and it was by you!" Johnson came sidearm, lunging forward slightly as he released the ball. He claimed that this "buggy whip" delivery had always been his natural style: "If I should rear back in the box as Dazzy Vance does and swing overhanded, I doubt if I could pitch at all." Grover Cleveland Alexander, the great Phillies' and Cubs' star of the 1910s and 1920s, also used a sidearm motion, one so simplified that it was close to the modern no-windup delivery.

Throwing sidearm may actually subtract one or two miles per hour from the fastball, and it imposes a slight additional strain on the elbow. But it is much easier on the shoulder, especially at the rotator cuff, and baseball folklore claims that "sidearmers last longer."

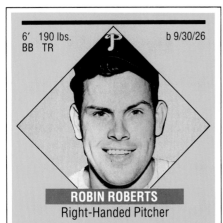

6′ 190 lbs.   b 9/30/26
BB   TR

ROBIN ROBERTS
Right-Handed Pitcher

The key to life and pitching, according to Robin Roberts, was to keep things "real simple." "There's a fine line between winning a game and putting on a show." For Roberts, winning was enough, and he took the mound every fourth day—sometimes more often—and gave his teams a chance to win and the bullpen a chance to rest. Roberts won 286 games, despite playing for just one pennant-winner in 19 years.

A $25,000 "bonus baby" in 1948, Roberts became the ace of Philadelphia's 1950 Whiz Kids at the age of 23. The Phillies rode his strong arm, live fastball and outstanding control down the stretch against the Dodgers, and he started three of the season's last five games. In a ten-inning thriller on the season's final day, Roberts won 2–1 to clinch the pennant for the Phillies, then lost his only World Series start to the Yankees, 2–1 in ten innings.

From 1950 to 1956, Roberts won more games than any pitcher in baseball, averaging 22 wins per season. He walked an average of just 1.7 hitters per nine innings during his career. Roberts was also the most durable pitcher of his time. He led the NL in starts from 1950 to 1955, complete games from 1952 to 1956, innings pitched from 1951 to 1956, and wins from 1952 to 1955. His finest season was 1952, as he went 28–7 with a 2.59 ERA, 30 complete games and just 45 walks in 330 innings.

"I was never impressive as a pitcher," Roberts said. "I just got them out."

Throughout his 20-year career, Tom Seaver provided a textbook example of proper pitching mechanics. He wasted no motion, and his low and powerful leg drive made his right knee dirty and famous. He won 311 games and three Cy Young Awards.

A special technique of classically smooth pitching is the "drop and drive" style. Unlike Jim Palmer, who held both back and front legs fairly straight, right-hander Robin Roberts seemed to thrust himself down and straight at the hitter by bending his back leg and landing on a flexed or "collapsed" front leg. After an inning or so, Roberts' right knee was usually dirty from hitting the ground.

Tom Seaver's dirty right knee became famous, and he checked it to make sure he was throwing correctly. In fact, with the New York Mets in the late 1960s and early 1970s, Seaver was the anchor of a whole drop-and-drive pitching staff—Jerry Koosman, Tug McGraw and Nolan Ryan. The great longevity of this foursome—each of whom pitched at least 19 major league seasons—suggests that they were doing something fundamentally sound. The drop-and-drive method permeated the Mets' organization, from general manager Johnny Murphy—who had been the Yankees' relief ace in the 1930s and 1940s—to pitching coach Rube Walker and even to the scouts, who began to look for that certain kind of amateur pitcher.

Dropping and driving was supposed to maximize speed and, more importantly, to alleviate strain on the throwing shoulder during follow-through. If a pitcher lands on a stiff front leg, Seaver says, his arm is likely to coil back on itself, to "bullwhip," at the end of the pitching motion. By contrast, a flexible front leg allows the throwing arm to arc easily to the outside, providing extra space and time for deceleration. The pivot foot acts as a brace to begin a strong hip rotation, and the move toward home is less a push than a natural fall, gaining mechanical advantage by moving from high to low. The most distinctive feature of this technique is a long stride, which brings the back knee down automatically. Jerry Koosman, 6′2″, had a pitching stride of over five

feet. The method itself is well exemplified today by Bret Saberhagen and by a one-of-a-kind hurler named Nolan Ryan, who entered the 1989 season throwing smoke at 42.

Among the most memorable pitching stylists have been the high kickers, with knee raises that keep on going, sometimes until the toe of the front foot is higher than the head. Such a motion can add momentum as the pitcher moves toward launch, but it can also create new problems. "Few pitchers," Carl Hubbell once observed, "are able to kick the foot high and still have control." Another liability may be poor fielding position on follow-through.

A high kick is often the pitcher's individual solution to a universal problem of throwing: how to synchronize the top and bottom halves of the body. Typically, the bottom half moves a little faster, and some pitchers must find a way to slow it down and reset the timing of the delivery. In the history of pitching, two men—Warren Spahn of the Braves and Juan Marichal of the Giants—made the kick into a Hall of Fame art form. Both used it for deception as well as for leverage. Both were able to maintain superb control. Both threw overhand, and the high kick gave their arms more time to get on top of the pitch. Both were only average height, but their dynamic deliveries made them look like giants on the mound.

Spahn perfected his motion in boyhood, through endless games of catch with his father. His windup began with a big arm pump, swinging both hands back dramatically to head height. In mid-delivery he hid the ball behind a straight front leg, but that leg flexed rapidly and led into a graceful drop-and-drive launch. Spahn's follow-through was perfectly balanced, and

San Francisco's Juan Marichal threw a one-hitter against Philadelphia in his first major league start on July 19, 1960. Marichal had great velocity and movement, the highest leg kick in baseball, and a killer instinct. "Put your club a run ahead in the late innings," said Giants' manager Alvin Dark, "and there's no better pitcher in baseball."

Facing Rich "Goose" Gossage in the 1970s and 1980s was downright scary. The 6'3", 226-pound right-hander glared at hitters, then reared far back to unleash a rising fastball once measured at 99.5 mph.

he ended his motion in perfect fielding position. Not surprisingly, for 21 seasons he remained one of the best fielders in the game.

Marichal kicked higher than Spahn but with less backward tilt and a distinctive whirling effect. When Marichal rotated away from the plate, batters caught sight of the big Number 27 on the back of his uniform, then had to locate a ball that seemed to come from somewhere between Marichal's left knee and the sky. Unlike Spahn, Marichal landed somewhat stiffly, falling toward first base, and he was only an average fielder. But his delivery generated speed without sacrificing control, and his ratio of strikeouts to walks was outstanding. In 1963, for example, Marichal pitched $321\frac{1}{3}$ innings, striking out 248 and walking 61.

"In the early stages of my career," Bob Feller says, "I used an extraordinarily high left leg kick, but I gave it up. It tended to destroy balance and it added little speed, if any." Feller didn't need more speed. He was one of the fastest pitchers ever to toe a rubber, the kind of power pitcher that might be called an "exploder."

Feller says that the only contemporary pitcher whose motion resembles his own is Goose Gossage. But Dwight Gooden and Lee Smith use similar power principles, as did the big pitchers of the 1960s—Jim Bunning, Don Drysdale and Bob Gibson. They all catapult the ball toward home plate by extremely powerful hip and torso rotation, and they tend to drop to a three-quarter arm angle so that the motion has less "whip" and more "pull." This leads to an unorthodox follow-through, as in the sweeping fall of a Gibson or a Bunning toward first base.

Feller's body was what used to be called "country strong." He grew up on an Iowa farm and, like Walter Johnson and Grover Cleveland Alexander,

For 21 years NL hitters had to face the swirling motion and varied pitches of Warren Spahn. The Braves' left-hander pitched his first no-hitter at the age of 39, and at 42 he went 23–7. "I don't think Spahn will ever get into the Hall of Fame," said Cardinal great Stan Musial. "He'll never stop pitching."

had spent much of his youth pitching hay and digging post holes. He was a "chesty" pitcher whose three-quarter motion was especially intimidating to right-handed hitters. One such hitter was George Case, who stood in against Feller in 1937 when that "big rawboned kid" was 18 years old. "He'd scare the hell out of you," Case said. "He had a little nervous twitch in his eyes and he'd stand out there on that mound with those eyes twitching and you'd be up there saying to yourself, 'I hope the son of a gun sees me all right.' "

Compared to these pitchers, Sandy Koufax was an "imploder." His back leg and throwing arm were so coiled in mid-delivery that he seemed to compress the energy stored in his own body. Koufax's arm angle was unusually high, especially for a left-hander, and he whipped the arm through with exceptional torque and thrust. The follow-through was smooth, a continuous downward sweep over a flexible front leg, but his extra momentum often left Koufax in poor fielding position. The torsion in Koufax's delivery put strain on the elbow, where pressure eventually broke down tissue and contributed to "traumatic arthritis," diagnosed in 1964 by Dr. Robert Kerlan, a pioneer in sports medicine. For the next two years it was medicated with cortisone, ice and prayer.

Koufax retired at the end of the 1966 season, 30 years old. His last two years of pain, swelling and courage were among the most magnificent seasons in all of pitching. In 1965 and 1966 Koufax won 26 and 27 games, respectively, and the Dodgers won two pennants. He had 82 starts, completed 54, and didn't miss a single turn in the rotation. He usually pitched with three days rest, but he won Game 7 of the 1965 Series with only two. Even in pain, Koufax did not compromise his dynamic motion. He remained a power

HALL OF FAME

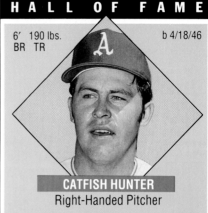

6' 190 lbs.
BR TR

b 4/18/46

CATFISH HUNTER
Right-Handed Pitcher

Upon his graduation from high school in 1965, Jim Hunter was approached by the Kansas City Athletics. Hunter asked for a Thunderbird and the same contract as Blue Moon Odom. Instead, he received $75,000 and a nickname to outlast the money.

Catfish Hunter was one of the most consistent pitchers of his era. For five consecutive seasons, 1971 to 1975, Hunter won 20 or more games, including 13 straight in 1973. From 1970–76, he averaged 21 wins a year. In 1974, in his tenth season with the Athletics, Hunter led the league with 25 wins and a 2.49 ERA en route to the Cy Young Award. In 1975, his first of five seasons with the Yankees, he led the American League with 23 wins, 30 complete games, and 328 innings pitched. His winning percentages of .750 and .808 were the league's best in 1972 and 1973, respectively.

Hunter's pitching philosophy remained the same throughout his career. By "just letting them hit it," Hunter won 224 major league games in 15 seasons. On May 8, 1968, not a Twin "hit it," and Hunter, at the age of 23, became one of the youngest pitchers in history to pitch a perfect game. Hunter was no slouch as a hitter, and in 1971 he became the last AL pitcher ever to hit .300 and win 20 games in the same year.

Hunter won four World Series games for the 1972, 1973 and 1974 world champion Oakland Athletics and a fifth for the Yankees in 1978. Those five Series wins rank eighth on the all-time list.

pitcher to the end, coiling and whipping in the same implosive style. In 1965 he pitched a perfect game—his fourth career no-hitter—and set a new record by striking out 382 batters; the next year he whiffed another 317. In those last two years, his ratio of strikeouts to walks was almost 5 to 1, and his ERA was 1.87.

Koufax redefined an old baseball expression: "pitching with pain." He went out blazing because he knew his arthritic condition was incurable, and because—like most pitchers of his generation—he believed in a traditional code of endurance. "We didn't baby our arms," said Warren Spahn, who pitched in the major leagues for 21 years. "A sore arm is like a headache or a toothache. It can make you feel bad, but if you just forget about it and do what you have to do, it will go away. If you really like to pitch and want to pitch, that's what you'll do." Spahn was talking about "natural" soreness—the stiffness that persists for several days after sustained pitching.

Tough as he was, even Spahn would never have ignored chronic tendinitis, or an impingement of the elbow or shoulder, or a soreness severe enough to alter his pitching motion. He was all too aware of other National League pitchers of his day, like Curt Simmons or Don Newcombe, who ruined their arms by trying to pitch through pain.

Sparky Lyle, the Yankee relief ace of the late 1970s, disagreed with the conventional wisdom that pitchers should arrive early at spring training and only gradually start to throw harder. "I like to go down there late, throw as hard as I can the first day, and get the adhesions broken. My arm is sore for a few days, but after that I'm ready to throw in a game." An adhesion is the sticking together of separate muscle tissues after a period of disuse. Lyle said that it took him less than three weeks to rebuild the strength in his left arm

A group of four muscles holds the human arm snugly in the shoulder socket. Together these muscles guide and control the arm's internal rotation, fine tuning all overhand motion from a scratch of the head to a swimming stroke. All four muscles, three at the back of the shoulder and one at the front, taper into broad, flat tendons that form a single fibrous sheath, or cuff, around the ball at the top of the upper arm bone.

The rotator cuff makes baseball pitching possible. It is at once a stabilizer and a shock absorber, directing the whip of the hurler's arm at 85 mph and then slowing it to a smooth stop. The rotator cuff is strong yet delicate. Heavy and repeated strain can cause inflammation, swelling, pinching within the shoulder joint, or actual tearing of tissue.

Whereas curveball specialists are more likely to have elbow problems, rotator cuff injuries are the bane of hard-throwing fastball pitchers. The pitching careers of Mel Stottlemyre, Don Drysdale, Ron Perranoski, Jim Bibby, Don Gullett and

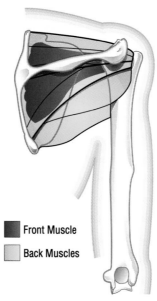

RIGHT SHOULDER BACK VIEW

■ Front Muscle

□ Back Muscles

Steve Busby were all cut short by damage to the rotator cuff.

Busby was a Kansas City Royals' phenom in 1973 and 1974, hurling two no-hitters and winning 38 games. The following year he experienced "a gradual erosion process in the back of the right shoulder." Busby pitched through the pain, won another 18 games, and never appeared in the majors again. He was 25.

Dr. Frank Jobe, who operated on Busby, says that full recovery is rare after a major tear in the cuff, because the injury usually means permanent deterioration of the shoulder socket. The surgeon can relieve pain, but he may not be able to improve the hurler's range of motion. Jobe, who does rotator cuff surgery, stresses prevention: "The rotator cuff needs to be cared for separately, with different kinds of exercises from those done for the arm." Tom Seaver believes that such a program, based on exercises using light weights and slow stretches, added years to his career.

Sandy Koufax (opposite) endured great pain from an arthritic elbow that ended a brilliant pitching career after 12 years. When he tried to bend his arm the day after he pitched, Koufax said it "sounded as if I were squeezing a soggy sponge."

for his money pitch, the slider, and he was annoyed that spring training lasted twice that long. "John McGraw said it should be six weeks, so it's six weeks. But McGraw's been dead for fifty years."

McGraw managed in the major leagues from 1899 to 1932. For the first two decades of his career, before the introduction of the lively ball, his pitchers could pace themselves through a game. With little fear of the home run, they would bear down only with men on base. Christy Mathewson called it "pitching in a pinch." Modern mound strategy, based on the availability of relief pitchers, dictates that a starter throw hard for as long as he can. That makes him far more likely to rupture tiny blood vessels and muscle fibers in the throwing arm. To reduce swelling and hemorrhaging, he may have the arm in ice for as long as 30 minutes after a game. "A pitcher's life," says sportswriter Tom Boswell, "is one day of deliberate self-injury, followed by three days of healing, then a fresh injury."

Specialists in sports medicine sometimes describe overhand pitching as "an unnatural act." They point out that an underhand delivery is really more natural, whereas overhand hurling creates a whipping effect so extreme that the arm assumes positions impossible to reproduce when it is stationary. In a deeper sense, the act of pitching is supremely natural. The motions of pitchers from Walter Johnson to Lew Burdette to Nolan Ryan are mirrored in any child's intuitive way of throwing rocks or dirt clods. At the heart of pitching is a functional elegance in the individual style of each pitcher's delivery. Baseball is a game wonderfully open to the eye, and its action always begins at the center of the diamond in the rhythms and forms of the hurler. ◗

Dizzy Dean

Dizzy Dean never made it past the third grade, but in the 1930s he taught the game of baseball a thing or two about pitching, self-promotion and the English language. How great Dean might have been had he not tried to come back too soon after an injury in 1937 is impossible to predict, but from 1932 to 1937 he was one of the the National League's best pitchers, and hands down baseball's most colorful personality.

Born Jay Hanna Dean in Lucas, Arkansas in 1911, Dizzy won 25 games—for two minor league teams—in 1930, his first pro season in the Cardinal organization. Relying on a rising fastball, a hard curve and excellent control, Dean excelled in the minors, and all the while kept Cardinal general manager Branch Rickey informed of his progress by mail, signing his letters "The Great Dean."

Dizzy did finally make it to the majors late in 1930, and gave up just one run and three hits in a complete-game win for St. Louis. But he was back in the minors in 1931, and responded with a 26–10 mark, a 1.57 ERA and 303 strikeouts. The following year he opened the season with the Cardinals, and stayed, winning 18 games and leading the league in innings pitched with 286, and in strikeouts with 191. His strikeout total was the highest by a National League rookie since Grover Cleveland Alexander struck out 227 in 1911, and he went on to lead the NL in strikeouts in his first four years in the majors. And Dean, while an affable personality, was an intimidating pitcher. When hitters dug in against him, he would yell in, "That's right, podnuh, dig a nice big hole up there so they can bury you."

In 1933 Dean had the first of four straight seasons with 20 or more wins. He led the NL in complete games with 26 and struck out 199. Against the Cubs on July 30, 1933, he struck out 17 batters, at the time a 20th-century record for strikeouts in a nine-inning game, but still the team could do no better than fifth.

In 1934, things were different. Dean exploded as a pitcher and a personality, his younger brother Paul joined the club, and the Cardinals—with talent like shortstop Leo Durocher, third baseman Pepper Martin and left fielder Ducky Medwick—became the Gashouse Gang. Dean, who always said "it ain't braggin' if yuh can do it," made some bold predictions a month before the season started. He said that he had sat down with pencil and paper and figured out that the Cardinals would win the pennant. "It will require 95 games to win the pennant, and the [defending champion] Giants can't take that many. That's why we will win," Dean said. He also predicted that he and Paul would combine for between 45 and 50 wins. He was right.

Dean opened the season with a six-hit win against Pittsburgh. The Cardinals kept on playing well, but stayed behind the Giants and Cubs late into the summer. Throughout the season Dean and Pepper Martin spread a litany of practical jokes across the country, one of the simplest of which was rigging smoke bombs in a row of limousines outside the team's hotel.

On August 24 Dean shut out the Giants and stole a base in a 5–0 win that vaulted St. Louis past the Cubs into second place. On September 28—with only two days rest—Dean won his 29th, blanking Cincinnati 4–0, taking the Cards into a tie for first with the Giants. The next day, Paul beat Cincinnati 6–1 for his 19th win, and on the last day of the season, Dizzy, pitching with just one day of rest, shut out Cincinnati again, earning his 30th win and clinching the pennant for St. Louis.

Dean and the Cardinals strode confidently into the World Series against Mickey Cochrane's Detroit Tigers. "We're gonna win," he said as the team's train left for Detroit. And in Game 1 the Cardinals did win, 8–3, behind Dizzy's eight-hit complete game. After Detroit won Game 2, Paul led the Cards to a 4–1 win in St. Louis. Detroit beat Tex

Everything about Dean was exaggerated, including his leg kick. "Anybody who's had the privilege of seein' me play ball knows that I am the greatest pitcher in the world," Dean said.

DIZZY DEAN

Right-Handed Pitcher
St. Louis Cardinals 1930, 1932-1937
Chicago Cubs 1938-1941
St. Louis Browns 1947
Hall of Fame 1953

GAMES	317
INNINGS	
Career	1,966⅓
Season High	324⅓
WINS	
Career	150
Season High	30
LOSSES	
Career	83
Season High	18
WINNING PERCENTAGE	
Career	.644
Season High	.875
ERA	
Career	3.03
Season Low	1.81
GAMES STARTED	
Career	230
Season High	36
COMPLETE GAMES	
Career	154
Season High	29
SHUTOUTS	
Career	26
Season High	7
STRIKEOUTS	
Career	1,155
Season High	199
WALKS	
Career	458
Season High	102
WORLD SERIES	1934,1938
MOST VALUABLE PLAYER	1934

Carleton 10–4 in Game 4, and manager Frankie Frisch made a move that almost wound up costing the Cardinals the Series. Frisch sent Dizzy in as a pinch-runner in the fourth. Pepper Martin grounded to short, and when Dean came in to break up the double play standing up, second baseman Bill Rogell's relay throw cracked into Dizzy's skull. "The great Dizzy crumpled and fell like a marionette whose string had snapped," wrote Grantland Rice, and Dizzy spent the night in the hospital. The next day's headline said, X-RAY OF DEAN'S HEAD REVEALS NOTHING.

Remarkably, Dizzy started the next day, but lost 3–1 and the Tigers took a 3–2 lead in the Series. Paul came back in Game 6 to out-duel School-boy Rowe 4–3, sending the Series to a seventh game, and afterward the Dean brothers demanded that Frisch allow one or both of them to pitch Game 7. "This is a family matter," Dizzy said. So for the third time in seven days, Dizzy took the mound to start Game 7. And in the most lopsided Game 7 in Series history, he blanked Detroit on six hits and the Cardinals drilled six Tiger pitchers for 17 hits and an 11–0 win.

Dean won 28 in 1935 and 24 in 1936, but in the 1937 All-Star Game he was struck on the toe by a line drive off the bat of Earl Averill. Told by a doctor his toe was fractured, Dean replied, "Fractured, hell, the damn thing's broke." Dean came back too soon after the injury, and in changing his motion to compensate for his broken toe, he ruined his arm, and finished the season at 13–10. At the beginning of the 1938 season, Dean was traded to the Cubs for three players and $185,000, and while he didn't pitch often in Chicago, he pitched very well. Late in the season, even though Dean's arm was sore and he hadn't started a game for a month, Cub manager Gabby Street picked Dean to pitch the opener of a critical three-game series against Pittsburgh. Dizzy responded with a 2-1 win, and the Cubs went on to win the pennant. "I banked on his heart," Street said. "I knew they wouldn't scare him." Dean finished the season with a 7–1 record and a 1.81 ERA.

Dean pitched sparingly until his release in mid-May of 1941, then began a broadcasting career that lasted for 17 years. With his colorful vocabulary and country charm, Dean was an instant success on the airwaves, and spoke of batters who

"swang," runners who "slud" into bases, and pitchers who "throwed" the ball. In 1947, after Dean joked about how bad the St. Louis Browns were, president Bill DeWitt challenged him to get on the mound and do better, so as a publicity stunt, Dizzy pitched four innings against the White Sox on the final day of the season. Despite being quite a bit heavier than in his playing days, he shut them out, but had to leave the game when, after pounding a line drive deep to left, he pulled his hamstring rounding first base.

Although he won just 150 games in his career, Dean was elected to the Hall of Fame in 1953. He is credited as having turned in the NL's last 30-win season, a landmark achievement that many say got Dean into the Hall. In reality Dean didn't win 30 games in 1934. He was given credit for a win after coming in as a reliever with the Cardinals already ahead. The official scorer gave Dizzy the win, and so in the record books it says he won 30.

But for six years he was brilliant. He gave baseball a unique spark, and drove Branch Rickey to distraction in the process. "If there was one more like him," Rickey said, "I'd get out of the game."

The Dean brothers returned to St. Louis in style after combining for all four wins in the Cardinals' seven-game 1934 World Series victory over Detroit. Paul is at left in the back seat of the car, Dizzy is at right, and in the middle is Dizzy's wife, Pat.

Carl Hubbell may have been baseball's best pitcher in the mid-1930s, but Dizzy Dean was its most marketable commodity. A watch was just a small piece of the promotional packaging of Old Diz.

WILD PITCH

The Balancing Act

Baseball games are duels on several levels. Pitchers challenge the batters on every pitch, while dueling each other inning after inning. The heart of the game is the contest between pitcher and batter, and as the game has changed over the decades, the advantage of being at the plate or on the mound has regularly tilted in favor of one or the other.

In the original baseball rules drafted in 1845 by Alexander Cartwright for New York's Knickerbocker Club, the job of the "feeder" was to help the batter put the ball in play. From a pitching box 45 feet from the hitter, he was required to use a smooth underhand delivery with no wrist snap, and to pitch "for the bat." To thwart the batter through deception or brute power was considered unsporting.

All very nice for gentlemen's sporting clubs, but amateur ball had become serious business even before the Civil War. The next generation of hurlers began to rely on finesse and change of speed. Some, like Harry Wright, who organized and managed one of baseball's first professional teams, the Cincinnati Red Stockings of 1869, were experienced cricket bowlers noted for "dodgy" techniques. Wright was especially good at varying pace and location, teasing the batter with faster pitches away from the plate, then tossing an arching "dewdrop" as a change of pace.

In 1860 the Brooklyn Excelsiors paid cash for the services of young Jim Creighton, who had perfected a baffling "twist" delivery that imparted extra speed and spin. Purists objected that his motion, incorporating a subtle wrist

Control was less of a factor for a pitcher in baseball's early years (opposite). In 1880, for example, pitches were thrown underhand and wherever the batter wanted, and it took eight called balls to produce one walk.

Even in death, pitcher Jim Creighton (top, center) dominated the baseball landscape, as this print from the November 4, 1865 edition of Leslie's *magazine illustrates. Creighton's wrist snap so changed the nature of pitching that after his death in 1862 some clubs adopted his name.*

Ace underhand pitcher A.G. Spalding (above) had a pretty good year in 1876. After jumping from Boston of the National Association to Chicago of the National League, he won 47 games and managed the team to the pennant. He also announced the opening of his sporting goods company, which flourishes today.

snap, was illegal, but umpires allowed it. The Excelsiors dominated baseball in the Northeast, and Creighton became one of the game's first heroes, and its first martyr. In October 1862 he somehow "strained himself" hitting a home run, suffered through two days of internal bleeding, and died at 21.

Shutouts were so rare in the 1860s that Creighton became famous for the few he hurled. Baseball of that era—combining underhand pitching, high scoring, and bare-handed fielding—was a lot like modern amateur softball. On June 18, 1868, for example, Harvard University defeated the Lowell Club of Boston 39–28. The box score notes 71 errors, but many of the miscues resulted from interference by the huge crowd. Both pitchers went the distance, giving up a total of 48 hits and one walk. Henry Chadwick, the first true baseball writer, honored in his own lifetime as "Father of the Game," called it "the finest played game we ever witnessed in New England."

The Boston Red Stockings, managed by the same Harry Wright, were champions of the National Association for four of its five seasons, 1871 to 1875. Boston's premier pitcher was a strapping midwesterner named Albert Goodwill Spalding. According to one sportswriter, Spalding had developed "a peculiar manner of delivering the ball to the batsman suddenly, calculating to bother or deceive him." He recorded 207 victories in five seasons, finishing 57–5 in 1875.

In 1876 Spalding went 47–12 and pitched Chicago to a pennant, but ambition led him elsewhere. At 26 he founded the sporting goods business that still bears his name, obtaining a monopoly on supplying official balls for the league and publishing its annual log, *Spalding's Official Base Ball Guide.*

You needed a *Guide* if you wanted to keep up with the rules, which were in constant turmoil, evolving through trial and error toward a livelier game

Alexander Joy Cartwright — shown in the back row center of this 1846 metal-backed daguerreotype — is often called the father of modern baseball. Cartwright founded the Knickerbocker Base Ball Club, and his Knickerbocker Rules, written in 1845 and adopted by many clubs, established the nine-inning game, 90-foot baselines and the fixed batting order.

based on speed, precision, and offensive/defensive balance. Legalizing the wrist snap in 1872 led to development of the curveball, which changed the very nature of the war between pitcher and hitter. Moving the front edge of the pitcher's box to 50 feet from home plate in 1881 helped batters. Allowing an overhand delivery in 1884 tipped the scales again toward pitching.

Similar tinkering led to redefinition of the strike zone, the number of balls required for a walk, and the dimensions of the pitching box. Complaints about such changes were minimal. Players and officials seemed to accept that baseball was evolving toward the fulfillment of a natural form.

Strong pitching dominated play in the early 1890s. In 1892, for example, the league batting average was .245, league ERA was 3.28, and six hurlers won 30 or more games. Among them were the two big fastballers of the decade, right-handers Denton True "Cy" Young of Cleveland and New York's Amos Rusie. While Young was a brilliant control artist, Rusie remained a wild intimidator. In four seasons Rusie led the NL in both strikeouts and walks. Known as "The Hoosier Thunderbolt," he was a big man at 6'1" and 200 lbs., with short, powerful arms. His delivery was "a simple piston motion," said sportswriter Hugh Fullerton. "Rusie just swung back and threw, and defied anyone to guess whether it was a fastball or a curve."

I n 1893 rulemakers tried to restore offensive balance by eliminating the pitcher's box, and requiring the pitcher to throw with his foot touching a hard rubber slab 60'6" from home plate. The results were immediate. Batting averages rose about 14 percent, league ERA rose 30 percent, and strikeouts fell 44 percent. Young and Rusie still won games at the new distance but, like every other pitcher in the league, they worked fewer innings.

Amos Rusie's blistering fastball was no fun to hit or to catch. Richard Buckley, Rusie's catcher with the New York Giants in the 1890s, wrapped a piece of lead and a sponge in a handkerchief, and put it in his mitt to dull the sting of Rusie's fastball.

The 1911 World Series was a rematch of the 1905 Series between Connie Mack's Athletics and John McGraw's Giants, and no one was neutral. Game 1, a pitching showdown between Philadelphia's Chief Bender and New York's Christy Mathewson, drew a Series-record 38,281 fans to the Polo Grounds (above). Mathewson beat Bender 2–1, but the A's won the Series in six games.

At once, teams had to add more arms. In fact, the most lasting effect of the longer distance was development of the modern pitching staff. That and a burst of new pitches, a new kind of ball, new fielding tactics, and more rule changes once again swung the pendulum back toward the mound.

By the turn of the century, the screwball, then called a "fadeaway," had arrived, notably in the repertoire of Christy Mathewson of the New York Giants. A few years later came two aerodynamic wonders, the knuckleball and spitball. The "damp delivery" did well in the slick fingers of Jack Chesbro, 41 victories for the New York Highlanders in 1904, and Ed Walsh, 40 in 1908 for the White Sox. It was a legal pitch until 1920.

Until 1910 the standard Spalding baseball had a rubber core. A cork-centered model was introduced to revive hitting, but by modern standards it was still a dead ball. Pitchers retained the edge, not because of the ball's insides, but its exterior. It was hard to see. "Pitchers would use dirt and tobacco juice and licorice and make the ball as black as your hat," recalled Lefty O'Doul, who began his professional career during World War I. A ball was almost certain to be scuffed, because only three or four balls were used in the course of a typical game. Only *one* ball was used during a full nine-inning contest between the Dodgers and Cardinals on August 15, 1908. "It looked as if I would have to take it out in the eighth inning," umpire Bill Klem said, "but I saw the ball was game and always coming back for more."

Pitchers were also getting more support on the field, with better gloves and better groundskeeping. After 1900, the catcher was coming into his own. Officially required to work close behind the batter, and shielded by mask, shin guards, and a chest protector, the catcher was more than ever the pitcher's collaborator. Foul bunts and caught foul tips counted as strikes

In what turned out to be one of the most lopsided trades ever, Cincinnati got Amos Rusie from New York in exchange for the rights to Christy Mathewson (left) in 1900. Rusie never won another game in the majors, while Mathewson went on to win 373 for the Giants.

Enlarged from original photograph, © by International News Service, N. Y.

CHRISTY MATHEWSON

Rube Waddell

George Edward "Rube" Waddell had as much raw talent as anyone who ever toed a pitching rubber. Connie Mack, Waddell's manager with Philadelphia from 1902 to 1907 and a man with 64 years of baseball experience, said Waddell "had more natural stuff than any other pitcher I've seen, the best combination of speed and curve." The problem was, Waddell found too many things he liked better than playing baseball, and often he'd be doing them when he was supposed to be on the mound.

Waddell liked to fish, hunt, drink, tend bar, chase fire trucks, and lead parades. He was probably the most undependable pitcher in the game's history. Once he showed up ten minutes before the start of a game in which he was scheduled to pitch. "I'm sorry, Mr. Mack," he said. "I was umpiring this game between some 12-year-olds, and I kinda forgot what time it was."

Waddell once left the mound in the middle of an inning and raced over the center field fence in pursuit of a fire truck. Another time he was missing for three days and turned up leading a parade down Broad Street, Philadelphia, twirling a baton. Whether Waddell was merely a man of simple tastes and childlike pleasures, a drunken buffoon, or the unfortunate victim of some mental deficiency depends on whose account you read. What no one argues about, however, is how good he was at making hitters miss.

In 1903 Waddell became the first man to strike out 300 batters, and the following season he struck out 349, a record that stood for 61 years. He led the American League in strikeouts from 1902 to 1907, and on July 2, 1902, he became the first pitcher in recorded history to strike out the side on nine pitches.

What makes Waddell's strikeout totals all the more exceptional is that he pitched in the dead-ball era, when most hitters were contact hitters. Waddell's lifetime average of 7.04 strikeouts per nine innings is 13th on the all-time list, but he is the only one among the top 20 to have pitched before 1950. He was the first ever to fan 16 batters in a game, and in 70 games he struck out ten or more, a feat that ties him with Tom Seaver for sixth on the all-time list.

Born into a poor farm family in Bradford, Pennsylvania, in 1876, Waddell's strikeout feats as a teenager soon gained him attention from big-league scouts. He signed with Louisville of the National League in 1897, but pitched in just two games before one of his disappearing acts landed him in the minors at Detroit. But when the Detroit manager fined him $50 for some offense, Waddell packed his bag and left on a whirlwind tour of major and minor league teams in the U.S. and Canada.

Waddell moved around so much between 1897 and 1902 that no two accounts of his travels match up. He spent time in the majors with Louisville, Pittsburgh and the Chicago Cubs. He played for Connie Mack in Milwaukee of the Western League in 1900, but pitched so well—winning ten of 13 decisions—that Pittsburgh demanded him back. He began the 1902 season with Los Angeles of the Pacific Coast League. Mack, by then manager of the Philadelphia Athletics, convinced Waddell to come east, and sent two Pinkerton detectives to make sure he didn't get lost along the way.

It was with the Athletics that Waddell pitched his way into the Hall of Fame. He was an instant star in 1902, going 24–7 with a 2.05 ERA and a league-high 210 strikeouts, as Philadelphia went from fourth place to first, despite losing star second baseman Napoleon Lajoie to Cleveland. Waddell won ten games in the month of July, an unprecedented

In order to keep Rube Waddell out of trouble in the off-season, the St. Louis Browns hired him in 1908 to hunt game. Waddell got a paycheck and a chance to hunt, and Browns' officials got duck, venison and other game for their tables.

and still unmatched feat. He averaged 22 wins from 1902 to 1907, and his ERA never climbed above 2.44. Though this was the most stable period of Waddell's career, it was far from uneventful.

Money, marriage and alcohol were always problems for Waddell. In 1905 he sat out the World Series, claiming to have hurt his arm tripping over a suitcase. Allegations were made, however, that he was bribed $17,000—of which he reportedly received only $500—not to play. He married three times and spent several stints in jail for failure to pay alimony. In 1903, disciplinary fines—including $1,000 for breaking a non-drinking pledge in his contract—and loans for alimony payments equaled more than his annual salary.

The most famous story about Waddell tells of his calling in his outfielders and infielders, and having them sit down on the grass around him while he struck out the side on nine pitches. While he never did it in a major league game, it was one of his favorite stunts during the many exhibition games he pitched.

How great Waddell might have been had he taken a more serious approach to the game is unknown, but baseball historian Bill James ventured a guess. "Rube Waddell would have been as great a pitcher as Walter Johnson if only he had the sense God give a rabbit."

RUBE
WADDELL

Left-Handed Pitcher
Louisville Eclipses 1897, 1899
Pittsburgh Pirates 1900–1901
Chicago Cubs 1901
Philadelphia Athletics 1902–1907
St. Louis Browns 1908–1910
Hall of Fame 1946

GAMES	**407**
INNINGS	
Career	**2,961⅓**
Season High	**383**
WINS	
Career	**191**
Season High	**26**
LOSSES	
Career	**145**
Season High	**19**
WINNING PERCENTAGE	
Career	**.568**
Season High	**.778**
ERA	
Career *(6th all time)*	**2.16**
Season Low	**1.48**
GAMES STARTED	
Career	**340**
Season High	**46**
COMPLETE GAMES	
Career	**261**
Season High	**39**
SHUTOUTS	
Career	**50**
Season High	**8**
STRIKEOUTS	
Career	**2,316**
Season High *(4th all time)*	**349**
WALKS	
Career	**803**
Season High	**92**

6'3" 180 lbs. b 10/09/1889
BB TL d 6/1/80

RUBE MARQUARD
Left-Handed Pitcher

In 1908 the New York Giants outbid several other clubs for the services of 19-year-old southpaw Rube Marquard. Labeled "the $11,000 beauty" for the record price his contract demanded, Marquard proceeded to go 5–13 in his first full season, changing his label to "the $11,000 lemon."

With considerable help from coach and mentor Wilbert Robinson, Marquard finally silenced his critics in 1911 with a 24–7 record and a league-leading 237 strikeouts. He combined with Christy Mathewson to lead the Giants to the first of three straight pennants, and he averaged 24 wins from 1911 to 1913. The rangy Marquard had a blazing fastball, which Chicago shortstop Joe Tinker described this way: "You can't hit what you can't see."

In 1912 Marquard won his first 19 decisions, matching the major league record set 24 years earlier by the Giants' Tim Keefe. Marquard actually won 20 straight, but was denied a win in relief by rules that existed then. He finished the season at 26–11 with a 2.57 ERA. Though the Giants lost the World Series to Boston, Marquard pitched two brilliant seven-hitters and allowed just one earned run. Marquard pitched in five fall classics, but his team never won a Series.

Marquard, who once went the distance in a 21-inning, 3–1 win over Pittsburgh, had career marks of 201 wins, a 3.08 ERA, 1,593 strikeouts and 30 shutouts.

In 1907, the Giants' Roger Bresnahan (above, center) lessened the pain of being a catcher by introducing shin guards. He had to endure a few taunts from the fans, but the guards quickly became standard equipment.

before the turn of the century, but regular foul balls carried no penalty. A clever batter like Willie Keeler could simply swat one foul after another while waiting for a perfect pitch. By calling the first two foul balls strikes in 1901, the NL batting average dropped 12 points; Keeler's dropped 13. The fledgling AL adopted the modern rule in 1903, with equally negative effects on hitting.

The masters of dead-ball pitching relied on pacing and pinpoint control. Home runs, remember, hardly happened. A savvy pitcher could keep the ball in the strike zone and bear down only when there were men on base. Christy Mathewson called it "pitching in a pinch." Mathewson's control was even better than Young's. In 1913 he walked only 21 batters in 291 innings, including one stretch of 68 innings without a single base on balls. "You could catch Matty sittin' in a chair," said Roger Bresnahan, Mathewson's batterymate in the World Series of 1905, a World Series in which each of the five games was a shutout, no home runs were hit, the winning Giants gave up no earned runs, the Athletics recorded a 1.47 ERA in defeat, and Christy Mathewson had the greatest week of his or any pitcher's career. He won three of the six games pitching 27 innings, hurled 18 strikeouts, gave up 14 hits, one walk, and not a single run. On October 15, 1905, the *New York Times* said: "His almost superhuman accomplishment will stand as a mark for all pitchers of the future." The mark still stands.

The World Series of 1905 and the offensive slump of 1908—the first modern "Year of the Pitcher"—raised troubling questions about the game's strategic balance. An editorial writer drew a parallel with chess: "The pitcher is really of too much account, and the rest of the outfit too little. They are the pawns and he is the queen."

Eddie Plank's World Series woes pretty much summed up the dead-ball era. Plank (left), a 327-game winner for the Philadelphia Athletics, got no runs to work with in four of his six Series starts. His lifetime Series ERA was a sparkling 1.32; his won-loss record a dull 2–5. In his $5\frac{1}{2}$ years with the Cubs, Orval Overall (below) pitched in four World Series. Overall gave up just two earned runs in $36\frac{1}{3}$ innings and held Detroit's Ty Cobb to two hits in 15 at-bats as the Cubs won back-to-back Series over the Tigers in 1907 and 1908.

Some believed that offense was in the doldrums because hitters were too concerned with "slugging for homers" instead of working to get on base. In 1905 the two leagues combined hit all of 339 home runs. That was a new record, but still an average of only one homer in every four games. Even after the cork-centered ball was introduced in late 1910, home runs averaged well under one every two games until the ball was livened again in 1919. New aces appeared—Walter Johnson in the American League, Grover Cleveland Alexander in the National—and hurlers benefitted again when major league talent was diluted by the Federal League, from 1914 to 1915, and the World War, from 1917 to 1918.

At the same time, black athletes, the biggest untapped pool of baseball talent, were inaccessible—and almost invisible. The Boston Braves signed Adolfo Luque, a Cuban pitcher, in 1913. Newspapers repeatedly described him as "very light skinned," in order to allay fears that black players might infiltrate the major leagues.

Luque often used his fists to answer innuendos about his ancestry. He had great pride and a quick temper. When a teammate's error cost Luque a game, he chased the offender around the clubhouse with an ice pick. He was famous for brushing back hitters—but when Brooklyn's Tiny Osborne brushed *him* back, Luque hurled his bat toward the mound like a bolo.

At 5'7" and 160 pounds, Luque relied on finesse more than power. His best pitch was a sharp downward curve called a "twizzler." He was confident enough to throw to the corners of the plate: "Some pitchers with the count three and two will cut loose through the center of the plate. I never do." Luque said that he had learned his craft by studying Christy Mathewson. Many years later, New York Giant Sal Maglie said that he had learned his craft by studying Adolfo Luque.

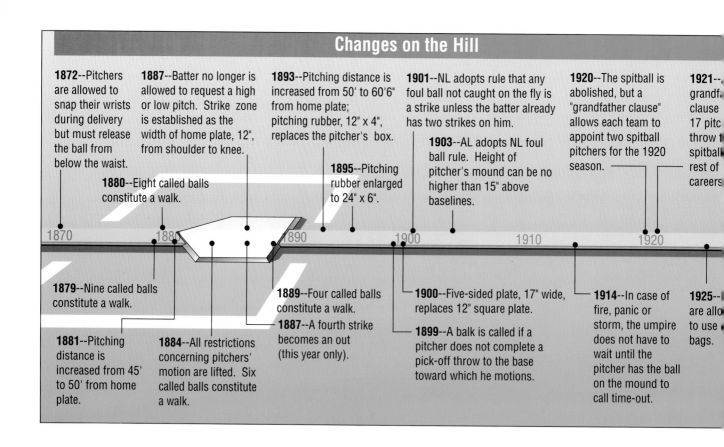

Changes on the Hill

1872--Pitchers are allowed to snap their wrists during delivery but must release the ball from below the waist.

1887--Batter no longer is allowed to request a high or low pitch. Strike zone is established as the width of home plate, 12", from shoulder to knee.

1893--Pitching distance is increased from 50' to 60'6" from home plate; pitching rubber, 12" x 4", replaces the pitcher's box.

1901--NL adopts rule that any foul ball not caught on the fly is a strike unless the batter already has two strikes on him.

1920--The spitball is abolished, but a "grandfather clause" allows each team to appoint two spitball pitchers for the 1920 season.

1921--grandf. clause 17 pitc throw t spitbal rest of careers

1880--Eight called balls constitute a walk.

1895--Pitching rubber enlarged to 24" x 6".

1903--AL adopts NL foul ball rule. Height of pitcher's mound can be no higher than 15" above baselines.

1870   1880   1890   1900   1910   1920

1879--Nine called balls constitute a walk.

1889--Four called balls constitute a walk.

1887--A fourth strike becomes an out (this year only).

1900--Five-sided plate, 17" wide, replaces 12" square plate.

1914--In case of fire, panic or storm, the umpire does not have to wait until the pitcher has the ball on the mound to call time-out.

1925-- are allo to use bags.

1881--Pitching distance is increased from 45' to 50' from home plate.

1884--All restrictions concerning pitchers' motion are lifted. Six called balls constitute a walk.

1899--A balk is called if a pitcher does not complete a pick-off throw to the base toward which he motions.

After being a starter for 19 years, Dolf Luque became the Giants' relief ace in 1932. The following season, at age 43, he led the NL in relief wins with eight, and clinched the World Series for New York with 4 1/3 innings of shutout relief in Game 5 against Washington.

In his big year, 1923, Luque led the NL with 27 victories and a 1.93 ERA. He remained a steady starter until 1932, when he was bought by the Giants and made a reliever by John McGraw. In the 1933 World Series, Luque saved the final game in grand style with 4 1/3 innings of shutout pitching.

Luque pitched in Cuba every winter and often managed teams with black American players. He left the majors in 1935, his 20th season, with a record of 194–179 and 28 saves. He kept pitching in Cuba until 1940 when, at 49, he walked off the mound and hung his glove on a nail in the dugout. "No hay mas," he said. "Luque está terminado." ("There's no more. Luque is finished.") Known throughout his career as "The Pride of Havana," Luque was still a hero in Cuba when he died in 1957.

The "big bang" era began in the major leagues after World War I. In 1919 the major league ERA rose from 2.76 to 3.11, and Babe Ruth, in his last year pitching for the Red Sox, hit a record 29 home runs, a preview of the slugging era that followed with the introduction of the livelier ball.

Catcher Moe Berg, probably the most scholarly big leaguer of all time, once explained the change as an indirect result of the World War. In 1917 and 1918 baseball manufacturers were unable to obtain Australian wool. "To make up for the lack of superior yarn," Berg said, "our machines were adjusted to wind the domestic product tighter. In 1919, when the war was over, the foreign yarn was again available, but the same machines were used." Because the ball was now more resilient, it traveled farther when hit.

The rules also were changed in 1920 to ban the use of dirty or scuffed balls. Enforcement came slowly, until Ray Chapman was killed that season by a pitch from Carl Mays which he probably didn't see. Dozens of fresh

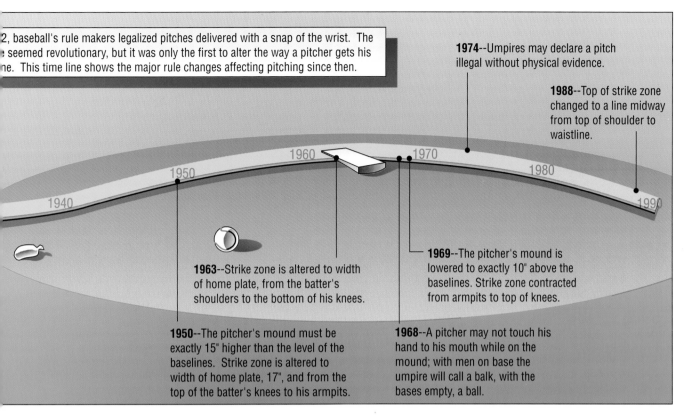

2, baseball's rule makers legalized pitches delivered with a snap of the wrist. The ‌ seemed revolutionary, but it was only the first to alter the way a pitcher gets his ‌e. This time line shows the major rule changes affecting pitching since then.

1974--Umpires may declare a pitch illegal without physical evidence.

1988--Top of strike zone changed to a line midway from top of shoulder to waistline.

1940 1950 1960 1970 1980 1990

1963--Strike zone is altered to width of home plate, from the batter's shoulders to the bottom of his knees.

1969--The pitcher's mound is lowered to exactly 10" above the baselines. Strike zone contracted from armpits to top of knees.

1950--The pitcher's mound must be exactly 15" higher than the level of the baselines. Strike zone is altered to width of home plate, 17", and from the top of the batter's knees to his armpits.

1968--A pitcher may not touch his hand to his mouth while on the mound; with men on base the umpire will call a balk, with the bases empty, a ball.

baseballs a game and the ban on spitballs and foreign-substance pitches once again gave the game back to the hitters. When the ball was juiced again in 1926, this time with a cushion-cork center, offensive numbers climbed more rapidly. Baseball reached the plateau of one home run per game in 1929, and the following year broke all records for run production. Just as 1908 was the Year of the Pitcher, 1930 was the Year of the Hitter.

For the pitchers, it was a war of retrenchment. There were no new weapons—the slider was evolving slowly and did not become widespread until the 1940s—but they were adapting the old ones. As more would-be sluggers dug in at home plate, more pitchers used the brushback to loosen them up. The number of hit batsmen per game actually decreased, mainly because the ball was easier to see—but the "purpose pitch," the warning shot, was more purposeful than ever.

Hitters who swung for the fences were also vulnerable to the strikeout and, in the big-bang decades, strikeout pitchers came into their own. Walter Johnson was succeeded by Lefty Grove, Dazzy Vance, Wild Bill Hallahan, Johnny Allen, Bob Feller, Bobo Newsom, and Van Lingle Mungo. The archetype of power pitching was Dizzy Dean, who led the NL in strikeouts in his first four major league seasons with the Cardinals, 1932 to 1935.

In the early days of the Depression, Dean seemed like a natural force springing up from the Arkansas cotton fields. In hard times, he brought a playful style to the difficult business of pitching. Always a showman, he once put a cake of ice on home plate to cool off his fastball. He was 6'2" and lean, and he threw with a graceful, sweeping motion. But after a liner off the bat of Earl Averill broke his toe in the 1937 All-Star Game, Dean tried to come

In 1920, Cleveland's Ray Chapman was the AL's best shortstop. On August 17, he became baseball's only on-field fatality, killed by a pitch from Carl Mays of the Yankees.

The Ball

The earliest baseballs—those used from the 1840s to the Civil War—were anything but standard. Some had lead cores, others rubber, wrapped in twine or rubber strips with sheepskin or chamois covers. Covers were cut and stitched in several styles, among them the "half moon", "lemon peel" and "belt ball" as well as the familiar "figure-eight" pattern. Size and weight also varied, ranging from balls as light as three ounces to some over ten inches around weighing six ounces or more.

New York's Knickerbocker Club introduced baseball's first Code of Rules in 1845, but it made no mention of ball specifications. In 1854, additions were made to the Code, one requiring a weight of $5\frac{1}{2}$ to 6 ounces and a circumference of $8\frac{5}{8}$ to 11 inches, at least for club play.

These baseballs were quite lively, and in a deliberate move to control wildly high-scoring games, specifications were altered greatly—and often—until 1872, when rule changes brought the weight to between 5 and $5\frac{1}{4}$ ounces, the circumference 9 to $9\frac{1}{4}$ inches, where they remain. The 1-ounce rubber center was wrapped in yarn, and horsehide replaced sheepskin. This was by definition a "dead ball," and that fact was emphasized in contemporary advertising.

Since 1872, the most significant change has been to the ball's center, and the difference defines an era. In 1910 the cork-center ball was introduced, and the ball was made even more lively in 1926 with a core of cork molded to rubber, or "cushioned cork." In 1930, it was determined that the NL ball had too much hop—eight of ten teams hit at least .300—and it was toned down at season's end.

The earliest "official" baseball was the Mahn brand, which was adopted by numerous clubs in the 1860s and 1870s, and by the American Association in 1882. The NL ball carried the Spalding name for nearly a century, from 1879 to 1977. The AL's choice was the Reach baseball from 1901 to 1974. Spalding produced the AL ball in 1975 and 1976, Rawlings in 1977. The NL adopted the Rawlings baseball a year later and today it remains the official ball of both leagues.

The nucleus of a modern baseball is the "pill" or cushioned cork center surrounded by coverings of black and red natural rubber. Four windings of yarn, three wool and one cotton, totaling about a quarter-mile in length, envelop the pill.

Next comes a film of rubber cement, and finally the cover, held together by 108 stitches of waxed red thread. NL balls used red and black thread until 1934 and AL balls used red and blue until 1935; cowhide replaced horsehide in 1974.

Today the pill is produced in the US, and the pill, yarn, cowhide and thread are sent to Haiti, where baseballs are manufactured, including the hand-stitched cover. Baseballs then endure a Major League-sanctioned test to measure "coefficient restitution"—in other words, to see if they have enough bounce.

Many people believe the ball had a little extra bounce in 1987, when home runs were hit at a record pace. Even though Major League Baseball and Rawlings deny any livening of the ball, 4,458 homers were hit that year, breaking the previous mark set a year earlier by a whopping 645. Nonetheless, numerous tests failed to prove that the ball was any livelier than before.

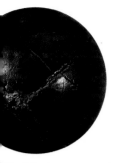

...5 ball features a one-piece
...n cover.

In 1868 the ball's weight went
from $5\frac{3}{4}$ to $5\frac{1}{4}$ ounces, its
fourth change in ten years.

1876 saw balls with figure-eight
stitching grow in popularity.

..., some balls were stitched . . .

Before a modern baseball is made, the yarn
used to make it is climate-controlled. Before
it is put into play, the home plate umpire
dabs it with Lena Blackburne's Baseball
Rubbing Mud.

. . . and some were seamless.

...center in 1910 meant a
...ball. Pitchers retaliated by
...and slathering its surface.

The Federal League ball became a
collector's item when the league
folded in 1916.

In 1974 cowhide replaced
horsehide as the ball's cover
material.

6'1" 185 lbs.   b 2/26/1887
BR TR   d 11/4/50

GROVER ALEXANDER
Right-Handed Pitcher

By the time Game 7 of the 1926 World Series rolled around, Grover Cleveland Alexander's place in the Hall of Fame was secure. The 39-year-old wizard of control and changing speeds had already won 327 games and led the NL in innings pitched and shutouts seven times; in wins, complete games and strikeouts six times; and in ERA five times.

Alexander had already thrown two complete game victories in the Series, one the day before to knot his Cardinals and the Yankees at three games each. But with a one-run lead, two outs and the bases full of Yankees in the bottom of the seventh, St. Louis manager Rogers Hornsby called on Alexander to face rookie sensation Tony Lazzeri, who'd driven in 114 runs during the season. Four knee-high curves later, Lazzeri had struck out, and the man they called "Old Low-and-Away" was on his way to a save and his first world championship.

Despite recurring battles with alcoholism, Alexander remained spectacular throughout his career. He set the modern record for wins by a rookie with 28 in 1911, including a 12-inning, one-hit, 1–0 win over Cy Young. On the way to 373 career wins—third highest of all time—he won 30 or more games three times. His 16 shutouts in 1916 tied him with George Bradley for the major league record, as he shut out every team in the NL at least once.

Brooklyn's Dazzy Vance used his 83-inch reach to become the National League's Most Valuable Player in 1924, the first year the award was given. Vance's 28 wins beat out Rogers Hornsby's .424 average.

back too soon and developed a herky-jerky delivery that ruined his arm. He won his last major league game at the age of 29.

Hitters enjoyed a power surge after World War II, thanks to a livelier ball and a smaller strike zone. Ever since the abolition of the high-low rule in 1887, the strike zone had been between the batter's knees and shoulders. In 1950 the zone was compressed to the area between the *top* of the knees and the *armpits*. As pitchers were squeezed, sluggers flourished. Home runs rose by 20 percent in one season, inaugurating a long-ball decade.

In fact, the scale was beginning to tip in favor of the pitchers—not through rule changes, but through a convergence of trends: night games, specialized relief pitching, proliferation of the slider, and evolution of stadium architecture. Two California parks—Candlestick in San Francisco, Dodger Stadium in Los Angeles—set the style for new stadiums of the expansion era, in which faraway fences and large swatches of foul ground produced fewer homers and many more pop-outs.

In 1963 the Rules Committee reacted to another power surge—epitomized by Roger Maris' record-setting 61 homers in 1961—raising the strike zone to the shoulders and lowering it to the bottom of the knee, the deepest threshold ever. For a hitter who stood six feet tall, the new rule added six big inches of vertical vulnerability. In 1963 batting averages dropped ten points and homers fell off ten percent as the hurlers again took command.

By 1968 the imbalance was so extreme that *Sports Illustrated* dubbed it "the season of the zero hero." One game out of five was a shutout. The collective ERA in each league was under 3.00, and seven pitchers finished under 2.00. Don Drysdale set a record, broken in 1988 by Orel Hershiser, of $58^2/_3$ consecutive scoreless innings.

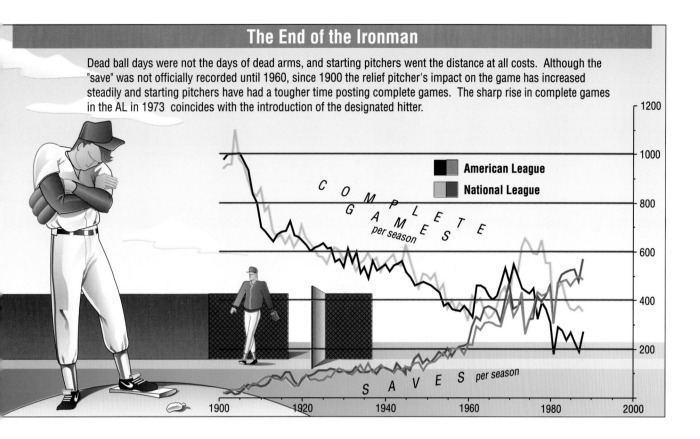

The End of the Ironman

Dead ball days were not the days of dead arms, and starting pitchers went the distance at all costs. Although the "save" was not officially recorded until 1960, since 1900 the relief pitcher's impact on the game has increased steadily and starting pitchers have had a tougher time posting complete games. The sharp rise in complete games in the AL in 1973 coincides with the introduction of the designated hitter.

American League
National League

C O M P L E T E G A M E S *per season*

S A V E S *per season*

1900   1920   1940   1960   1980   2000

1200   1000   800   600   400   200

In 1969 Paul Richards, the Braves' general manager, recommended that the pitchers be moved back five feet to 65′6″. Jim Fregosi, the Angels' young shortstop, suggested making them pitch from a hole in the ground. The rule-makers were less severe, simply lowering the mound from 15 inches to 10, but they also shrank the strike zone back to the limits of 1950: top of knees to armpits. Moreover, umpires began to penalize blatant intimidators and to give pitchers little or nothing on the inside edge of the plate. In effect, the strike zone was being squeezed on three sides.

Although the rule changes provided a quick fix for hitters, pitchers still controlled the game—especially in the American League, where by 1972 the batting average fell to .239. The AL responded with a designated-hitter rule making AL pitchers super specialists. Ironically, the DH had first been proposed in 1929, a hitter's heyday, by NL President John Heydler, but the proposal was blocked by the AL and Commissioner Kenesaw Mountain Landis. Adoption of the DH in 1973 immediately boosted American League ERA by 23 percent and home runs by 32 percent. Since 1973 the AL batting average has stabilized between .258 and .270 every season; the NL average has run one to ten points lower.

In the 1970s and 1980s, three other factors have affected the hitting-pitching balance. First, umpires in both leagues gradually brought the upper strike zone limit down almost to the navel. "If we called strikes up around the letters," said NL umpire Dick Stello, "the hitters wouldn't hit." Then in 1988 the Rules Committee changed the upper limit to a point midway between shoulders and waist, in hopes that the umpires would bring it *up* that high. Batting averages for the season fell by 13 points in the NL and 6 in the AL, possibly warning of a new imbalance.

In 1934 Dizzy Dean, the king of St. Louis' Gashouse Gang, won 30 games at the age of 23. He added two wins in the World Series, including a Game 7 shutout. But arm trouble cut short his career, and from 1938 to his release in 1941 Dean won just 16 games.

Brooklyn's Van Lingle Mungo had a great fastball, but little control, either on or off the mound. He led the NL three times in walks, and according to teammate Leo Durocher, Mungo "drank a bit. A bit of everything."

Second, the ball seems to have gone through several phases of liveliness, even after its cover changed from horsehide to cowhide in 1974. In 1987 major league hitters whacked a record 4,458 home runs; in 1988 homers fell off to 3,180, a drop of almost 30 percent—more than the new strike zone alone could account for.

Third, bigger parks, artificial turf, and the emergence of the running game have most obviously helped the offense, prompting a new preoccupation with the balk rules, in order to protect base stealers from the pitcher's other weapon—the pick-off throw.

The large strike zone of 1963 to 1968 was another exception that proved the point: hitters are usually the ones who need help. In the future, the larger zone of 1988 and domed stadiums may necessitate more fine tuning to restrict the hurlers' advantage. In 1935 the venerable sportswriter Hugh Fullerton gave a succinct account of baseball's balancing act. "The history of pitching is simple," Fullerton said. "The pitcher always has held the ascendency over the batter—so much so that every rule (except the foul strike rule) governing the delivery of the ball has been passed to handicap the pitcher and prevent him from becoming too great an element in the sport." ◗

The Mound

A pitcher's mound was not part of baseball's original design. Old photographs suggest that it developed after 1884, when overhand pitching was legalized. At first the pitcher worked from a box, its back edge 45, later 50, feet from home plate. Shoveling earth or sand over that heavily used area after a rain kept it from becoming a quagmire and may have created, in time, a little hill that gave an overhander just a bit of an edge.

The pitching rubber appeared when the modern pitching distance of 60′6″ was established in 1893. The solid slab replaced the chalk line at the back of the box, providing a starting block for the pitcher. At first the rubber was only 4″ by 12″; in 1895 it was enlarged to its present size of 6″ by 24″, giving the pitcher a broader angle to work a hitter.

The modern mound has precise specifications: a circle with a nine-foot radius centered 59 feet from the point where the foul lines meet at the back tip of home plate. The front edge of the rubber is fixed 18 inches behind the center of the mound—and therefore 60′6″ from home. Six inches in front of the rubber, the mound slopes down toward the edge of the infield grass ten feet away.

When baseball rules mentioned the mound for the first time in 1904, its maximum height was 15 inches; in 1950 that became a fixed height. But rules are not always observed. The mound at Cleveland's Municipal Stadium was built high for fastball pitchers like Bob Feller, Herb Score and Sam McDowell. Some National League mounds in the 1960s were as high as 25 inches, while the mound at Philadelphia's old Connie Mack Stadium was kept low to favor sidearmers like Jim Bunning.

The mound at Philadelphia's new Veterans Stadium is still reputed to be the lowest in the NL, even though—after a 1968 season that belonged totally to pitchers—rulemakers reduced the strike zone and fixed the height of mounds in both leagues at ten inches, where it supposedly remains.

A universal accessory on the mound is a small cloth bag full of powdered resin. In 1921, with the introduction of the lively ball, umpires began putting fresh baseballs in play throughout the game. Pitchers complained that the new balls were too slick, so in 1925 the NL let pitchers use resin, the only permissible "foreign substance" on the ball; the AL followed suit a year later.

Gone from the baseball scene is one of the most intriguing features of old baseball diamonds: the pathway that used to connect the mound to home plate. Phased out after World War II, this alley varied from decade to decade and ballpark to ballpark. Groundskeepers at the turn of the century sometimes outlined it with chalk. By the 1940s the pathway at the Polo Grounds had become a mere ribbon, about 2 feet wide; the pathway at Yankee Stadium was closer to 4 feet.

The alley was a holdover from the days when baseball was played on cricket fields. In cricket, the path between the two bases, or wickets, is also the alley where the bowler delivers the ball to the batsman. A clear path between pitcher and batter stayed in baseball long after its origin was forgotten. It was not functional, only symbolic, but the pathway linking pitcher's circle to batter's box made the field look more like a giant game board, emphasizing the power struggle at the heart of the game: pitcher vs. hitter.

YOUNG, CLEVELAND

Cy Young

Long after his playing days were over, Cy Young was asked by a young reporter how many games he had won. "Son," he said, "I won more games than you'll ever see." And, almost surely, more than any other pitcher ever will.

Denton True "Cy" Young was the winning pitcher 511 times in his 22-year career, an average of 23 wins a season. He won 20 or more games 16 times, 30 or more games five times. His durability was unparalleled, as he pitched 7,356 innings in his career, and completed all but 64 of the 815 games he started.

Born in 1867, two years after the end of the Civil War, Young grew up tall and strong on his parents' farm in Gilmore, Ohio. At the age of 23, the 6'2", 210-pound right-hander began his professional baseball career for $40 a month with the Canton, Ohio team in the Tri-State League. He threw a three-hitter in his first start, and added a no-hitter in July on his way to a 15–15 record.

Cleveland manager Patsy Tebeau bought Young's contract from Canton for $250, and Young finished the 1890 season with the NL Spiders. In his first start with Cleveland, Young struck out Cap Anson, who was then player/manager for the Chicago Cubs. Anson, who struck out just 23 times in 504 at-bats that season, was so impressed with Young's blazing fastball and sharp-breaking curve that he offered Tebeau $2,000 for Young, but the Spiders' skipper refused.

Young finished the season with a 9–7 record, and completed all 16 of his starts. In 1891 he won 27 games to kick off an unprecedented string of 14 straight seasons with at least 20 wins. Young had one of his best seasons the following year, going 36–11 with a 1.93 ERA, and nine shutouts; he recorded career highs in innings pitched with 453 and complete games with 48. The Spiders placed second in the National League that year, their highest finish ever.

In 1895 Young went 35–10, including a 7–0 record in relief, and led the Spiders to another second-place finish, earning the team a spot in the second Temple Cup, a postseason showdown between the National League's top two teams. The NL had expanded to 12 teams in 1892, and William Temple, part owner of the Pittsburgh Pirates, had proposed the idea of a postseason challenge as a way of stimulating interest in the league. The Pirates finished second to Boston in 1892, but unfortunately for Temple, his concept didn't become a reality until 1894 when the Pirates sank to seventh. But in 1895 Young won three games in the series with Baltimore, leading Cleveland to a 4–1 win in the series and giving him and his teammates the winner's share of $600 each.

Although he allowed a league-leading 477 hits in 1896, Young won 29 games and led the NL in shutouts with five and in saves with three. He pitched in an era when home runs were rare—Bill Joyce led the NL with 14 homers in 1896—so a pitcher didn't necessarily give up lots of runs if he gave up lots of hits. Young knew how to pace himself throughout a game, how to coast when he could afford to, and bear down when the game was on the line. He never overworked his arm, and usually needed only a dozen warmup throws before he was ready to pitch.

In 1908 Young's waistline gave him some trouble but his 41-year-old right arm was as sound as ever. He won 21 games and posted a career-best 1.26 ERA, the tenth best single-season ERA ever.

Young suffered through what was for him a sub-par season in 1897, going 21–18 with a 3.79 ERA, but on September 18 he pitched his first of three major league no-hitters, walking just one in a 6–0 win over Cincinnati. Now past 30 and with a waning fastball, Young turned to the slider, or "nickel curve," as he called it, and was rewarded with 25 wins and a 2.58 ERA in 1898. St. Louis offered a higher financial reward for his services in 1899, so Young packed up his favorite catcher, Lou Criger, rejoined manager Tebeau and won 46 games in the next two years for St. Louis.

In 1901 Young joined second baseman Napoleon Lajoie and other top players in jumping to the newly formed American League. Persuaded by AL president Ban Johnson and a $3,500 salary, Young—again bringing Criger with him—joined the Boston Pilgrims. The formation of the new league had diluted the talent pool available to both leagues, and the revitalized Young took advantage of the situation in 1901, pacing the AL with 33 wins, a 1.62 ERA, 158 strikeouts and five shutouts. In his first four years with Boston, Young averaged 30 wins and his ERA never rose above 2.15. In 1903 he

CY YOUYOUNG

Right-Handed Pitcher
Cleveland Spiders 1890–1898
St. Louis Cardinals 1899–1900
Boston Red Sox 1901–1908
Cleveland Indians 1909–1911
Boston Braves 1911
Hall of Fame 1937

GAMES *(5th all time)*	906
INNINGS	
Career *(1st all time)*	7,356
Season High *(4th all time)*	453
WINS	
Career *(1st all time)*	511
Season High *(4th all time)*	36
LOSSES	
Career *(1st all time)*	313
Season High	22
WINNING PERCENTAGE	
Career	.620
Season High	.778
ERA	
Career	2.63
Season Low *(10th all time)*	1.26
GAMES STARTED	
Career *(1st all time)*	815
Season High *(8th all time)*	49
COMPLETE GAMES	
Career *(1st all time)*	751
Season High *(2nd all time)*	48
SHUTOUTS	
Career *(4th all time)*	76
Season High	10
STRIKEOUTS	
Career	2,799
Season High	208
WALKS	
Career	1,217
Season High	140
NO-HITTERS *(3rd all time)*	
	1897, 1904, 1908
WORLD SERIES	1903

A lifetime .221 hitter, Lou Criger (below, left, with former Red Sox batting champ Hugh Duffy) lasted 16 years in the majors because he was Young's favorite catcher. Young won many trophies (right) for his pitching, then lent his name to today's most prestigious pitching award.

won 28 games and even hit .321 while leading Boston to the AL pennant and into baseball's first World Series.

The loser in Game 1 of the best-of-nine Series, Young threw a six-hitter and tripled in three runs in Game 5 to cut Pittsburgh's margin to 3–2. Boston swept the next three games to win the Series, with Young again going the distance in Game 7. Young's 26 wins led Boston to another pennant in 1904, but manager John McGraw and owner John T. Brush of the NL champion New York Giants refused to allow their teams to play in the World Series, not recognizing the 1902 agreement that was meant to mend a rift between the two leagues. Their decision cost Young a chance to pitch in another World Series.

The 1904 season held other highlights for the 37-year-old Young. On April 25 Young finished a game with two hitless innings. On April 30 he pitched seven hitless innings in relief. On May 5 he was matched up against Philadelphia ace Rube Waddell, who had pitched a one-hitter against Boston just a few days earlier. On this day, Young was better. He went into the ninth inning having al-

lowed no baserunners, and with two outs Athletics' manager Connie Mack let Waddell—whose average was .122—hit for himself. Waddell hit the ball hard, but shortstop Fred Parent snared the line drive and Young had the first perfect game of the modern era. "I don't think I ever had more stuff," Young said years later. But Young wasn't through. In his next start he gave up no hits for six innings against the New York Highlanders before his hitless streak was snapped at 24 innings, still a major league record.

Young continued to pitch well into his 40s, and pitched his third no-hitter in 1908 at the age of 41, coming within one walk of becoming the only man ever to pitch two perfect games. When he retired in the spring of 1912, he claimed it was more because of his stomach—which kept him from fielding bunts—than his arm. But after 906 games—a major league record until reliever Hoyt Wilhelm broke it in 1968—his strong right arm was tired. "It's no use," he told Boston Braves' catcher Johnny Kling, "the arm feels like a pump handle." Young returned to his Ohio farm—which he worked until he was in his 80s. After his death in

Nineteen years after he started his major league career there, Young returned to Cleveland in 1909 (right) and had his last good season—19 wins, a 2.26 ERA and 30 complete games. Young was a master at controlling the dead ball (above).

1955 the annual award for major league baseball's best pitcher was named in his honor.

For more than two decades Young was consistently among baseball's elite pitchers, and he attributed it mostly to his ability to put the ball where he wanted to. "Control is what kept me in the big leagues for 22 years," he said. In 1904 he walked just 29 batters in 380 innings—one every 13 innings.

He had great control as a person as well as a pitcher. He never argued with umpires, and was a gracious, clean-living gentleman in an era when few ballplayers answered that description.

Constellations

In spring training, all pitchers run, regardless of wins, losses or ERA. The Kansas City Royals' 1989 staff (above) promised to be one of baseball's best, but in order to stay in contention in the dog days of August and September, a staff must build up its legs in March.

In 1915, (from left to right) Babe Ruth, Ernie Shore and Rube Foster combined for 56 wins for the world champion Red Sox. First baseman Del Gainor (far right) rounded out this photograph, but Dutch Leonard and Smoky Joe Wood rounded out Boston's five-man rotation with 15 wins each.

Old Hoss Radbourn accounted for 60 of Providence's 84 wins in leading the team to the NL pennant in 1884. In a postseason series against the New York Highlanders, champions of the American Association, Radbourn pitched every inning in the Grays' three-game sweep.

P itching is an isolated and lonely job. Over the course of a season, however, the individual hurler must find a niche in the pitching staff, which is in itself a team within a team. A strong pitching staff blends and balances component skills, like a team of horses or a company of actors. Christy Mathewson was lucky enough to pitch on two great staffs; Walter Johnson didn't get to pitch on one good one until the end of his career.

A staff is built around the starting rotation, the alternating nucleus of pitchers who start games. Today a five-man starting rotation is typical, with a smaller sequence of top talent for the close of a pennant race or the postseason crucible. A modern staff, ten men in all, normally includes a "swing man"—a backup starter who doubles in relief—as well as a ministaff of bullpen specialists: the "long man" good for four or five innings, a "set-up man" who can come in for one or two innings late in the game, and a "closer" to slam the door in the ninth.

Such roles were beyond conception in the days of underhand pitching, when one man could do it all. In the National League's opening season, 1876, George "Grin" Bradley of St. Louis, Bobby Mathews of New York, and Jim Devlin of Louisville pitched almost every inning their teams played. The last one-man staff was Charles "Old Hoss" Radbourn of the Providence Grays.

In 1884, the year overhand pitching became legal, Radbourn pitched $678\frac{2}{3}$ innings. Early in the season he worked in tandem with Charlie Sweeney, said to be the fastest pitcher of the day; on June 7, Sweeney struck out 19 batters in a nine-inning game. Radbourn, still using a modified underhand delivery, relied on curves and change-ups. The two pitchers were rivals more than partners, and both were temperamental. In July, with Radbourn

In the 1870s and 1880s, Bobby Mathews
had a greater assortment of pitches than did
most staffs. He won 30 games each season
from 1883 to 1885 for Philadelphia in the
American Association, and is credited by
some as having invented both the curve and
the spitball.

suspended for drunkenness, Sweeney quit the team and jumped to the Union
Association. Bargaining to get his suspension lifted and his contract renego-
tiated, Radbourn declared that he would pitch every remaining Grays' game.
And he almost did, hurling 35 of the team's 37 games during a stretch drive.
Radbourn led Providence to a pennant, earned himself a 60–12 record, and
then won three more games in postseason play.

The best duo of the era was the New York Giants' tandem of Tim Keefe
and Mickey Welch. In five seasons, 1885 through 1889, Keefe won 172 games
and Welch 153. Each averaged over 400 innings a year. Keefe, nicknamed
"Sir Timothy," was quiet and thoughtful, an ambitious businessman and players' rights advocate. "Smilin' Mickey" Welch was a famous carouser who
credited his pitching success to plenty of beer. They began their pro careers
together in 1880 with the Troy Haymakers. Reunited in New York, Keefe and
Welch led the Giants to pennants and championships in 1888 and 1889. The
term rotation was unknown, but that's what Keefe and Welch were.

When the modern pitching distance was established in 1893, staffs
expanded because greater strain on arms reduced the number of
innings that any ace could work. In the last year at the old distance, Chicago's Wild Bill Hutchison led the NL in innings pitched with 627.
Next season, hurling from 60 feet, 6 inches, Amos Rusie of the Giants led with
482—and no one since has pitched so many. The last hurler to go over 400
was Ed Walsh in 1908.

Out of necessity, most clubs developed a three-man rotation, often with
the third slot alternating spot starters. A few had four-man rotations. On
Brooklyn's 1899 championship team, managed by Ned Hanlon, four pitchers

Great Dead-Ball Staffs

In the first two decades of the 20th century—the dead-ball era—nine pennant-winning teams boasted pitching staffs of three 20-game winners.

	W	L	G	IP	ERA
Pittsburgh, NL, 1902					
Jack Chesbro	**28**	6	35	286	2.17
Jesse Tannehill	20	6	26	231	1.95
Deacon Phillippe	20	9	31	272	2.05
Boston, AL, 1903					
Cy Young	**28**	9	40	**342**	2.08
Bill Dinneen	21	13	37	299	2.26
Long Tom Hughes	20	7	33	245	2.57
New York, NL, 1904					
Joe McGinnity	**35**	8	**51**	**408**	**1.61**
Christy Mathewson	33	12	48	368	2.03
Dummy Taylor	21	15	37	296	2.34
Boston, AL, 1904					
Cy Young	26	16	43	380	1.97
Bill Dinneen	23	14	37	336	2.20
Jesse Tannehill	21	11	33	282	2.04
New York, NL, 1905					
Christy Mathewson	**31**	8	43	339	**1.27**
Red Ames	22	8	34	263	2.74
Joe McGinnity	21	15	**46**	320	2.87
Philadelphia, AL, 1905					
Rube Waddell	**26**	11	**46**	329	**1.48**
Eddie Plank	25	12	41	347	2.26
Andy Coakley	20	7	35	255	1.84
Detroit, AL, 1907					
Wild Bill Donovan	25	4	32	271	2.19
Ed Killian	25	13	41	314	1.78
George Mullin	20	20	46	357	2.59
Boston, AL, 1912					
Smoky Joe Wood	**34**	5	43	344	1.91
Hugh Bedient	20	9	41	231	2.92
Buck O'Brien	20	13	37	276	2.58
New York, NL, 1913					
Christy Mathewson	25	11	40	306	**2.06**
Rube Marquard	23	10	42	288	2.50
Jeff Tesreau	22	13	41	282	2.17

Boldface indicates league leader.

The Giants' Tim Keefe (above) celebrated on July 4, 1883 by winning both ends of a doubleheader against Columbus, allowing a total of three hits. In 1903 Joe McGinnity (opposite, right), won three doubleheaders by himself in the same month, and still topped teammate Christy Mathewson (left) by just one win, 31–30. All John McGraw (center) did was manage their brilliance.

threw between 275 and 300 innings each: Jim Hughes, Brickyard Kennedy, Doc McJames and Jack Dunn, the man who later discovered Babe Ruth and Lefty Grove. In his last season as a player, 1904, Dunn appeared in one game with John McGraw's New York Giants. For a fleeting four innings, Dunn was a reliever on one of the greatest staffs in the history of the game.

All of John McGraw's staffs had control, cunning and guts—just like the Old Man. Among McGraw's greatest rotations were Christy Mathewson, Rube Marquard and Jeff Tesreau, from 1912 to 1915, and Carl Hubbell, Freddie Fitzsimmons and Rube Walker, from 1929 to 1932. But in his first seven years with the Giants, 1902 to 1908, McGraw came up with the *idea* of a rotation and started the concept of a real pitching staff. Of course, it helped that he began with Joe McGinnity and Christy Mathewson.

As a boy, McGinnity had worked in a foundry, and he was already nicknamed "Iron Man" when he reached the majors in 1899, a 28-year-old rookie. On the mound McGinnity gave the name new meaning. Three times in August 1903 he pitched—and won—both games of a doubleheader. Over a ten-year career he averaged almost 350 innings and 25 wins a season, and he continued to pitch in the minor leagues until he was 54.

This remarkable endurance was the result of an easy sidearm delivery, almost underhand, that let McGinnity curve the ball with a minimum snap of the wrist. He called his curve "Old Sal." Others described it as a "nickel rocket" because it had a sweeping roundhouse trajectory instead of a sharp break, and it seemed to rise as it passed the hitter. McGinnity relied on the pitch so heavily that Giant catcher Roger Bresnahan didn't bother to use signs.

Christy Mathewson mixed a fastball and drop curve with his famous screwball. Artful pitch selection and supreme control made him the very em-

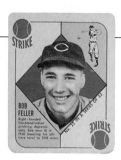

Bob Feller

According to Ted Williams, who wasn't in the habit of handing out idle compliments to pitchers, Bob Feller "had more stuff than anybody."

Feller's "stuff" included a near 100-mile-per-hour fastball and a curve that is considered among the game's best. He won 266 games in his 18-year career, leading the American League six times in wins and seven times in strikeouts. He also lost four years of his prime—and probably 80 to 100 wins and 1,200 strikeouts—to military service in World War II. But during those 18 years, Feller was one of the winningest pitchers in baseball.

Feller was a very good pitcher at an early age. His father bought him a new Rogers Hornsby glove every two years, and built him—at age 12—a playing field complete with a grandstand and scoreboard on their farm in Van Meter, Iowa. In 1936 Feller threw five no-hitters for his high school team, then started pitching for the Cleveland Indians. By signing him, Cleveland broke the rules forbidding the signing of pre-college amateurs, but Feller's parents convinced Commissioner Kenesaw Mountain Landis to allow their son to stay with the Indians.

In his first major league start in 1936, Feller struck out 15 St. Louis Browns. Wild and unschooled early in his career, he had a nervous twitch in his eyes that—along with his blinding speed—scared many hitters. Washington manager Bucky Harris told his players, "Go up and hit what you see, and if you don't see it come on back." In 1938 he won 17 games and led the American League with 240 strikeouts, including a record-breaking 18 in a game against Detroit. But he also set a league record with 208 walks. He settled down in 1939, winning 24 games and his third straight strikeout title.

He started the 1940 season by throwing baseball's only Opening Day no-hitter April 16 against Chicago. He finished the season with a career-high 27 wins, and led the league in complete games, innings pitched, strikeouts, shutouts, and starts. Feller won 25 games in 1941, but then joined the Navy. When he left for World War II at age 23, he had struck out 1,233 batters, more than any other pitcher his age.

Feller returned from World War II with five campaign ribbons and eight battle stars earned in the Pacific theater aboard the battleship *Alabama*. His fastball had lost nothing while at sea. He rejoined the Indians late in 1945. The next year was his best season, as he won 26 games, had a career-low 2.18 ERA, threw ten shutouts, and came within one of Rube Waddell's AL record of 349 strikeouts. His 36 complete games are the most since Walter Johnson's 38 in 1910. He also threw his second no-hitter.

In 1948 Feller and fellow pitchers Bob Lemon and rookie Gene Bearden led the Indians to the AL pennant. In his first World Series appearance, Feller threw a two-hitter in Game 1, but lost 1–0 to the Boston Braves and Johnny Sain's four-hitter. Feller was hit hard in an 11–5 loss in Game 5, but the Indians won the Series in six.

In 1951 Feller had his last 20-win season and threw his third no-hitter, tying him at the time with Cy Young for the all-time lead. He retired after the 1956 season, and was elected to the Hall of Fame in 1962.

Satchel Paige played against Feller during barnstorming tours Feller organized of major league stars against negro league stars in 1946 and 1947. Paige said of Feller, "If anybody threw that ball any harder than Rapid Robert, the human eye couldn't follow it."

Throughout his career, Feller was hit hard by Yankee great Joe DiMaggio. "Feller tried everything against him," said catcher Jim Hegan. "Nothing helped." But on April 30, 1946, against DiMaggio and the Yankees, Feller tossed his second —and sweetest—no-hitter.

BOB
FELLER

Right-Handed Pitcher
Cleveland Indians 1936–1941,
  1945–1956
Hall of Fame 1962

GAMES	**570**
INNINGS	
Career	3,827
Season High	371⅓
WINS	
Career	266
Season High	27
LOSSES	
Career	162
Season High	15
WINNING PERCENTAGE	
Career	.621
Season High	.813
ERA	
Career	3.25
Season Low	2.18
GAMES STARTED	
Career	484
Season High	42
COMPLETE GAMES	
Career	279
Season High	36
SHUTOUTS	
Career	46
Season High	10
STRIKEOUTS	
Career	2,581
Season High *(5th all time)*	348
WALKS	
Career *(3rd all time)*	1,764
Season High *(3rd all time)*	208
NO-HITTERS *(3rd all time)*	
	1940, 1946
	1951
WORLD SERIES	**1948**

In 1910, any seat was a good one as long as fans could watch the Athletics' brilliant starting rotation pitch at Philadelphia's Shibe Park. Eddie Plank, Chief Bender, Jack Coombs and Cy Morgan combined for 88 of Philly's 102 regular-season wins, then Coombs and Bender polished off the Giants in five games in the World Series.

Red Ames probably deserved a better fate than pitching in the shadow of Mathewson, McGinnity, Rube Marquard and Jeff Tesreau with the Giants from 1903 to 1913. His ERA never rose above 2.74, and from 1904 to 1907 he led the NL in strikeouts per game.

bodiment of what old-time sportswriters called a "twirler." After one Mathewson masterpiece, a Cincinnati reporter wrote: "He toyed with the sphere as a cat would with a ball of yarn, putting it where he pleased." In four of his seven seasons as McGinnity's partner, Mathewson recorded 30 or more wins.

Not satisfied, McGraw tried to expand the rotation and spread out the pitching load. His original third man was right-hander Luther "Dummy" Taylor, who won 27 games in 1904. Taylor was deaf and mute, and because of him most of the team could use sign language. "McGraw would sit there on the bench," Fred Snodgrass said, "and spell out S-T-E-A-L so plain that anyone in the park who could read deaf-and-dumb language would know what was happening." Umpire Hank O'Day also read signing, and he once ejected Taylor from a game for "cursing" with his hands.

The following season McGraw established a four-man rotation—providing spot starts for Red Ames, a stocky righty, and Hooks Wiltse, a lanky lefty—and the result was 15 or more wins for five pitchers, a record that has never been equaled.

Hooks Wiltse had a good curve, but his nickname came from a prominent nose. Described as "elongated" and "cadaverous," he threw with a cross-fire motion like Eddie Plank's, his body a moving background against which hitters had to pick up the flight of the ball. Wiltse was the first southpaw McGraw ever liked, mainly because he had sharp control.

Taylor and McGinnity pitched bravely in 1908, in a mad pennant race with the Cubs, but it was the last season for both. From July to September, Mathewson and Wiltse had to start every third day, winning 37 and 23 games, respectively. Mathewson had 12 shutouts; Wiltse a ten-inning no-hitter. But the Giants fell one game short as a tired Matty lost 4–2 to the Cubs

Before Game 1 of the 1929 World Series against the Cubs, Athletics' manager Connie Mack (center) had to wrap up prize pitchers George Earnshaw (left) and Lefty Grove (right) to keep them warm. But in the winter of 1933 the cold-hearted Mack traded them both on the same day.

and Three Finger Brown on the last day of the season and the final game for McGraw's first great staff.

There never was, and may never be, another duo like McGinnity and Mathewson. With a combined 346 wins and 32 saves in six seasons, they were the archetypes of "iron man" and "twirler," king and ace, grizzled veteran and golden youth. They were ideal complements, with skills ideally suited to the master plans of "Little Napoleon," John McGraw.

In Connie Mack's 53 years as a manager, 50 at the helm of the Philadelphia Athletics, he assembled several brilliant staffs. From 1903 to 1914 Eddie Plank and Chief Bender—supported by the likes of Rube Waddell, Jack Coombs and Herb Pennock—collaborated for five pennants. But Mack's best staff was the one that coalesced around Lefty Grove, George Earnshaw and Rube Walberg. In three seasons, 1929 to 1931, pitching in a hitter's era and a hitter's stadium, Shibe Park, the Philadelphia trio won 197 games. More impressive than the statistics were the pennants, three in a row, wrested from the Yankees of Babe Ruth, Lou Gehrig and Bill Dickey.

Mack, a horse trader by nature, had no farm system. In 1924 he invested in the Pacific Coast League's Portland franchise just to obtain catcher Mickey Cochrane, but almost all of his stars were bought outright from independent minor league teams. His best buy may have been Lefty Grove.

Grove joined the Athletics in 1925. After solving a control problem, he became a 20-game winner in 1927, led the AL in strikeouts in his first seven seasons, and in the pennant years of 1929 to 1931 had a winning percentage of .840 (79–15). Grove was lean and mean. His main pitching partner, Moose Earnshaw, was heavy-set and urbane. Like Grove, Earnshaw came from

In 1927 the Chicago American Giants had a stellar pitching staff whose brightest star was Willie Foster (third from left). Often called the greatest left-hander in negro league history, Foster led the Giants to the pennant and won two games in Chicago's postseason sweep over the Birmingham Black Barons.

Baltimore's International League franchise with a blazing fastball. Mack bought his third starter, Rube Walberg, from the Giants in 1923. What Connie Mack saw, and what John McGraw missed, was a southpaw who could shuttle easily between starting and relieving, and who could change speeds, disconcerting left-handed hitters.

Philadelphia's bullpen ace was knuckleballer Ed Rommel. In 1922 Rommel won 27 games as a starter, although the Athletics finished seventh. By the end of the decade he was a tireless reliever. "I could pitch the knuckleball every day from eight o'clock in the morning till six o'clock at night," Rommel said. In 1925, John Picus Quinn joined the team at age 41, earning 63 wins and 11 saves over his next five full seasons.

In 1929 Mack's rejuvenated hero was 35-year-old Howard Ehmke, 7–2 in spot starts. In September, Ehmke took on a secret scouting assignment. The Chicago Cubs were winning almost as easily in the NL as the Athletics were in the AL, and Mack wanted a detailed "book" on their murderous right-handed hitters: Rogers Hornsby, Hack Wilson and Kiki Cuyler. After debriefing Ehmke, Mack decided to start only right-handed pitchers in the Series, using southpaws Grove and Walberg as relievers. But instead of starting Moose Earnshaw in Game 1, Mack stunned both teams by sending Ehmke to the mound. The Cubs, who feasted on fastballs, were befuddled by Ehmke's sidearm breaking pitches. He struck out 13, a Series record, as Philadelphia took the opener, 3–1. It was Ehmke's last major league victory.

Mack's Athletics took that Series handily and repeated as champions in 1930 against St. Louis. In 1931, pacing the Athletics' 107 regular-season victories, Grove led the league in wins, winning percentage, complete games, shutouts, strikeouts and ERA. His record was 31–4; the losses were

by scores of 7–5, 4–3, 2–1 and 1–0. Earnshaw and Walberg were also 20-game winners, and the club went into the 1931 World Series against the Cardinals overwhelming favorites. The Philadelphia staff posted a Series ERA of 2.66, but they couldn't harness "The Wild Horse of the Osage," Pepper Martin. St. Louis upset them in seven games, thanks to Martin's twelve hits and five steals.

The 1931 Series was the high-water mark for the staff, the team, and Connie Mack himself. Finishing second to the Yankees in 1932, Mack coped with the Great Depression the same way he had coped with financial troubles in 1914: he broke up a dynasty by selling off his stars. By 1934 Cochrane was in Detroit, Earnshaw in Chicago, Grove and Walberg in Boston. In Mack's final 17 years as a Philadelphia manager, he had three winning seasons and ten trips to the cellar. He never won another pennant.

T he photograph above shows the Cleveland Big Four and that triumphant gesture so familiar nowadays: "We're number one." In the more modest 1950s such self-promotion was rare, but the Indians were justifiably proud. They had just clinched the 1954 AL pennant, finally dethroning the tyrant Yankees, world champions for five consecutive years.

Bob Lemon, Early Wynn, Mike Garcia and Bob Feller may have been the greatest pitching rotation of all time. In seven years together, 1949 to 1955, they combined for 443 wins and 278 losses, a winning percentage of .614 and almost 17 victories per man per season. Three of the Big Four, all but Garcia, are in the Hall of Fame.

Feller's years with this staff wrapped up his major league career. His last great season was 1951, when, at age 32, he went 22–8 and pitched his

In 1954 Cleveland's Big Four—from left, Mike Garcia, Early Wynn, Bob Feller and Bob Lemon—led a staff that posted a 2.78 ERA, the lowest for an American League team since the dead-ball era's 1919 Yankees.

Don Mossi's ears earned him the nickname "The Sphinx," but his six wins, seven saves and 1.94 ERA as a rookie for Cleveland in 1954 earned him greater respect.

Satchel Paige

Satchel Paige loved nothing better than a good showdown, and on July 21, 1942, he orchestrated one of the best. Paige was pitching for the Kansas City Monarchs against the Homestead Grays and Josh Gibson, the greatest slugger in negro league history. The Monarchs led 4–0 with a runner on third and two outs in the seventh, when Paige decided to walk the next two batters intentionally to load the bases for Gibson. Paige had presaged the confrontation in the early 1930s when he and Gibson were teammates on the Pittsburgh Crawfords. "Someday we're gonna meet," Paige told Gibson. "You're the greatest hitter in negro baseball, and I'm the greatest pitcher, and we're gonna see who's best."

The crowd fell silent as Gibson stepped to the plate. Paige yelled to Gibson that a fastball was on its way, but Gibson took strike one at the knees. Again Paige announced his intention to throw a fastball, and again Gibson took it for a strike. "Now I'm not going to trick you," Paige yelled in. "I'm gonna throw a pea on your knee, only it's gonna be faster than the last one." Paige nipped the outside corner at Gibson's knees for strike three. "I told you I was the greatest in the world," he said.

If he wasn't the greatest pitcher ever—and many will argue he was—Paige was certainly a unique combination of pitcher, showman and personality. According to teammate Jimmy Crutchfield, "When Satchel got to the ballpark, it was like the sun just came out." Paige's career spanned 44 years, 2,500 games, 300 shutouts and 55 no-hitters. He pitched for 250 teams—many on a one-day freelance basis—in the United States, Canada, Mexico and the Caribbean against sandlot, semi-pro, negro league and all-star major league teams. He once struck out Hall of Famer Rogers Hornsby five times in a game, and once he even rescued the political fortunes of Rafael Trujillo, dictator of the Dominican Republic, by pitching Trujillo's team to the league championship in 1937.

Paige began his pro career with Birmingham of the National Negro League in 1926. He went 63–11 in 1932–1933 with the legendary Pittsburgh Crawfords. Paige hurt his arm pitching in Mexico in 1938, and was told he couldn't pitch again, but in 1939 he earned a spot with the Kansas City Monarchs and wound up winning three games in the 1942 Negro League World Series against the Homestead Grays.

In 1948, Cleveland Indians' owner Bill Veeck signed Paige, who at age 42 became baseball's oldest rookie. Paige went 6–1 for the Indians as they won the AL pennant in a playoff against Boston. In his first three starts, Paige drew more than 200,000 fans to set night-game attendance records in Cleveland and Chicago. He pitched in the majors until 1953, and then in 1965—in order to qualify for a major league pension—pitched three shutout innings for Kansas City.

Paige's early pitching repertoire was limited to a blistering fastball, using a windmill windup with a high leg kick. His control was so good he'd show off by throwing strike after strike using chewing gum wrappers for home plate. He later developed his famous hesitation pitch, which so disrupted a hitter's timing that it was banned shortly after Paige reached the majors.

Joe DiMaggio called him the greatest pitcher he ever faced. One player said Paige's fastball looked like "a white dot on a sunshiny day," while another complained about a called third strike this way: "That one sounded a little low, didn't it ump?"

Veeck, one of Paige's greatest fans, was second-guessed when he signed the 42-year-old pitcher. "Everybody kept telling me he was through. That was understandable. They thought he was human."

SATCHEL PAIGE

(major league records only)
Right-Handed Pitcher
Cleveland Indians 1948-1949
St. Louis Browns 1951-1953
Kansas City Athletics 1965
Hall of Fame 1971

GAMES		179
INNINGS		
Career		476
Season High		138
WINS		
Career		28
Season High		12
LOSSES		
Career		31
Season High		10
WINNING PERCENTAGE		
Career		.475
Season High		.857
ERA		
Career		3.29
Season Low		2.48
GAMES STARTED		
Career		26
Season High		7
COMPLETE GAMES		
Career		7
Season High		3
SHUTOUTS		
Career		4
Season High		2
STRIKEOUTS		
Career		290
Season High		91
WALKS		
Career		183
Season High		57
WORLD SERIES		1948

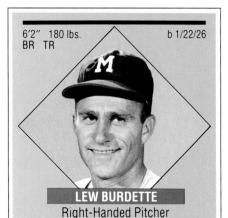

6'2" 180 lbs. b 1/22/26
BR TR

LEW BURDETTE
Right-Handed Pitcher

Even before he released the ball, Lew Burdette had hitters in trouble. The prime spitball suspect of the 1950s, Burdette would put his fingers to his mouth before every pitch, then wipe the excess moisture off on his pants. Or did he? Hitters could never be sure. Then he would go into one of the game's most fidgety motions, heightening the hitter's discomfort. Burdette used these diversions—and an assortment of pitches—to win 203 games in his 18-year career.

From 1953 to 1961 Burdette averaged 17 wins per year for the Milwaukee Braves, including 20 wins in 1958 and 21 in 1959. The right-hander from Nitro, West Virginia, was one of the greatest control pitchers ever, averaging less than two walks per nine innings. With Warren Spahn, he formed one of the most successful lefty-righty duos in history, combining for 392 wins from 1952 to 1962.

Burdette pitched a no-hitter in 1960 against the Phillies, but his long career had two bigger highlights, the first in the 1957 World Series against New York. Burdette beat the Yankees 4–2 in Game 2, then threw a pair of seven-hit shutouts in Games 5 and 7, finishing the Series with a 0.67 ERA and a share of Series records for wins and complete games. Then on May 26, 1959, Burdette locked up in a pitcher's duel with Pittsburgh's Harvey Haddix. Haddix pitched a perfect game for 12 innings, but Burdette kept the Pirates scoreless longer and won the game, 3-0 in the 13th.

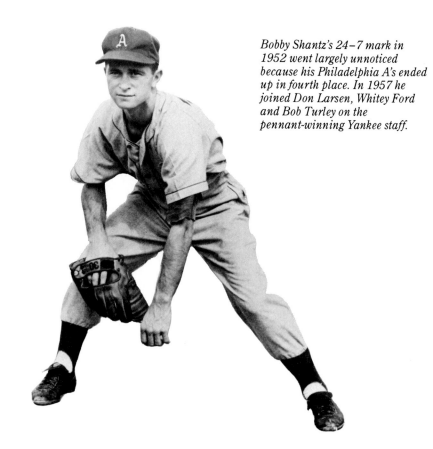

Bobby Shantz's 24–7 mark in 1952 went largely unnoticed because his Philadelphia A's ended up in fourth place. In 1957 he joined Don Larsen, Whitey Ford and Bob Turley on the pennant-winning Yankee staff.

third no-hitter. As the legendary fastball slowed into real time, Feller declined gradually from ace to fourth starter, but he still had one of the best curveballs in the game, and he was still smart. "I was over the hill by the time that photo was taken," Feller says. "But I wasn't too old to learn new tricks. Or teach them."

Bob Lemon matured quickly to become the bellwether of the staff. Before World War II he had been an infield prospect with the Indians, and as a pitcher he remained an excellent fielder and a good hitter, with 37 career homers. Lemon threw a natural sinker, and—under the tutelage of pitching coach Mel Harder—he developed one of the best sliders of the postwar era. In 1948, when the Indians acquired veteran Early Wynn from the Senators, Harder taught him a nasty curveball as a fifth pitch. The other weapons in Wynn's arsenal were fastball, slider, knuckler and brushback.

Mike Garcia was a 6'1", 195-pound, barrel-chested rookie in 1949. Nicknamed "The Big Bear," he might as well have been called "The Work Horse." In 1952, for example, Garcia led the league with 36 starts and relieved in another ten games. "Fastball hitters used to hit Mike pretty well," Bob Feller says, "but he had a first-class curve and change-up. And of the four of us, he had the best control."

In the early 1950s, the Indians often ranked last in the AL in doubles, triples, and stolen bases, and they turned 30 to 50 fewer double plays per season than the Yankees. But they led the league in homers every year from 1950 to 1954, once with eight double-figure sluggers. "Much of manager Al Lopez's strategy," author Robert Creamer says, "was to wait for the home run by holding the other team down with his magnificent pitching."

Why didn't that strategy lead to more than one pennant? One possibility

Early Wynn (left) was already one of baseball's meanest pitchers when he was traded to Cleveland in 1949. After pitching coach Mel Harder taught him a curve, he became one of its best.

is that the magnificent pitching was overworked. Either Lemon or Wynn led the league in innings pitched every year from 1950 through 1954, and in 1952 Lemon-Garcia-Wynn finished 1-2-3. Yankee southpaw Ed Lopat says: "We always thought that if we could just stay close to the Indians through each August, we could beat them in the last month of the season. Their main guys seemed to get tired. The Yankees were working on more of a five-man rotation, and we never pitched as many complete games. We'd let the relievers earn their paychecks." Lopat's lifetime record against Cleveland was 40–12.

When the Indians took the pennant in 1954, winning a record 111 games, their saves jumped from 15 to 36. They finally had a relief corps. Seven saves and seven wins came from "Prince Hal" Newhouser, pitching beautifully in his last full major league season. Another 20 saves and nine wins came from a pair of rookies, Ray Narleski and Don Mossi, who ushered in a whole era of righty-lefty relief duos.

Even with southpaws Newhouser and Mossi in the bullpen, a full 90 percent of the team's innings in 1954 were pitched by right-handers. The Indians had no left-hander in the starting rotation between Gene Bearden in 1948 and Herb Score in 1955—which may be another reason that the team so often finished second. In a short series Cleveland gave up an edge, however slight, to a club with good left-handed hitters, like the Yankees. Or like the Giants, who swept the Indians four straight in the 1954 World Series.

A rookie in 1955, Herb Score displaced Feller as the fourth starter. One doubleheader in May was especially symbolic. In a spot start against the Red Sox in Cleveland, Feller pitched the 12th and last one-hitter of his career. It would have been his fourth no-hitter, but Sammy White broke it up with a single in the eighth inning. In the second game, Score struck out 16. At that

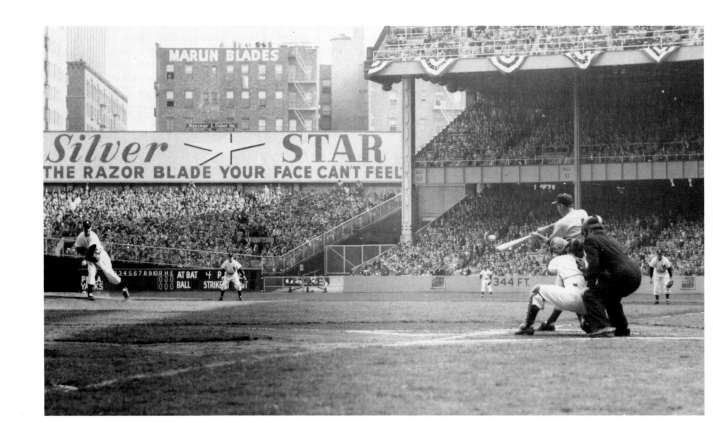

Ed Lopat didn't get the decision in Game 3 of the 1950 World Series (above), but with staffmates like Whitey Ford, Vic Raschi and Allie Reynolds, it hardly mattered. Lopat was 4–1 lifetime in World Series play, and pitched on five straight Yankee world champions from 1949 to 1953.

The way things were going for the Cleveland pitching staff in 1948, Bob Lemon (opposite) no longer needed his glove. On August 21 Lemon ran the Indians' string of scoreless innings to 47, a new AL record.

time the record was 18, and Bob Feller owned it. "I thought Herb was going to break it," Feller says, "because all of his strikeouts came in the first seven innings." Score cooled off in the eighth and ninth, but it was clear that a torch had been passed.

In 1956 the transition was complete. Feller retired and Score joined Lemon and Wynn as a 20-game winner—but that was the staff's last season of glory. On May 7 of the following year, Score's career was shattered by a line drive off the bat of Gil McDougald. As the Indians fell to sixth place, the Yankees kept winning. The excellence of the Yankees' own staff —balancing a team of power hitters—may be the best explanation for the Indians' record as runners-up.

Even before Whitey Ford became a regular starter in 1953, the Yankee rotation of Vic Raschi, Allie Reynolds and Ed Lopat provided a model of consistent, complementary talent. Raschi was "The Springfield Rifle," a fastballer whose ferocity intimidated even his own teammates. Reynolds, part Creek Indian, was "Superchief," another power pitcher who could double in relief. Lopat was "The Junk Man," a left-handed master of breaking pitches—curve, slider and screwball—who could change speeds on all of them. His approach was simple: "Never the same pitch twice, never the same place twice, never the same speed twice." In home doubleheaders, Lopat started the first game, disrupting opposing hitters' timing. Reynolds or Raschi would pitch the second game, firing bullets as shadows fell across Yankee Stadium's infield. The Yankee staff of the early 1950s may not have been among the best of all time, but it was good enough to contend with a Cleveland staff that was.

The Kingdome

Pro football had arrived in Seattle in 1976, and with it a glittering new domed stadium: King County Stadium, better known as the Kingdome. So when the American League expanded the following year, Seattle—in marked contrast to its first major league experience—had a truly major league facility in which to house the expansion team.

Back in 1969, after a last-place finish in the AL West and a first-year attendance of just 677,944, the Seattle Pilots were $800,000 in debt. A minor league city since the late 1800s, Seattle had finally gone major league, but was saddled with a tiny stadium and financially strapped owners. Sick's Stadium—the Pilots' home in 1969—afforded a lovely view of Mt. Rainier, but held just 25,000 fans and had bathrooms that club owner Dewey Soriano called "disgraceful." On March 30, 1970, AL owners voted to approve the franchise's move to Milwaukee, and by Opening Day, major league baseball was gone from the Pacific Northwest.

In fall 1972, a 35.9-acre plot—adjacent to the site where the city was founded—was marked for construction of a domed stadium. Three and a half years and $67 million later, the Kingdome opened. The Kingdome was an immediate success, while the new baseball club—which came in 1977—struggled.

The Mariners opened their inaugural 1977 season with a 7–0 loss to California in front of 57,762 fans. Seattle drew 1.3 million fans in 1977, but finished 64–98, just one-half game out of last place in the AL West. Through 1988, Seattle finished in last place five times, and had not yet had a winning season. Attendance topped one million five more times from 1978 to 1988, but stayed below the 1977 level.

Set against the Puget Sound and the Olympic Mountains, the Kingdome receives almost unanimous praise for its beauty from players and fans. Pitchers are less enthusiastic than most, however, as the ball carries very well in the climate-controlled, wind-free conditions of the Kingdome. And it doesn't have to carry very far to become a home run there, as the Kingdome has the shortest power alleys in baseball—357 feet—and foul poles just 316 feet away from home plate. In four of its twelve years as a major league ballpark, the Kingdome has been the site of more home runs than any other stadium—1979 to 1981, and 1988. Not surprisingly, the Mariners have produced more power hitters than Cy Young Award hopefuls. One of the most powerful was designated hitter Ken Phelps, who in six seasons with Seattle, 1983–1988, averaged one home run every 13.3 at-bats.

Thanks to the loudspeakers that hang from the underside of the roof, the Kingdome has seen its share of the unusual. Batted balls have periodically bounced off speakers. Some have been caught for outs, others have fallen for base hits, and still others never came down at all. In 1979 Ruppert Jones hit a foul ball that stuck in a speaker above the first base dugout, and in 1983 Ricky Nelson did the same. Both players were Mariner outfielders, and both balls were ruled foul and counted as strikes.

The Kingdome's biggest baseball crowd—58,905 fans—came on July 17, 1979, at the 50th All-Star Game. Another baseball highlight came on May 6, 1982, when Gaylord Perry won his 300th career game, 7–3, over the Yankees.

The Seattle Kingdome at dusk (above, left) is a dramatic sight, and even if the host Mariners haven't done very well inside the stadium (left), Seattle baseball has come a long way from humble Sick's Stadium (above, right), home of the 1969 Pilots.

The Kingdome

201 South King Street
Seattle, Washington

Built 1976

Seattle Mariners, AL
1977–present

Seating Capacity 59,438

Style
Multipurpose, symmetrical
dome with artificial turf

Height of Outfield Fences
Left field foul pole to left
  center field: 16½ feet
Left center field to right
  center field: 11½ feet
Right center field to right
  field foul pole: 23 feet

Dugouts
Home: 3rd base
Visitors: 1st base

Bullpens
Foul territory
Home: right field line
Visitors: left field line

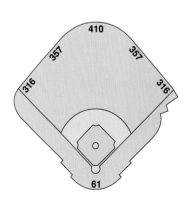

In the first six seasons of divisional play, 1969 to 1974, Baltimore won five AL East titles. The Orioles had fearsome hitting from Frank Robinson and Boog Powell, plus superb fielding from Brooks Robinson and Mark Belanger, but most of all it was a ballclub built on pitching. Oriole pitching routinely led both major leagues in ERA, and the Baltimore Big Three—Dave McNally, Jim Palmer and Mike Cuellar—won 342 games during that six-year span, an average of 57 per season.

The Orioles had been a pitching organization since arriving in Baltimore in 1954 as the transplanted St. Louis Browns. Paul Richards, both general manager and field manager, showed that a weak team could pull itself up to respectability on the strength of young arms. In the mid-1960s new executives like Frank Cashen and Harry Dalton showed that enough fresh pitching could carry a respectable team to a championship. Baltimore won the AL pennant in 1966 with the starting rotation of Dave McNally, Jim Palmer, Steve Barber and Wally Bunker—average age 23—and a veteran bullpen—Stu Miller, Moe Drabowsky, Ed Fisher—that led the league in saves. In the 1966 World Series the Orioles swept the Dodgers in four games, the last three with shutouts.

Earl Weaver took over as Baltimore manager in the middle of the 1968 season. Weaver's field strategy was "pitching and three-run homers," and he said that pitching always came first. His first dividend was the return of Dave McNally, fully recovered from elbow problems, who won 22 games in 1968 and was named Comeback Player of the Year. Because of strains in his arm and back, Jim Palmer had pitched only 49 major league innings in 1967 and 1968. Thanks to a specially padded shoe to correct a left leg shorter than his right, in 1969 Palmer returned to form at 16–4. Baltimore also acquired

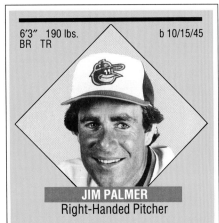

6'3" 190 lbs.
BR TR

b 10/15/45

JIM PALMER
Right-Handed Pitcher

On October 6, 1966, Baltimore rookie Jim Palmer pitched a four-hit shutout to beat Sandy Koufax and the Los Angeles Dodgers in Game 2 of the World Series, the last game of Koufax's brilliant career. A torch was passed that day, from Koufax, the dominant pitcher of the 1960s, to Palmer, the dominant pitcher of the 1970s.

Palmer, like Koufax, had a graceful motion, an active fastball and a sharp-breaking curve. The lanky right-hander overcame arm trouble early in his career to win 20 or more games in eight seasons during the 1970s. He was the centerpiece of an Oriole pitching staff that led the team to six division titles and four pennants from 1969 to 1979 under manager Earl Weaver. In postseason play, Palmer was 8–3.

The 20-year-old Palmer burst onto the scene in the 1966 Series, and his win over Koufax made him the youngest pitcher ever to throw a World Series shutout. He went on to win three Cy Young Awards and led the AL four times in innings pitched, three times in wins, and twice in ERA and shutouts.

Palmer put his pitching philosophy this way: "You must accept that you'll give up runs. The pitcher who gives up runs one at a time wins, while the pitcher who gives them up two, three and four at a time loses. I've given up long home runs that I turned around and admired like a fan. But the ones I admired were all solos." In nearly 4,000 career innings, Palmer never once gave up a grand-slam home run.

Although his brilliant career was cut short by a stroke in 1980, Houston's J.R. Richard's average of 8.37 strikeouts per game earned him fourth place in career standings.

southpaw Mike Cuellar from Houston, thereby turning an excellent staff into a great one.

Sportswriters sometimes referred to the Big Three as "McCuelmer," a collective name connoting common virtues: control, intelligence, fielding skill, and enough hitting ability to remain in close games instead of leaving for a pinch-hitter. But the three hurlers also provided studies in contrast. Palmer, severely logical, was a fastball-curveball pitcher with a classically smooth delivery. Cuellar had an angular motion and superstitions. To start each inning, Cuellar circled the mound and walked up the front of it with his back to the hitter. Always. Cuellar's major league record over six previous seasons was 42–41, but Weaver discovered Cuellar's "devastating" screwball while managing in the Puerto Rican winter leagues. "I had such hitters as Orlando Cepeda, Tony Perez, Paul Blair, and Dave Johnson. Mike made them look silly." Weaver also knew that Cuellar, born in Cuba, was not fluent in English. "A lot of people talked to Mike, and he would just nod at them and say OK, but actually he didn't understand." When Cuellar came over to the Orioles, Weaver teamed him with catcher Elrod Hendricks, who spoke both Spanish and English. In 1969 Cuellar went 23–11 and tied Denny McLain for the Cy Young Award.

Dave McNally lacked Palmer's speed and Cuellar's off-speed assortment, but was called "McLucky" because of the Orioles' remarkable offensive support. "When he's pitching," Brooks Robinson said, "we always seem to get him five or six runs early in the game." Earl Weaver was happy: "All Dave really does well is win."

In effect, the Orioles had three stoppers. Through the whole 1970 season the team's longest losing streak was three games. And in three

In their first 17 seasons in the AL East, the Red Sox won one division title. Since Roger Clemens became the ace of the staff in 1986, they've won two in three years.

Great Rotations

1920 Chicago White Sox

Pitcher	W	L	ERA
Red Faber	23	13	2.99
Lefty Williams	22	14	3.91
Dickie Kerr	21	9	3.37
Ed Cicotte	21	10	3.26
Roy Wilkinson	7	9	4.03

1931 Philadelphia Athletics

Pitcher	W	L	ERA
Lefty Grove	31	4	2.06
George Earnshaw	21	7	3.67
Rube Walberg	20	12	3.74
Roy Mahaffey	15	4	4.21
Waite Hoyt	10	5	4.22
Ed Rommel	7	5	2.97

1948 Cleveland Indians

Pitcher	W	L	ERA
Gene Bearden	20	7	2.43
Bob Lemon	20	14	2.82
Bob Feller	19	15	3.56
Steve Gromek	9	3	2.84
Sam Zoldak	9	6	2.81

1954 Cleveland Indians

Pitcher	W	L	ERA
Bob Lemon	23	7	2.72
Early Wynn	23	11	2.73
Mike Garcia	19	8	2.64
Art Houtteman	15	7	3.35
Bob Feller	13	3	3.09

1968 St. Louis Cardinals

Pitcher	W	L	ERA
Bob Gibson	22	9	1.12
Nelson Briles	19	11	2.81
Ray Washburn	14	8	2.26
Steve Carlton	13	11	2.99
Larry Jaster	9	13	3.51

1971 Baltimore Orioles

Pitcher	W	L	ERA
Dave McNally	21	5	2.89
Pat Dobson	20	8	2.90
Jim Palmer	20	9	2.68
Mike Cuellar	20	9	3.08

1986 New York Mets

Pitcher	W	L	ERA
Bob Ojeda	18	5	2.57
Dwight Gooden	17	6	2.84
Sid Fernandez	16	6	3.52
Ron Darling	15	6	2.81
Rick Aguilera	10	7	3.88

consecutive league playoffs, 1969 to 1971, the Orioles swept their AL West opponents, surrendering only 63 hits in those nine victories.

Weaver's fourth starter in 1969 and 1970 was Tom Phoebus, a 5′8″ right-hander with a deceptive motion. Before the 1971 season the Orioles landed Pat Dobson from San Diego. In 1971 Dobson went 20–8, giving the Orioles four 20-game winners, a record matched by only one other staff in baseball history, the 1920 White Sox of Ed Cicotte, Lefty Williams, Red Faber and Dickie Kerr.

George Bamberger, Weaver's pitching coach, said that the 1971 Orioles had "the greatest rotation I ever saw. From the seventh inning on, if they had a one-run lead, they smelled victory and wiped them out." The fact is that the team didn't have an ace reliever. Eddie Watt led the 1971 club with 11 saves, and the whole bullpen had only 22. The four starters threw three-quarters of the team's innings.

"Where pitching staffs really make a difference," Frank Cashen says, "is with your third or fourth starters. Practically everybody has two good ones. When the Indians would come into Baltimore, they'd pitch Sudden Sam McDowell one day and Luis Tiant the next. And we'd match up with McNally and Palmer. But by the time we got to the third game, they were starting a guy whose record was 5–11 and we were countering with someone 11–5. And the percentages really kinda wore 'em down."

By the end of the 1980s, that same philosophy was best exemplified by the New York Mets. And why not? The Mets' general manager, Frank Cashen, and field manager, Davey Johnson, traced their baseball lineage to Baltimore. Johnson had played second base behind the pitching of "McCuelmer," Dobson and Company. In 1988, when the Mets' pitchers car-

In 1986 Met starting pitchers—from left, Ron Darling, Dwight Gooden, Bob Ojeda and Sid Fernandez—combined for a 66–23 record and had the top four winning percentages in the NL. The team won 108 games and a world championship.

ried the team through offensive slumps to a division title, Johnson claimed that his staff was even better than the Orioles' constellation, mainly because it was younger.

The 1988 Mets used a five-man rotation—Dwight Gooden, Ron Darling, Bob Ojeda, David Cone, Sid Fernandez—with an average age of 26. New York pitchers led the NL in fewest walks, fewest homers, most strikeouts and lowest ERA. But unlike Earl Weaver, Johnson relied heavily on relievers Roger McDowell, Randy Myers and Terry Leach. The 1988 Mets recorded only 31 complete games; the 1971 Orioles had recorded 71.

While the modern pitching staff has evolved toward more starters and larger roles for relievers, the best teams still show family resemblances to the great pitching ballclubs of the past, especially in questing endlessly for more hurlers. At the end of 1988 the Mets were looking at new arms, like David West from their own system and Mark Langston from outside. "I'm a pitching guy," Frank Cashen says. "It's the one commodity everybody needs and nobody ever has in excess. You *never* have too much pitching." ◗

Starting pitchers rarely go the distance for manager Sparky Anderson (opposite, 11), who has one of the quickest hooks in baseball. This time it was Eric King (right), who completed just three of 25 starts in his first three years with Detroit, giving way to a reliever.

Christy Mathewson

John McGraw became manager of the New York Giants on July 16, 1902. He recalled that day many years later: "The club at that time was in last place by 14 games—a good, safe margin. The attendance was almost nothing. And when I walked onto the field to see my team, I found Christy Mathewson playing first base."

Although he had been hired as a pitcher in 1900, Mathewson alternated as first baseman and outfielder while the Giants suffered under a succession of luckless managers. Under McGraw, "Matty" ripened into the dominant pitcher of his era. He won 22 or more games for 12 consecutive seasons, at least 30 games in four of them.

Mathewson, born August 12, 1880 in Factoryville, Pennsylvania, joined the Giants in 1900 after graduating from Bucknell College and serving a short stint in the minors. As a ballplayer, he was unlike most others of the era. He neither drank nor smoked and he disdained playing on Sunday. He was clean-cut and handsome, college-educated and articulate—the all-American boy. It was said of Mathewson, "All at once the game received a new respectability. Young ladies could now ask their escorts to take them to the Polo Grounds to see a college boy play."

There's little question that Mathewson would have become one of the great pitchers whether or not he had ever met McGraw or had played on such a superb and well-rounded team as the pre–World War I New York Giants. McGraw, however, was

little short of a baseball genius. He transformed a last-place team into a pennant winner in less than three seasons; into a World Series champion in four. Mathewson benefited not only from McGraw's genius at recruiting strong players, but from McGraw's overall knowledge of the game. The relationship was close off the field as well: McGraw, Mathewson and their wives—also best friends—shared a Manhattan apartment for a short while.

The 6'1½" right-hander won 20 games in 1901. He won 30, 33 and 31 games in 1903 to 1905 respectively, McGraw's first three full years at the helm. New York finished second in 1903 before capturing back-to-back pennants. To John McGraw, the NL pennant was the ultimate in baseball. The idea of being challenged by a rival from the upstart American League, founded in 1901, was beneath McGraw's dignity.

Refusing to play the World Series against the AL champion Boston team in 1904, the Giants yielded a year later, thrashing the Philadelphia Athletics in five games. Mathewson staged what is still the preeminent pitching performance in Series history: shutouts in Games 1, 3 and 5; 27 innings, 14 hits, one walk, 18 strikeouts and, obviously, an 0.00 ERA.

His "pitch in a pinch" was the fade-away, a forerunner of the screwball. Despite his career 2,502 strikeouts, Matty believed in conserving his arm. He once won a complete game throwing only 67

In 1909 Mathewson posted the best ERA and winning percentage of his career, 1.14 and .806, respectively.

CHRISTY MATHEWSON

Right-Handed Pitcher
New York Giants 1900-1916
Cincinnati Reds 1916
Hall of Fame 1936

GAMES	**636**
INNINGS	
Career	**4,782**
Season High	**390⅔**
WINS	
Career *(3rd all time)*	**373**
Season High *(3rd all time)*	**37**
LOSSES	
Career	**188**
Season High	**17**
WINNING PERCENTAGE	
Career *(6th all time)*	**.665**
Season High	**.806**
ERA	
Career *(5th all time)*	**2.13**
Season Low *(5th all time)*	**1.14**
GAMES STARTED	
Career	**552**
Season High	**46**
COMPLETE GAMES	
Career	**435**
Season High	**37**
SHUTOUTS	
Career *(3rd all time)*	**80**
Season High *(4th all time)*	**12**
STRIKEOUTS	
Career	**2,502**
Season High	**267**
WALKS	
Career	**846**
Season High	**100**
NO HITTERS	**1901,1905**
WORLD SERIES	**1905,1911**
	1912,1913

Mathewson was more than a ballplayer, he was an American hero. After his death, one magazine wrote that men like Mathewson "realize and typify in a fashion the ideal of sport—clean power in the hands of a clean and vigorous personality."

pitches. In 1908 he led the NL in innings pitched with 391, setting the season's high mark for strikeouts with 259 and a low of 42 walks. Through his career he walked an average of only 1.58 men per nine innings. In 1913, he yielded a record-sharing .62 walks a game and went 68 straight innings without issuing a base on balls, a mark that endured for nearly half a century until broken by Kansas City's Bill Fischer in 1962.

He threw two no-hitters; one on June 13, 1905 missed being a perfect game only because of two errors from his teammates. His 373 wins tie him with Grover Cleveland Alexander, who played three more seasons than Matty, for most in NL history.

In 1908 Mathewson had a career-best 37 wins. That season ended in what he described as "the most dramatic and important contest in the history of baseball," a one-game playoff against the Cubs for the pennant. He surrendered three runs in the third inning of a 4-2 Chicago triumph. "I never had less on the ball in my life."

Mathewson and the Giants went to the World Series three more times, in 1911, 1912 and 1913.

They lost each time. In a Game 3 loss to the A's in 1911, Mathewson, with a 1-0 lead, gave up a home run to Frank Baker in the ninth. Philadelphia won in the 11th and Baker—who also homered off Rube Marquard in Game 2—emerged a national hero with an immortal nickname: "Home Run" Baker. In those three Series, Mathewson could do no better than 2-5. Nonetheless, his four shutouts and ten complete games remain Series records.

Christy Mathewson was the greatest pitcher of the dead-ball era, if not the best pitcher in baseball history. He pitched at a time when baseball was a hit-and-run game, not a power contest. A pitcher was expected to go nine innings, and more if necessary. In his 14 full pitching seasons, he threw fewer than 300 innings only twice. In 636 career games, he gave up only 91 home runs, and he hit seven himself.

He showcased his love and understanding of the game in a 1912 book, *Pitching in a Pinch*. A collaboration with John Wheeler of the New York *Herald,* it detailed such intricacies of the sport as situational pitching; the psychology of managing;

Right up to the end of his career, Mathewson was still the game's greatest control pitcher. In 1916, his final season, he averaged less than one walk per game.

stealing signs; and ballplayer superstitions. The book is accurately subtitled *Baseball from the Inside,* and it was a genuine first. Not only was an athlete/author virtually unheard of then, but most fans viewed baseball as the simplest of games, until Matty explained otherwise.

Mathewson won only 11 games from 1915 to mid-1916. McGraw then traded him to Cincinnati where he managed the Reds, pitching one final game in 1916. Matty quit the Reds midway through the 1918 season to become an Army captain in a chemical warfare division. Exposed to poisonous gas in France, he never returned to baseball. Tuberculosis eventually killed him on October 7, 1925, a few months after his 45th birthday.

Christy Mathewson is one of five players who in 1936 were selected charter members of the Hall of Fame. "To me, he was pretty much the perfect type of pitching machine," said McGraw of his star player and close friend. "He had the stature and strength, and he had tremendous speed. There never was another pitcher like Mathewson."

Though the all-American Mathewson didn't smoke, his clean-cut image graced a three-foot tall cardboard ad for Hassan cigarettes in 1911.

Southpaws

Left-hander John Tudor has an answer for every hitter. He jams and unnerves left-handed hitters with his sidearm delivery, uses his great control to carve small portions of the outside corner against righties, and keeps all hitters off balance by changing speeds.

Kansas City's Charlie Leibrandt doesn't throw particularly hard, and there are better breaking–ball pitchers, but Leibrandt's control and intelligence have made him a consistent winner. He won 58 games from 1984 to 1987, second only to Minnesota's Frank Viola among AL left-handers.

Baseball is the left-hander's revenge. Lefties make up just about ten percent of the population, but in major league baseball southpaws account for one-sixth of the position players and one-third of the pitchers. In fact, thanks to baseball, the word "southpaw" is part of the language. The earliest recorded use of the word is 1885, in the journal *Sporting Life*. In those days, diamonds were customarily laid out so hitters would not have the afternoon sun in their eyes. The pitcher therefore faced west, and if he was a lefty, his throwing hand was also his "south paw."

At first glance, baseball seems designed for the convenience of righties. We run the bases counterclockwise, apparently to favor right-handed infielders, who throw more easily across the diamond to first. More by custom than logic, the lefty tends not to play catcher, although he has an edge at first base because, unlike a righty, he does not have to pivot before throwing to second and third base.

As a hitter, the lefty stands closer to first base, and his swing takes him another half step nearer. In the majors he averages 4.05 seconds going down the line to first base; the righty averages 4.15. The breaking pitches of right-handed hurlers come more directly toward the power of a hitter on the left-hand side of the plate, rather than across his body—and he's facing those righties about two-thirds of the time.

The advantages of being a southpaw on the mound are many. The most obvious is the relative unfamiliarity to righties of a left-handed opponent. Then there's the lefty's natural ease in throwing to—and therefore holding runners at—first base. Most important, a lefty's fastball tails away from the right-handed batter, making it decidedly tougher to hit.

In 1978 Ron Guidry (left) had a season most pitchers only dream about. The 5'11", 161-pound southpaw rode his stinging slider to a 25–3 mark, a 1.74 ERA and nine shutouts. His .893 winning percentage was the highest ever for a pitcher with more than 20 wins.

O ne myth about the left-hander is that his pitches have more natural movement than a right-hander's. Whether or not it's true, hitters aren't the only ones who think so; umpires and catchers believe it, too. The late Tom Gorman, who had a brief stint as a New York Giant southpaw in 1939 and a long career as a National League umpire, said: "I've never seen a left-hander who could throw a ball straight. That's why they call them 'crooked arms.' The ball dips and sails and jumps all over. I've always tried to be extra patient with young left-handers who have trouble throwing strikes. I guess it's because I had the same problem myself."

Former Phillies' catcher Tim McCarver agrees: "Every left-hander I've ever seen just can't throw a ball straight. They've got a natural tail on balls that they throw. . . . Believe me, I'm not talking myth here." But McCarver may be talking myth, because no test has ever borne out the claim of "extra movement." It's simply been accepted since the early days of baseball, and the lingering bias against lefty catchers may reflect some instinctive doubt about the "trueness" of their pegs to second base.

According to Tug McGraw, there is a tendency to exaggerate the impressions of left-handed pitchers by players used to seeing right-handed deliveries. McGraw remembers sitting in the home team bullpen at Philadelphia's Veterans Stadium, which is topped with a plexiglass shield. "In that plexiglass," McGraw says, "I could see reflections from the other end of the pen. I was seeing Ron Reed or Gene Garber as *lefties*. And you know what? They looked just as weird as I did!"

If lefty pitchers do have extra movement, baseball people say, it must be because their arm angle is typically lower than righties', less overhand, more three-quarter to sidearm. That description fits southpaws like Tommy John,

One of the game's shrewdest southpaws, New York's Whitey Ford was dangerous whether you were at the plate or on the bases. In 16 years with the Yankees between 1950 and 1967, he won more than twice as often as he lost.

Herb Score threw with a classic overhand motion and a follow-through so complete that his left elbow would crash against his right knee after every pitch. The Cleveland fireballer wore a sponge-rubber pad on his knee to cushion the blow. Score was struck in the right eye by a Gil McDougald line drive on May 7, 1957. He returned to the mound on April 16, 1958 (above), but never regained his former brilliance.

Sid Fernandez and Danny Jackson, but it also raises a new question. When they do throw overhand, do lefty pitchers exploit some secret advantage? This special subcategory of southpaws—over-the-top lefties—includes pitchers like Warren Spahn, Herb Score, Sandy Koufax and Sam McDowell: some of the most devastating hurlers of the postwar era.

The real mystery, of course, is why the lefty's arm angle should be different at all. Pirate pitching coach Ray Miller says that it might be due to southpaws growing up in a right-handed world. Recalling group sprints at spring training, Miller says, "there would be big gaps in the line where some players had run crooked—and those players would always be left-handers."

A few major league observers, including Miller, believe that as more and more lefty pitchers enter the majors, hitters may be getting used to them. But many lefty hitters remain stymied, and the "familiarity factor" doesn't explain why they are more susceptible than righty hitters to being neutralized by a same-handed opponent. The answer might be that lefty pitchers are coming at them by way of the first-base dugout. According to John Matlack, the former Met southpaw, "It's easy for the ordinary left-handed batter to feel that my inside pitch is going to hit him in the ribs, or that my outside pitch is going way off the plate. These guys are bailing out. They're baffled."

Another myth about the lefthander is that he is notoriously wild, that his lack of control on the mound mirrors his lack of control in life, the dark side, of his "oddball" or "sinister" personality. Some lefties have indeed been legendary wild men, none more so than Steve Dalkowski, a minor leaguer in the Oriole system from 1957 to 1965. More than one scout claimed that Dalkowski was the fastest pitcher he'd ever seen. In his first

With a 174–150 lifetime record, Ken Holtzman (left) won't make the Hall of Fame, but his 15-year career did have its highlights. He pitched two no-hitters—in 1969 and 1971—with the Cubs, one in Wrigley Field. After being traded to Oakland in 1972, Holtzman compiled a 4–1 record and a .333 batting average in A's World Series wins in 1972, 1973 and 1974.

professional season, Dalkowski averaged almost two strikeouts—and more than two walks—per inning, giving support to the "wild lefty" theory. Actually, statistics dispute the myth. In 1988, for example, right-handers averaged 3.14 walks per nine innings, lefthanders only 3.02.

A baseball axiom is that "left-handed pitchers mature late." Sandy Koufax is often cited as an example. When he came up as a teenager, he was notoriously wild. Not until 1961, at age 25, did his walks per nine innings go from 5.1 to 3.4 and his won-lost record from 8–13 to 18–13. Koufax attributed the breakthrough to catcher Norm Sherry, who persuaded him not to force his fastball, and to coach Joe Becker, who taught him a slight rocking motion in the delivery as a way of establishing initial rhythm.

Right-handed hitters are supposed to feel baffled by southpaws, especially by control pitchers like John Tudor or Bruce Hurst. "Right-handed hitters try to pull them," says Pat Gillick, himself a former lefty pitcher and now Blue Jays' general manager. "Guys like Kenny Holtzman and Scott McGregor can sit on the outside corner and let right-handed hitters pull them all day. Guys like Charlie Leibrandt or Bud Black—they can just work the outside half of the plate, and right-handers who try to pull them hit ground balls to third or fly balls instead of going up the middle. That kind of pitcher doesn't really need speed, and size isn't even an issue."

Gillick's comments are echoed by many scouts, especially when the question is whether to draft or sign a short pitcher. In modern baseball "short" means under six feet. Before the turn of the century, when most Americans were smaller, nobody thought Old Hoss Radbourn was little at

When he threw his first pitch in the Yankees' season opener April 4, 1989, Tommy John—at age 45—entered his 26th season, a record for pitchers. The ageless sinkerball pitcher beat Minnesota on Opening Day for his 287th career win.

BABE RUTH
Left-Handed Pitcher

| 6'2" 215 lbs. | b 2/6/1895 |
| BL TL | d 8/16/48 |

After watching a 19-year-old pitcher named George Herman "Babe" Ruth hold the Phillies to two runs and six hits in $6^2/_3$ innings of a 1914 exhibition game, Philadelphia pitching coach Pat Moran said, "Ruth is a marvel for a kid just breaking in. He has the build, the curves and can hit quite a bit himself. I predict within the course of a few years Ruth will be one of the best southpaws in baseball."

Moran was right. By 1915 Ruth was mowing them down for the Red Sox; he went 18–8 that season. In 1916 he won 23 games, led the AL with a 1.75 ERA and nine shutouts, and hit three home runs while allowing none in 324 innings. Then, in his first World Series appearance, Ruth pitched the longest single-game stint in Series history, allowing only six hits in 14 innings in a 2–1 win over Brooklyn.

Ruth won 24 games in 1917, but by 1918 Boston needed his bat in the lineup more often. He went 13–7 that season and played 59 games in the outfield. But when Boston faced the Cubs in the World Series, Ruth found himself on the mound for Game 1. The Babe shut Chicago out on six hits, then extended his Series scoreless-innings streak to $29^2/_3$ in Game 4 before winning, 3–2.

Ruth's pitching career came to a virtual end after he was sold to the Yankees in 1920. He pitched in only five games in his 15-year Yankee career, and won all five. But he remains one of the most successful World Series pitchers of all time: 3–0 and a 0.87 ERA.

Despite his nickname, "Goofy," New York's Lefty Gomez was a serious obstacle for AL hitters in the 1930s and early 1940s. The Yankee southpaw led the AL three times in strikeouts and shutouts, twice in wins and ERA.

5'9" and 168 pounds. Right-hander Ed Cicotte and Claude "Lefty" Williams—the dishonest mainstays of the Black Sox pitching staff in 1919—were both 5'9". Over the last two generations, as all athletes have tended to become larger, small pitchers in general have become an endangered species. But little lefties seem better equipped to survive than little righties. At 5'10" and 185 pounds, Eddie Lopat looked as if he were "throwing wads of tissue paper," Casey Stengel once said. "Every time he wins a game, fans come down out of the stands asking for contracts." Stengel described Yankee ace Whitey Ford—the same height but a few pounds lighter—as a "banty rooster" who stuck out his chest and walked cockily out to the mound to outduel the big guys. Most of the little lefties have indeed been gutsy. Most have also been excellent fielders—and Harry Brecheen and Harvey Haddix, "The Cat" and "The Kitten," were among the best fielding pitchers ever. And a pitcher like Baltimore reliever Tippy Martinez, no bigger than Lopat or Ford, held his own from 1974 to 1986, posting a 55–42 career record, and a solid 3.38 ERA.

Before overhand pitching became legal, lefties showed no particular advantage over right-handers. Many 19th-century pitchers cannot be identified as either lefty or righty, but in the first 13 years of professional league baseball, 1871 to 1883, the combined winning percentage of known left-handers was .437 (150–193). From 1884 to 1899 the combined winning percentage for lefties improved to .503 (2,173–2,145), and since the turn of the century it has consistently stayed over .500.

The honor of being the first southpaw in the record books belongs to John McMullen—nicknamed "Lefty," of course—who compiled a 15–16

St. Louis' Harry "The Cat" Brecheen was known to wet his paw now and again to expand his pitching arsenal. Brecheen, who pitched with the Cardinals from 1943 to 1952, was especially tough in the World Series, where he went 4–1 with a 0.83 ERA in seven games.

Top Ten Southpaws

Pitcher	Years	W	L	ERA
Warren Spahn	1942-65	363	245	3.09
Steve Carlton	1965-88	329	244	3.19
Eddie Plank	1901-17	327*	193	2.34
Lefty Grove	1925-41	300	141	3.06
Tommy John	1963-	286	224	3.27
Jim Kaat	1959-83	283	237	3.45
Eppa Rixey	1912-33	266	251	3.15
Carl Hubbell	1928-43	253	154	2.97
Herb Pennock	1912-34	240	162	3.61
Whitey Ford	1950-67	236	106	2.75

*21 wins with Federal League, 1915

record in 1871, the charter season of the National Association. McMullen stood 5′9″, which was probably above average at the time. The first true "little lefty" may be Bobby Mitchell, 5′5″ and 135 pounds, who went 20–22 in the NL from 1877 to 1879. John Francis Smith, at 5′6″ and 162 pounds another little lefty, earned the nickname "Phenomenal" in 1885 when he pitched a no-hitter in which not a single ball was hit out of the infield; he also struck out 16 and picked off the only two baserunners.

In those days the name "Phenomenal" was particularly associated with pitchers who threw the screwball—and most of them were lefties. This pitch became most famous as the money pitch of right-hander Christy Mathewson, but Mathewson credited southpaw Davey Williams for helping him learn it, and it has always been a favorite of southpaws. And when Matty played minor league ball at Norfolk in 1900, his manager was none other than Phenomenal Smith.

Southpaws Eddie Plank and Rube Waddell paced the Philadelphia Athletics in their heyday from 1902 through 1907. For those seasons *each* pitcher averaged over 20 wins a year. Waddell, a notorious flake, never failed to lead the AL in strikeouts. Plank was the very opposite of Waddell—steady, colorless, a college man, very fidgety on the mound. Plank maddened hitters with endless little delays. He was a very slow worker with a sneaky fast delivery. Plank made famous a "crossfire" used later by many lefties, most notably Curt Simmons. Claude "Lefty" Williams later gave this description of the crossfire as Plank perfected it:

"It consists mainly of throwing your body behind the sweep of your arm so that you keep the ball between you and the batter. As he looks out across

In 1961, New York's Luis Arroyo set new standards for productivity out of the bullpen. In 65 appearances—all in relief—Arroyo was involved in 44 of the Yankees' 109 wins as he went 15–5 with 29 saves.

Fastballer Richard "Rube" Marquard averaged 24 wins a season for pennant-winning Giants' teams from 1911 to 1913. But in 1914 Marquard slumped to 12–22 and was released in 1915 by manager John McGraw.

the diamond he sees the ball coming at him against the background of the pitcher's body and the background is very confusing because it is vague and indistinct and continually moving. Then too, the ball will come sweeping in across the corner of the plate and is, all in all, a most effective delivery."

Plank and Waddell represent the first phase in Connie Mack's long career as the best manager of southpaws in the history of baseball. For most of his 50 seasons with Philadelphia, the "Tall Tactician" tried to build his staffs around left-handed pitching. His great 1914 Athletics included southpaws Plank, Herb Pennock and Rube Bressler. In his next dynasty, from 1928 to 1933, Mack's one-two punch was Lefty Grove and Rube Walberg. At the very end of his career, in 1949 and 1950, the Philadelphia staff had a lefty nucleus of Alex Kellner, Lou Brissie and Bobby Shantz.

By contrast, John McGraw, who managed 33 seasons for the New York Giants, had little use for left-handed hurlers. He supposedly said that if you split open a southpaw's head, all that would fall out would be bases on balls. The few left-handers who pitched for McGraw had remarkable control: Hall of Famers Rube Marquard and Carl Hubbell, Hooks Wiltse, Art Nehf, Slim Sallee and Rube Benton. In general, though, McGraw's Giants seem to have been vulnerable to lefty pitching. In 1903 Frank "Noodles" Hahn of the Reds, famous for cleverness and speed, notched five wins over the Giants, three of them shutouts. Two other southpaws—Harry Coveleski of the Phillies and Jack Pfiester of the Pirates and Cubs—were both called "Giant Killer" because of their success in big games against McGraw.

A New York sportswriter wrote in 1916, "His name is Babe Ruth. He is

built like a bale of cotton and pitches lefthanded for the Boston Red Sox. All lefthanders are peculiar and Babe is no exception, because he can also bat." Ruth did everything left-handed except for writing. He also did most everything well, or to excess. He is remembered as a Yankee slugger, the best of the breed. But had he stayed pitching for the Red Sox instead of being sold to New York in 1920, he might have been remembered for other reasons. The stats say it all: by the time he was 22, his pitching record was 67 and 34. His career stats were 94 wins, 46 losses, a .671 winning percentage and a 2.28 ERA; he averaged 3.25 walks and 3.59 strikeouts per nine innings. In World Series play he went 3–0 with an 0.87 ERA, and threw $29\frac{1}{3}$ consecutive scoreless innings, at the time a record.

In 1921 Ruth took a series of physical tests at Columbia University. The tests concluded that Ruth's eyesight and hearing were much "faster" than average, that his efficiency of coordination was almost twice normal, and that his nerves were steadier than those of 499 out of 500 persons. In retrospect, no one said it better than former Philadelphia A's pitcher Rube Bressler, in Lawrence Ritter's *The Glory of Their Times*: "Nature! That was Ruth."

As staffs grew in size and platooning became more common, more lefty pitchers appeared. In 1930 about 23 percent of major league pitchers were southpaws, trying to neutralize lefty hitters. Many ballparks of this era, especially Yankee Stadium, built shorter right field fences. The Yankees started adding left-handed pitching in the mid-1920s, but the Athletics were still able to outplay the Yankees of Ruth and Gehrig three years in a row, 1929 to 1931, mostly on the strength of two big left-handed pitchers: Lefty Grove and Rube Walberg.

During the 1940s, the Cardinals' staff included four lefties: Max Lanier,

The trend toward specialization in pitching in the 1980s has made it imperative for teams to have a southpaw available for all key pitching roles—starter, long man, set-up man, and closer. And lefties are rising to the occasion. In 1988 both leagues' ERA champs were lefties—Minnesota's Allan Anderson in the AL, and St. Louis' Joe Magrane in the NL.

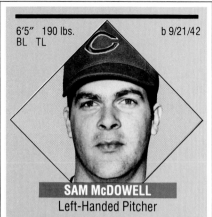

6'5" 190 lbs.
BL TL   b 9/21/42

SAM McDOWELL
Left-Handed Pitcher

Reggie Jackson called him "Instant Heat," but the nickname that stuck was "Sudden Sam"—an apt title for one of the game's greatest fastballers. At 6'5" and 220 pounds, Sam McDowell seemed to pulverize the ball as he pitched it.

McDowell signed a $70,000 bonus contract with the Cleveland Indians in 1960. A little more than a year later, he started his first major league game. He was cruising along beautifully until the seventh inning, when he threw one pitch so hard that he cracked two of his own ribs.

In 1965, at age 23, McDowell went 17–11 with a 2.18 ERA and 325 strikeouts in 273 innings. In addition to his overpowering fastball, Mc-Dowell threw a darting slider and also played with a knuckler, screwball and change-up. He disliked striking out a batter twice with the same pitch. "Almost every batter guesses a few times a game," McDowell said. "This is an advantage for me. Hell, most of the time *I* don't know what I'm going to throw."

McDowell never conquered his control problems, however, and averaged almost five walks per game in his 15-year career. Although he was a six-time All-Star and a five-time league leader in strikeouts, he could not live up to all that his fastball seemed to promise. Oakland's Blue Moon Odom said, "Man, if I had Sudden's stuff I'd win 25 games every year." McDowell won 20 only once, in 1970, and retired in 1975 with a lifetime record of 141–134.

On April 15, 1987, Milwaukee's 22-year-old southpaw Juan Nieves rode a live fastball and hard slider to a no-hitter against Baltimore.

Harry Brecheen, Howie Pollet and Alpha Brazle. In 1943 the four had an incredible group ERA of 1.88. Their success took the Cards into the 1946 Series against the Boston Red Sox. In the postwar era southpaws represented 25 percent of major league pitchers and headed for 30. Left-handed supremacy flowered in the career of Warren Spahn, the greatest pitcher of the first postwar generation, and in the stellar achievements of Whitey Ford, Sandy Koufax and Steve Carlton. It also became essential to the whole strategy of staff building.

Since World War II, the only pennant-winning teams that did *not* have a lefty in the starting rotation were the 1954 Indians and the 1967 Red Sox. Both teams lost in the World Series. In 1965 the Dodgers' rotation included Johnny Podres, Koufax and Claude Osteen, with Ron Perranoski in the bullpen. In 1980, under left-handed owner Bill Veeck, the White Sox staff included five southpaws: Rich Wortham, Ross Baumgarten, Steve Trout, Ken Kravec and Britt Burns. One of the strongest group of lefty pitchers ever appeared with the 1988 Yankees: John Candelaria, Tommy John, Ron Guidry, Al Leiter and Dave Righetti, maybe because their ballpark demands left-handed pitching, just as Fenway Park discourages it.

The southpaw pitcher is an ultimate baseball phenomenon, an archetype. He has become ingrained in all our thinking about the game. Any serious baseball analyst who picks an all-time team, or any kind of imaginary team, selects ten players, not nine—including both a right-handed and a left-handed pitcher. That says it all. ◗

Steve Carlton is the only left-hander on the top ten lists for career innings pitched and strikeouts. The ageless southpaw pitched 5,217 innings and struck out 4,136 batters, more than any other left-hander.

Lefty Grove

For most of his career, Lefty Grove had only one pitch—a fastball as powerful as his temper. Just ask Al Simmons. On August 23, 1931, Grove was on the mound for the Philadelphia Athletics and going after an American League record of 17 straight victories. The unbroken record of 16 was held by Walter Johnson and Smoky Joe Wood. Grove pitched his usual stellar game, but on this day St. Louis' Dick Coffman—whose lifetime record was 72–95—was just as good.

The only run of the game scored when the A's Jimmy Moore, substituting for Simmons, misjudged a line drive in the third that allowed Goose Goslin to score. Denied the AL record for most consecutive wins, Grove flew into a rage and destroyed the clubhouse locker by locker. He screamed at Moore and team owner/manager Connie Mack, but saved the summit of his tantrum for Simmons, who had committed the unpardonable sin of taking the day off to tend to some nagging injuries.

But Grove was even tougher on hitters. "Never bothered me who was up there with the bat. I'd hit 'em in the middle of the back or hit 'em in the foot, it didn't make any difference to me. But I'd never throw at a man's head. Never believed in it," he said.

Still, Grove's talent was bigger than his temper. Pitching in the lively ball era and in two hitters' ballparks—Philadelphia's Shibe Park and Boston's Fenway Park—Grove led the American League in earned run average nine times. No one else won more than five ERA titles. He led the league in winning percentage five times, two more than any other pitcher. He led the AL in strikeouts his first seven years in the majors, and only he and

Sandy Koufax twice struck out the side on nine pitches. And for most of his career, he had only one pitch—an overpowering fastball.

Grove grew up the son of a coal miner in the mountains of western Maryland. He made his professional debut in 1920 with Martinsburg, West Virginia, in the Blue Ridge League, where he struck out 60 batters in 59 innings. But the Martinsburg team needed an outfield fence for its new field, and the money wasn't there, so Grove was sold for $3,000 to the Baltimore Orioles of the International League. Owned and managed by Jack Dunn, the man who discovered Babe Ruth, the Orioles became one of the finest minor league teams of all time with Grove on the mound. In $4^1/_2$ seasons in Baltimore, Grove won 109 games and lost just 36.

Ironically, Grove's great success in the minors delayed his ascent to the majors. Back then minor league teams operated independently, and players only reached the majors when and if their contracts were sold. Dunn had a good thing going in Baltimore; the Orioles won the pennant in each of Grove's four full seasons—years that the left-hander could have pitched in the big leagues. Grove won 300 games in the AL, but his lifetime total might have hit 400 had he reached the majors at age 21 instead of 25.

When Dunn finally decided to sell Grove's contract, it was for a record price. The Yankees had paid the Red Sox $100,000 for Babe Ruth's contract in 1920, and Dunn convinced Mack that for $600 more he could get thousands of dollars in publicity for breaking Ruth's record price. He did. Mack unveiled his new star before 22,000 fans on Opening Day at Shibe Park in 1925, along with newly

Brooklyn manager Wilbert Robinson spoke in admiration of Lefty Grove when he called him "pleasingly wild," but few AL hitters found Grove's wildness pleasant.

acquired catcher Mickey Cochrane. Grove and Cochrane—both of whom are in the Hall of Fame—became one of the game's greatest batteries and played together from 1925 to 1933. The Athletics won three pennants, two world championships, and never finished lower than third place during that period.

But on Opening Day, Mack's decision looked questionable as Grove walked four, hit a batter and was knocked out of the box in the fourth. Accustomed to blowing away minor league hitters with his speed, Grove found his transition to the majors rocky. He went 10–12 in 1925, and while he led the league in strikeouts with 116, he also led it with 131 walks, and posted a poor 4.75 ERA. He evened his record at 13–13 the following year, lowered his ERA to a league-best 2.51 and increased his strikeouts to 194.

Grove hit his stride in 1927 and began a string of seven straight 20-win seasons. In 1928 he won 24 games and walked an average of just 2.2 batters a game. In 1929 he won the first of four straight ERA titles, and the A's broke the Yankees' streak of three consecutive American League pennants. Connie

LEFTY GROVE

Left-Handed Pitcher
Philadelphia Athletics 1925–1933
Boston Red Sox 1934–1941
Hall of Fame 1947

GAMES	**616**
INNINGS	
Career	**3,940⅔**
Season High	**291⅔**
WINS	
Career	**300**
Season High	**31**
LOSSES	
Career	**141**
Season High	**13**
WINNING PERCENTAGE	
Career *(5th all time)*	**.680**
Season High *(5th all time)*	**.886**
ERA	
Career	**3.06**
Season Low	**2.06**
GAMES STARTED	
Career	**456**
Season High	**37**
COMPLETE GAMES	
Career	**300**
Season High	**27**
SHUTOUTS	
Career	**35**
Season High	**6**
STRIKEOUTS	
Career	**2,266**
Season High	**209**
WALKS	
Career	**1,187**
Season High	**131**
WORLD SERIES	**1929,1930 1931**
MOST VALUABLE PLAYER	**1931**

By 1941 Grove had lost his fastball, but was still crafty enough to go 7–7 in his final season. "I'm throwing the ball as fast as ever," he said. "It's just not getting there as fast."

Mack's troops were led by the pitching of Grove, Rube Walberg, Ed Rommel and George Earnshaw—the latter pitched with Grove in Baltimore—and the hitting of Simmons, Cochrane and Jimmie Foxx. The A's won 104 games. With incredible depth to his pitching staff, Mack used Grove only in relief in the World Series against the Cubs. He responded with $6\frac{1}{3}$ shutout innings as the A's won the Series in five games.

In 1930—often referred to as The Year of the Hitter—Grove went 28-5 and led the AL in wins, winning percentage, ERA, strikeouts and saves, as the A's cruised to another pennant. Grove scattered nine Cardinal hits to get his first Series win in Game 1, 5–2. He pitched even better in Game 4, but an error by third baseman Jimmy Dykes led to two unearned runs and a 3–1 St. Louis win. The following day Grove came on in relief of Earnshaw in the eighth inning of a scoreless tie. He held the Cardinals in check, and Foxx tagged Burleigh Grimes for a two-run homer in the ninth to give Grove his second win, and the A's won their second straight world championship two days later.

The AL Most Valuable Player Award and another World Series awaited Grove at the end of his marvelous 1931 season: a 31–4 record, a 2.06 ERA and his seventh straight AL strikeout title—as the Athletics won their third straight pennant. Grove pitched complete game victories in Games 1 and 6 of the World Series against St. Louis, but Grimes was better than Earnshaw in Game 7 and Philadelphia's two-year reign was ended.

Grove had two more outstanding seasons in Philadelphia then became part of Mack's warehouse sale. Mack sold Grove to Boston for $125,000 and Cochrane to Detroit for $100,000 after the 1933 season, a year after he sold Simmons, Dykes and outfielder Mule Haas, and a year before Foxx followed Grove to the Red Sox. Grove, whose middle name was Moses, became known as "Old Man Mose" with Boston, and won four more ERA titles, though he won 20 games just once in eight years. After several tries he won his 300th game on July 25, 1941 against Cleveland, and was given his unconditional release that winter, ending his career at the age of 41.

Grove mellowed over the years, and was described in his *New York Times* obituary as "a tall,

Told the Cardinals were going to bunt on him in the 1930 World Series, Grove (left)—a lifetime .148 hitter—found a better use for his bat.

genial gentleman of 75 with a head of lustrous white hair who loved to sit around at baseball gatherings cutting up old touches." But in his prime he was the fastest, meanest pitcher in baseball. Mack once brought Grove on in relief with the bases full of Yankees and none out. Ten pitches later, Babe Ruth, Lou Gehrig and Tony Lazzeri had struck out and the inning was over.

Detroit's Charlie Gehringer said Grove threw "much harder" than Cleveland's Bob Feller. Joe Cronin, who played against him for Washington and with him in Boston, said no one threw harder or wanted to play more than Lefty. "He was all baseball," Cronin said.

Years after his career ended, Grove still would rather play ball than eat. "If they said, 'Come on, here's a steak dinner,' and I had a chance to go out a play a game of ball, I'd go out and play the game and let the steak sit there," he said. "I would."

The Battery

"When Steve Carlton and I die we're going to be buried 60'6" apart."
—Tim McCarver

Game 7 of the 1926 World Series had come down to a classic confrontation: bottom of the ninth, two out, Cardinals leading Yankees 3–2, and Babe Ruth facing Grover Cleveland Alexander. The day before, Alexander had thrown nine full innings to even the Series at three games apiece. But when New York loaded the bases in this final game with two out in the seventh, Cardinal manager and second baseman Rogers Hornsby called again on the 39-year-old Alexander, who coolly struck out Tony Lazzeri to end the threat.

"Old Pete" coasted through the next inning and two thirds. Now it was a duel to the finish: Alexander and catcher Bob O'Farrell against the man who had just set a new home run record with 59. The moment was positively Ruthian, made to order for the big slugger. Cardinal fans clamored for nothing less than a strikeout. But the veteran St. Louis battery chose to work conservatively to Ruth, whose four Series home runs—three in Game 4—had carried New York this far.

The minds of the battery worked as one: Ruth would get nothing good to hit. O'Farrell crouched behind the plate and set his mitt as a target, low and outside. Pitching away from the Babe's power, Alexander ran the count to three and two before walking the slugger on the sixth pitch, a breaking ball that just missed the outside corner.

O'Farrell nodded encouragingly to his pitcher as New York's cleanup hitter, Bob Meusel, came to bat. In the fourth inning, Meusel had become the goat of the Series when he dropped a fly ball off O'Farrell's own bat,

When Met catchers like Barry Lyons (left) talked in 1988, reliever Randy Myers listened—and responded. Myers contributed seven wins, 26 saves and a 1.72 ERA to the Mets' division-winning effort.

In Game 4 of the 1926 World Series against St. Louis, Babe Ruth (above, right) smashed three home runs in a 10–5 Yankee romp. Ruth hit another in Game 7, but when he came up in the ninth, Cardinal catcher Bob O'Farrell (above, left) and pitcher Grover Alexander pitched around him. Then O'Farrell threw Ruth out trying to steal, and the Cards won the game, 3–2.

allowing the tying run to score. Meusel was more than ready to redeem himself, but he never had a chance. On the first pitch from Alexander, the Babe broke toward second. O'Farrell sprung from his crouch and whipped a perfect throw to Hornsby, who slapped the tag on the sliding Ruth. The World Series was over.

The 1926 Series is remembered for many things: Alexander's two wins, his strikeout of Lazzeri, Ruth's record four home runs, Meusel's error. What is entirely overlooked is how skillfully the St. Louis battery—Alexander and O'Farrell—worked the last seven Yankee batters they faced. Old Pete did what his catcher asked of him, and O'Farrell was alert and deadly accurate against Ruth's surprise steal attempt. The record credits Alexander with the "save" in Game 7, but O'Farrell deserves equal billing.

The relationship between pitcher and catcher is probably one of the least acknowledged aspects of the pitching game. "I always felt some resentment about not being appreciated," says Tim McCarver, who caught 21 seasons in the majors between 1959 and 1980, "but that was always balanced out by the pitchers who knew what I was doing back there. Some of them didn't appreciate me until the time came when they had to pitch to somebody else."

In 1915, when asked for his best advice on pitching, Hall of Famer Ed Walsh responded, "Hook up with some good catcher." Pitching for the White Sox, Walsh hooked up with catcher Billy Sullivan. In 14 full seasons between 1899 and 1916, Sullivan batted only .212, but he was considered one of the best catchers of the dead-ball era. More than 70 years after Sullivan played his last game for the White Sox, another Chicago catcher, Carlton Fisk, maintains the standards set by Sullivan. Fisk has been catching major league pitching since 1969. "I've caught for pitchers who thought that if they won

it's because they did such a great job," he says, "and if they lost it's because you called the wrong pitch. The good pitchers know that it isn't just their talent that's carrying them out there."

Like any relationship, a successful battery depends on clear communication. From his crouch, the catcher signals his pitcher for a particular pitch, a silent exchange that is basic to their success. In their simplest form, a catcher's signals are finger signs: one finger held down between his legs is a fastball; two fingers, a curve; and so on, depending on the pitcher's arsenal. But, because baserunners and coaches can steal signs and relay them to batters, catchers have devised ways to deceive the opposition. With runners on second, the catcher may flash several signs, only one indicating the desired pitch. For example, if the first sign the catcher holds down is two fingers, the pitcher knows that the *second* of the next few signs is the catcher's choice for the pitch. Signals may also indicate location: the catcher's palm held up or down tells the pitcher to throw either a high or low pitch. By touching the inside or outside of his thigh, the catcher can indicate whether he wants an inside or outside pitch.

When a smart pitcher is lucky enough to work with a good catcher, their communication is almost intuitive. Hall of Fame southpaw Sandy Koufax and catcher John Roseboro were a battery for the Dodgers from 1958 to 1966. According to Koufax, the two fell "into such a complete rapport that it was as if there were only one mind involved."

Howard Ehmke, who pitched for the Tigers, Red Sox and A's from 1916 to 1930, said that "pitching a game is really a memory test, like playing a game of cards where you must remember every card that has been played."

From their squat behind the plate, catchers must be ready to spring up and snag errant pitches. Boston's Elston Howard (above) couldn't snag Jim Lonborg's wild pitch to Orlando Cepeda in Game 7 of the 1967 World Series. Curt Flood scored from third to give St. Louis a 2–0 lead in a game the Cardinals won, 7–2.

In 1935 Detroit catcher-manager Mickey Cochrane hit .319 and led the Tigers to a world championship, so in 1936 he was cover material.

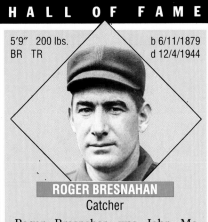

5′9″ 200 lbs.   b 6/11/1879
BR TR   d 12/4/1944

ROGER BRESNAHAN
Catcher

Roger Bresnahan was John Mc-Graw's kind of player—fiery and Irish. At 5′9″ and 200 pounds, Bresnahan was a fireplug of a catcher with a rocket arm, a palpable contempt for umpires, and a burning desire to win.

He began his career as a pitcher, and shut out St. Louis in his major league debut for Washington in 1897. In 1902 Bresnahan followed manager John McGraw from Baltimore to the New York Giants. He played outfield and hit .350 in 1903, as the team vaulted from last to second place. In 1905, at the suggestion of Christy Mathewson, McGraw made Bresnahan the starting catcher, and the Giants won their second straight pennant.

From 1905 to 1908, Bresnahan caught for the great duo of Mathewson and Joe McGinnity. In 1907, to the jeers of fans, he was the first major league catcher to wear shin guards, changing forever how catchers went about their work, and in 1908 he introduced padding to his catcher's mask.

Bresnahan managed in the majors for five years, and as a coach in the mid-1920s helped develop a young pitcher named Carl Hubbell. But he's remembered most for his judgment and tenacity behind the plate. One sportswriter wrote: "Watch him throw to bases. Absolute, unerring decision is his. Never a moment of hesitation, a second of doubt. He heaves the ball with a sort of cold, infallible ferocity. And he possesses that alacrity of taking a chance which differentiates soldiers of genius from the prudent plodder."

Jim Hegan (above, right) never hit better than .249 in 12 full seasons with Cleveland, but between 1946 and 1957 he caught a record 18 twenty-game winners, and was called by one of them, Hall of Famer Bob Feller "by far the best defensive catcher I ever pitched to."

What Ehmke neglected to say is that pitchers rarely have to rely solely on their own memory. One of the catcher's most important jobs is to know the weaknesses and strengths of the opposing lineup.

Moe Berg caught for 15 years in the 1920s and 1930s with the Dodgers, White Sox, Indians, Senators and Red Sox. Berg was known as an egghead, and after he left baseball, he earned a law degree and served in World War II with the Office of Strategic Services, forerunner of the CIA. Perhaps no one has waxed more eloquent about the role of a catcher than Berg did. "He is a poor catcher who doesn't know at least as well as the pitcher what a hitter likes or doesn't like, to which field he hits, what he did the last time, what he is likely to do this time at bat," Berg said. "The catcher is an on-the-spot witness, in a position to watch the hitter at firsthand."

Some pitchers like to review their opponents' hitting strengths and weaknesses with batterymates before the start of the game. Others rely on the catcher to call pitches. Bob Feller was confident enough to do just that. "If you believe that your catcher is intelligent and know that he has had considerable experience, it is a good thing to leave the game almost entirely in his hands." Of course, Feller worked with one of the best, Jim Hegan, who caught Feller, Bob Lemon, Allie Reynolds, Early Wynn, Satchel Paige, Mike Garcia and Herb Score for Cleveland teams from 1941 to 1957. Hegan caught 1,666 games in his career and batted just .228, yet he was the heart of Cleveland's powerful pitching game for nearly two decades.

In baseball's infancy, the catcher's only duty was to stop the ball—frequently with his body—whenever it passed the batter. He didn't help the pitcher much, and he wasn't very effective against speedy baserunners. He was, in the most literal sense of the term, a "backstop," and without padded

With pesky hitters like former Mets' second baseman Wally Backman at the plate, it helps to have an intelligent veteran like Mike Scioscia of the Dodgers behind it. In calling a game, Scioscia places his pitcher's strengths and weaknesses and the game situation ahead of the batter's strengths and weaknesses.

mitt, shin guards, chest protector or mask, he played way back. Even in the 1920s, Muddy Ruel, a catcher for the Washington Senators, referred to catchers' protective gear as "the tools of ignorance" because only a fool would opt to play catcher.

The term "battery," first used by Henry Chadwick in the 1860s, originally meant only the pitcher, likening his "fire power" to Civil War artillery. By the 1880s, "battery" had come to mean pitcher *and* catcher. Between the time A. G. Spalding outfitted his catcher with a fencing mask in 1875 and Roger Bresnahan introduced shin guards in 1907, the strategic significance of the catcher grew increasingly while men who excelled at the position—Deacon White, Buck Ewing, Wilbert Robinson—earned new respect among pitchers, players and fans.

Roger Bresnahan became a full-time batterymate for the likes of Christy Mathewson and Iron Man McGinnity for John McGraw's Giants. A pal of McGraw's from their Oriole days, Bresnahan, like McGraw, was both feisty and brainy. He was a former pitcher, a future manager, and a tough Toledo detective in the off-season. New York sportswriter J. W. McConaughy wrote, "In his clumsy shinguards and wind-pad, his head in a wire cage, through which comes a stream of reproof and comment as he fusses around the plate, he suggests a grotesque overgrown hen trying to get the family in out of the rain. And generally he succeeds."

Bresnahan intimidated umpires, or tried to, and he and McGinnity were notorious for "quick pitching"—legal in those days. On a prearranged signal, Bresnahan would return the ball to McGinnity on the mound, who would fire back without a windup before the hitter was ready. Teammate Fred Snodgrass recalled, "If you were looking at your feet or something, the way they

Rich Gedman (above, left) and Roger Clemens work together to keep opponents from scoring. In 1986 Clemens allowed just 6.3 hits per nine innings, and when those who did get on base tried to steal, Gedman threw them out 50 percent of the time.

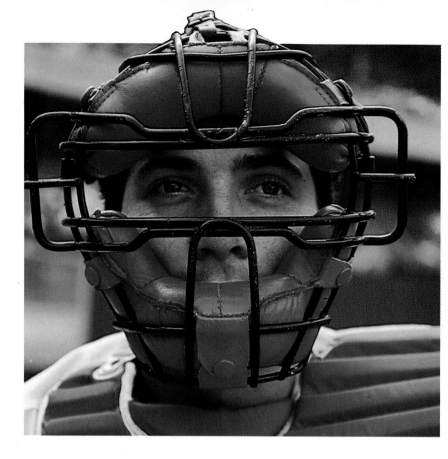

A team couldn't want much more from a catcher than Cincinnati got for 17 years from Johnny Bench. He hit more home runs—327—than any other catcher, won ten consecutive Gold Glove Awards for defense, and played at least 100 games for 13 straight seasons, an endurance record matched only by Mickey Cochrane.

Mickey Cochrane was a great hitter, defensive catcher, and psychic. "Before I'd even look at him, I had in mind what I was going to pitch, and I'd look up and there'd be Mickey's signal, just what I was thinking. Like he was reading my mind," said Athletics' great Lefty Grove.

do today to get just the right position and all, well, by that time the ball would already be in the catcher's mitt."

f a pitcher is like a racehorse—headstrong and powerful and spirited—the catcher is a combination trainer, jockey and broncobuster rolled into one. The catcher must always stay rational; under the worst conditions his must be the voice of reason, a calming influence for his pitcher. A good catcher knows the moods of his pitcher and the effect those moods have on his work; he knows when a pitcher's ego has grown bigger than his arm.

"As far as I'm concerned," says Detroit Tigers' manager Sparky Anderson, "the only responsibility a catcher has is to control his pitchers. He doesn't have to get a hit as long as he can do that." Easy to say for Anderson, who had the luxury of managing Johnny Bench for nine seasons, 1970–1978, with the Cincinnati Reds.

Bench is considered one of the finest all-around catchers of all time. In addition to hitting more home runs, 327, than any other catcher in history, Bench commanded the respect of his pitchers, yet knew how to "control" them. Bench's batterymate with the Reds, Jim Maloney, appreciated the way that Bench knew just how far to push his pitchers. "He'll come out to the mound and treat me like a two-year-old, but so help me, I like it."

One of the most effective catchers ever was Hall of Famer Mickey Cochrane. He and his Hall of Fame batterymate Lefty Grove broke into the majors on the same day, April 14, 1925. Fiery and confident, Cochrane was determined to understand and control his pitchers at all costs. And he learned quickly that no two pitchers are alike. In the late innings of a game, with Grove on the mound, Cochrane might quietly suggest that Lefty was tir-

Consistency behind the plate is often elusive, even for great catchers like the Yankees' Thurman Munson. In 1971 Munson committed just one error; in 1972 he led the AL with 15.

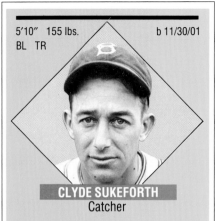

5'10" 155 lbs.   b 11/30/01
BL TR

CLYDE SUKEFORTH
Catcher

Like a lot of catchers, Clyde Sukeforth became a bullpen coach when his playing days were over. In ten seasons with Cincinnati and Brooklyn, he hit an unremarkable .264, with two home runs in 1,237 at-bats.

Until 1951 Sukeforth's most notable achievement was a one-day career as Dodger manager that happened to coincide with Jackie Robinson's breaking baseball's color line in 1947.

Sukeforth was Brooklyn's bullpen coach in 1951 as the playoff between the Dodgers and the Giants went to a third and deciding game. Brooklyn led 4–2 in the ninth, but the Giants put runners on second and third with just one out. Dodger starter Don Newcombe was tiring, and Ralph Branca and Carl Erskine were warming up under Sukeforth's watchful eye. Erskine bounced a curve in the dirt. "Carl didn't have anything," Sukeforth said later. "He was like that at times, and those times you had to bypass him. Branca was really firing."

So when Dressen made his move, it was Branca, who had given up a home run to Bobby Thomson in Game 1 of the playoff, who came on to face Thomson again. Thomson homered to win the pennant, and publicly Dressen blamed Sukeforth. "How dare anybody who is number one lay the fault on someone else?" said Dodger pitcher Clem Labine. "It wasn't Clyde Sukeforth who put Branca in; it was Charley who said, 'Give me Ralph Branca.'" That winter, Sukeforth was released by the Dodgers.

---

ing, that perhaps he should give in to a reliever. That would so fire up Grove that his fastball would "miraculously" return. Rube Walberg required a totally different tack. In one game against the powerful Yankees, Cochrane stalked out to the mound and confronted the tiring Walberg. "You remind me more of a gutless, washed-up old bum than a major league pitcher," shouted Cochrane. Walberg retired the next five Yankees in order and hung on to win.

But there are two sides to the psychological game between the catcher and the pitcher. "Catchers, like other players, can be temperamental," says Feller, "and they often show their temperament in firing the ball back to you as hard as they can. I've had some who threw almost as hard as I did."

"A catcher is the wife of the battery couple," Waite Hoyt once said. "He must jolly him along to make him think he is the big cheese." Not surprisingly, Hoyt earned his keep as a pitcher.

"I think the first thing I learned in the big leagues," recalled Tim McCarver, "was never to hang out with a pitcher, because for them every four days was either a wake or New Year's Eve. It can kill you."

Over the years the pitcher-catcher relationship has become the core of any winning team. The battery *is* like a marriage, with the personality of one player frequently becoming almost indistinguishable from that of the other. From 1903 to 1907, with the Philadelphia Athletics, Rube Waddell and Ossee Schreckengost teamed as a battery, were roommates, and shared a bed—the custom of the times. Each insisted that a clause be inserted into his contract that would prohibit the other from eating crackers in bed. The two had become that much alike. They died three months apart. ⚾

Candlestick Park

It seemed like a nice idea in 1958. With major league baseball in San Francisco, why not nestle its new stadium in a cove with a bayside view? There was ample parking, and adventurous fans could arrive by boat. Unfortunately, Candlestick Park was in trouble even before it opened. The city, team owner Horace Stoneham and building contractor Charles Harney fought running battles over money, scheduling and facilities for nearly two years while the stadium was being built. Grand juries ordered probes of the stadium's financing and parking contract, and a Teamster strike delayed the installation of seats. When the stadium finally opened on April 12, 1960, umpires complained because the foul poles were installed on the field of play.

But none of these problems compared with Candlestick Park's atmospheric woes. The stadium's location on Candlestick Point brought strong winds whipping in from left field, adding a nasty wind-chill factor to night game temperatures that could drop to the 40s. On chilly summer evenings, iron pipes carrying heated water underneath 20,000 reserved seats gave Candlestick the distinction of being the "only heated open-air stadium in the world," but brought little relief to shivering fans. One fan even sued the Giants, claiming he had to leave his seat during several exciting rallies because his feet were freezing. One game in 1960 had to be delayed for 30 minutes because of fog, and a nationwide television audience saw just how windy it got at Candlestick when Stu Miller, the Giants' 165-pound relief ace, was literally blown off the mound in the ninth inning of the 1961 All-Star Game. The unfortunate Miller was called for a balk.

By 1971 a $16.1 million renovation was completed, including 16,000 new seats, escalators to ease the long, uphill climb from the parking lot, synthetic turf, and conversion of the stadium into a bowl, which cut down somewhat on wind velocity. In 1979, grass replaced the synthetic turf, and in 1987 another $30 million was spent on renovations.

Despite its problems, Candlestick Park has been a successful home for the Giants over the years. Through 1988, the Giants had finished under .500 at home only eight times in 29 years. And while it's been the home park of great hitters like Willie Mays, Willie McCovey, Bobby Bonds and Will Clark, Candlestick is first and foremost a pitcher's park. The strong winds blowing in from left field turn potential home runs into fly outs, and as a result most of Candlestick's historic moments have been centered around pitchers.

Juan Marichal, the Giants' greatest pitcher since they moved to San Francisco, tossed a one-hit shutout in his major league debut on July 19, 1960. The 1962 World Series came down to a duel between the Giants' Jack Sanford, a 24-game winner, and the Yankees' Ralph Terry. Sanford and reliever Billy O'Dell held New York to a single run, but Terry held the Giants scoreless, and walked off the mound a winner after Willie McCovey's vicious line drive was caught by second baseman Bobby Richardson in the ninth, stranding Matty Alou at third base. On September 17 and 18, 1968, the Giants' Gaylord Perry and the Cardinals' Ray Washburn turned in back-to-back no-hitters. A pitcher even turned in some of Candlestick's greatest hitting fireworks. On July 3, 1966, Atlanta's Tony Cloninger became the first pitcher ever to hit two grand slams in a single game.

And while fans have to suffer through the wind and cold at Candlestick, rain is hardly ever a factor. The Giants have only had 21 games rained out since they moved to San Francisco in 1958, and once went 454 home games—from April 10, 1976, through October 2, 1981—without a rainout.

Sod from the Polo Grounds (above) was transferred from New York City to San Francisco's Candlestick Park (top), which opened in 1960 with a grass field, went to synthetic turf in 1971 and back to grass in 1979. Willie Mays (seated at back left of car) was the main attraction as the Giants paraded into San Francisco in 1958.

Candlestick Park

Candlestick Point, east
  of Bayshore Freeway
San Francisco, California

Built 1960

San Francisco Giants,
  1960–present

Seating Capacity 58,000

Style
Grass surface, symmetrical

Height of Outfield Fences
9 feet, foul pole to foul pole

Dugouts
Home: 1st base
Visitors: 3rd base

Bullpens:
Foul territory
Home: right field line
Visitors: left field foul line

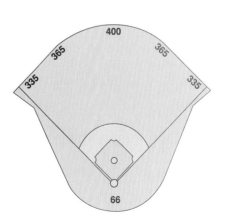

Helping Himself

Everybody moves on a sacrifice bunt. In Game 7 of the 1986 World Series, Met catcher Gary Carter (right) covered third as first baseman Keith Hernandez (left) charged the plate, then wheeled to watch pitcher Ron Darling (above) make the play at first.

When you're as good a pitcher but as bad a hitter—.115 lifetime—as Nolan Ryan, you lay down a lot of sacrifice bunts (right). In 1989 Ryan returned to the AL where, because of the designated hitter rule, pitchers don't hit.

Nineteenth-century wizard John Montgomery Ward could do it all. As a pitcher he completed 244 of his 261 career starts, then switched to shortstop and hit over .300 three times in the late 1800s for the New York Giants.

T he pitcher sometimes seems to be baseball's ultimate specialist. A starting pitcher appears in about one game out of five. A front-line reliever works more often but only in a narrowly defined role a few innings at a time. The duties of a hurler are so specific that less is expected of him as a fielder, runner or hitter. In the American League he almost never comes to bat; in the National, the most common managerial decision is when to take him out for a pinch-hitter.

Yet the enterprise of pitching has always encouraged and rewarded the all-around athlete. Throwing a ball with speed, control and consistency requires total body coordination. Small wonder that the same athletic skills carry to fielding and hitting. As a fielder the pitcher is the point man of the defense. As a hitter he can help the team by helping himself.

In the 19th century it was taken for granted that the pitcher should be a versatile team player. Rosters were smaller and the game itself was less specialized, especially before free substitution was permitted. Before 1891, substitutes could enter the game only because of an injury, or with permission of the opposing team. In 1884, when Old Hoss Radbourn won 60 games for Providence, he used his "off" days to play first base, second base, shortstop and left field. In 1886 Guy Hecker won 27 games for Louisville in the American Association, resting between starts by playing first base and the outfield. Hecker accrued enough at-bats to qualify for the league hitting title, and he claimed it with a .342 average.

The most multi-talented pitcher of last century was John Montgomery Ward. In 1879 Ward won 47 games and hit .286 to lead the Providence Grays to a National League pennant. With the New York Giants in 1883, he became the first pitcher ever to hit two home runs in a game. In 1887, playing as a

middle infielder, Ward stole 111 bases. He had been surpassed as a hurler when overhand deliveries became legal, but he continued to broaden his game as a team captain, labor leader and author. His *Base Ball: How to Become a Player* was a best-seller. After earning a law degree from Columbia in his off-seasons, Ward founded the Brotherhood of Professional Base Ball Players, a union that grew into the Players League of 1890. When that noble effort failed, Monte Ward completed his Hall of Fame career by returning to the NL as player-manager for the Dodgers and Giants.

Ward's lifetime record includes 161 pitching victories and 2,123 hits. No other major league player even comes close to that combination—and among those whose careers began after 1900, only three have had 100 victories and 500 hits. One was Smoky Joe Wood, whose pitching career was meteoric. In 1912, at 23, Wood went 34–5 for the Red Sox and won three more games in the World Series. But after he broke his thumb in 1913, Wood said, "the old zip was gone from that fastball." His arm became so sore that he needed two weeks between starts, and he retired in 1916. Then he resolved to try for a comeback: "I could hit and I could run and I could field. . . . Doggone it, I was a *ball player*, not just a pitcher." Wood played five more seasons as an outfielder for the Indians, and in 1921 he hit .366.

The other two pitchers to reach the 100/500 mark—Walter Johnson and Red Ruffing—did not do it by changing positions in mid-career. Each did it by playing more than 20 seasons and by batting well enough to be used as a pinch-hitter. Johnson's lifetime batting average was only .236, but in 1925 he hit .433 to set a single-season mark for pitchers. He also posted a 20–7 pitching record that year, the last of his 20-win seasons, leading the Senators to their second straight pennant. Ruffing batted over .300 eight times during

1988 Cy Young Award winner Orel Hershiser is a great all-around athlete. In addition to baseball, Hershiser played left wing for the Philadelphia Flyers Junior A hockey team, and he's also a four handicap golfer.

Mets' southpaw Bob Ojeda was a first baseman in high school, but was out of practice when this wide throw came his way in Game 6 of the 1986 World Series against Boston. Spike Owen (5) was safe on the play.

his long AL career, 1924 to 1947, and swatted 36 homers, only two fewer than the best hitting pitcher in major league history: Wes Ferrell. Ferrell still owns career records among pitchers for his .451 slugging average and 38 home runs, and season records for homers, nine in 1931 and hits, 52 in 1935. He batted .280 lifetime. His brother Rick, a Hall of Fame catcher, batted .281.

Wes Ferrell was 6'2", handsome, and high strung. He played the role of intimidator to the hilt. "I put an act on," Ferrell admitted after he retired. "I'd stomp and storm around out there like a bear cat, fight my way through a ball game, fight like the devil, do anything to win." Whenever he lost, Ferrell really *was* mean—and it was no act. One of his teammates, Doc Cramer, recalled: "I saw him stomp a brand-new wristwatch one day in the clubhouse after he'd got beat. He was putting the watch on, it slipped and fell, and he stomped it right there. 'Well, I won't drop you anymore!' he said."

Ferrell won 21 games for Cleveland in 1929, his rookie year, and a total of 91 in his first four seasons. The Indians used him as a starter, reliever, pinch-hitter, and reserve outfielder. In 1931 Ferrell hit .319 with nine homers and 30 RBI in 116 at-bats. That season he won 22 games, one of them a no-hitter. When he blanked the St. Louis Browns on April 29, he also hit a homer and a double and drove in four runs. The closest thing to a St. Louis hit was an eighth-inning grounder to deep short that was fumbled slightly, thrown late to first, and finally ruled an error. The batter was Rick Ferrell.

Wes and Rick played together for the Red Sox and Senators in the mid-1930s. They generally got along fine, but in one game against Detroit, when Wes kept shaking off his signs, Rick growled: "Throw any damn thing you please. You can't fool me. I know you well enough." The rest of that game, using no signs, he caught everything Wes threw and made it look easy. Wes

Wes Ferrell hit nine homers for Cleveland in 1931, which was not only a single-season record for pitchers, but third best on the entire Indian team. That year, Babe Ruth hit 46 homers, one every 11.6 times up. Ferrell's homers came once every 12.8 at-bats.

Slugging Hurlers

A good hitting pitcher is a double-barrelled asset. In a tight situation, a pitcher who can hit can win one for himself and his team. The following list ranks pitchers according to career home runs hit through the 1988 season.

		Career Statistics		
Pitcher	HR	BA	W	L
Wes Ferrell	38	.280	193	128
Bob Lemon	37	.232	207	128
Red Ruffing	36	.269	273	225
Warren Spahn	35	.194	363	245
Jack Stivetts	35	.297	207	131
Earl Wilson	35	.195	121	109
Don Drysdale	29	.186	209	166
John Clarkson	24	.219	327	177
Bob Gibson	24	.206	251	174
Walter Johnson	24	.231	416	279
Jack Harshman	21	.179	69	65
Milt Pappas	20	.123	209	164
Dizzy Trout	20	.213	170	161
Gary Peters	19	.214	124	103
Schoolboy Rowe	18	.263	158	101
Cy Young	18	.210	511	313
Jim Tobin	17	.264	105	112
Early Wynn	17	.214	300	244
Jim Kaat	16	.185	283	237
Johnny Antonelli	15	.178	126	110
Don Cardwell	15	.135	102	138
Dick Donovan	15	.163	122	99
Lefty Grove	15	.148	300	141
Jouett Meekin	15	.243	156	134
Don Newcombe	15	.271	149	90
Joe Nuxhall	15	.198	135	117
Claude Passeau	15	.192	162	150
Pedro Ramos	15	.155	117	160
Hal Schumacher	15	.202	158	120
Rick Wise	15	.195	188	181

hurled a two-hit shutout. After the game Rick told him: "Well, you pitched a pretty good ball game. But damn you, if you'd listened to me, you'd have pitched a *no*-hitter!"

At Boston in 1935 Wes had another season of manifold excellence: 25 pitching victories and a batting average of .347 with 7 home runs and 32 RBI. He remained a multiple threat even after he retired from the majors. In 1948, still playing in the minors at age 40, Ferrell hit .425 to lead the Western Carolina League.

He was always a tough athlete. As a pitcher he finished over 70 percent of his starts and led the AL three times in innings pitched. He posted a lifetime record of 193–128 with six seasons of 20 or more wins. And Ferrell picked up many of those victories for one simple reason: he helped himself.

The pitcher as all-around player was a mainstay of black baseball in the days before integration. Negro league teams maintained smaller rosters than their white counterparts, and economic conditions encouraged owners to look for players who could do double duty. Sportswriter Damon Runyon assigned Ted Radcliffe the nickname "Double Duty" in 1932 after watching the Homestead Grays play a doubleheader in Yankee Stadium. In the first game, with Radcliffe as his catcher, Satchel Paige threw a 5–0 shutout. In the second game Radcliffe took the mound himself and threw a 4–0 shutout. Runyon wrote: "It was worth the price of admission just to see Double Duty out there in action."

The best two-way shots in black baseball were Bullet Joe Rogan and Martin Dihigo. Rogan joined the Kansas City Monarchs in 1920 and remained a multiple star in the negro leagues for 19 years. In the first black

6'5" 205 lbs.   b 11/7/38
BL TL

JIM KAAT

Left-Handed Pitcher

Jim Kaat learned the importance of fielding his position the hard way. In 1962 a sharply hit grounder back to the mound relieved Kaat of six of his teeth. He went on that year to win his first of 16 straight Gold Glove Awards as the AL's best fielding pitcher.

But Kaat was much more than just a great fielder. His 25-year career spanned four decades, 1959 to 1983, and only Tommy John has pitched longer. The 6'5" southpaw won 283 games, with ten wins or more for 15 straight years, 1962 to 1976. Of course, when any player stays in the majors for that long, he's bound to pick up some less than flattering records. Kaat's include most AL losses by a left-hander, 191; most sacrifice flies allowed, 134; and he's tied for most career grand slams allowed, 9.

Kaat began his career with the Washington Senators, then became a mainstay of the Minnesota Twins' pitching staff in the 1960s. He out-dueled Sandy Koufax in Game 2 of the 1965 World Series with a seven-hitter, but wound up the loser in two subsequent meetings with Koufax in that Series. Kaat's finest season was 1966, when he led the AL with 25 wins, 19 complete games and 304⅔ innings pitched. He was an outstanding control pitcher throughout his career, averaging 2.15 walks per nine innings.

Kaat had two 20-win seasons with the White Sox in 1974 and 1975. He was a relief pitcher for Philadelphia, New York and St. Louis from 1979 until his retirement in 1983.

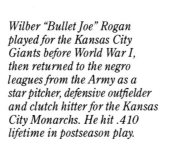

Wilber "Bullet Joe" Rogan played for the Kansas City Giants before World War I, then returned to the negro leagues from the Army as a star pitcher, defensive outfielder and clutch hitter for the Kansas City Monarchs. He hit .410 lifetime in postseason play.

World Series, a best-of-nine playoff in 1924 between the Monarchs and the Philadelphia Hilldales, Rogan went 2–1 as a pitcher, played six games in center field, and batted .325 with clutch hits in three Kansas City victories.

The stocky Rogan pitched with a no-windup delivery..Martin Dihigo, tall and graceful, threw with a long flowing motion—from center field as well as from the mound. Dihigo was an offensive-defensive titan in three countries: his native Cuba, the United States and Mexico. In the Mexican League in 1938, he went 18–2 with a 0.90 ERA, led the league in strikeouts, pitched a no-hitter, hit .387 and managed the Vera Cruz club to the pennant. Latin fans immortalized Dihigo as "El Maestro."

Don Newcombe, one of the first black pitchers in the major leagues, helped himself in sundry ways. In 1949, his rookie year with the Dodgers, Newcombe went 17–8 and led all NL pitchers with 22 hits and no errors. At 6'4" and 220 pounds, he generated power both as a hurler and a slugger— and big as he was, Newk could run. He stole home in 1955 against Elroy Face of the Pirates immediately after hitting a gapper and stretching it into a triple. That season Newcombe achieved a .632 slugging average, the highest ever by a pitcher.

One of Newcombe's contemporaries was Bob Lemon, a Cleveland infield prospect who returned from World War II as a formidable relief pitcher. By 1948, the Indians' championship season, Lemon had become a starter— and a 20-game winner—but he liked to take batting and infield practice as if he were a regular third baseman. When he retired in 1958, Lemon had 207 pitching victories, a career .291 average as a pinch-hitter, and 37 homers, one fewer than Wes Ferrell.

Two postwar pitchers, Harvey Haddix and Bob Gibson, won Gold Glove

Awards for fielding in the same season that they led all pitchers in hitting. Haddix did it in 1959 when he batted .309 for the Phillies, living up to his nickname "Kitten" by pouncing on everything hit up the middle. When Gibson did it in 1970, he also won the Cy Young Award with a 23–7 record. Originally signed by the Cardinals as a pitcher-outfielder, Gibson was a natural athlete who once played a year of basketball with the Harlem Globetrotters.

In the course of 25 major league seasons, from 1959 to 1983, Jim Kaat helped himself win 283 games. The big lefty was a fair hitter—.185 lifetime with 16 homers—and a superior bunter: he executed 134 sacrifices, a record for hurlers. The best fielding pitcher of his era, Kaat won 16 Gold Glove Awards—seven more than his nearest rival, Bob Gibson. Like Gibson, Kaat was an aggressor on the mound, a total athlete, a sharp analyst, and an incredibly fast worker.

Other pitchers—like Steve Carlton and Rick Rhoden—have also won Gold Gloves and led pitchers in hitting, but not in the same season. Three of the best hurlers of the 1980s at helping themselves have been Ron Darling, Fernando Valenzuela and Rick Reuschel. Darling's natural agility makes him a fifth infielder, and his quick feet give him a devastating pick-off move. Valenzuela has won games for himself with the bat as well as the glove. And Reuschel, according to Giants' manager Roger Craig, "may be big and ungainly looking, but he's refined a style with no waste motion and no waste *pitches.*" Reuschel works quickly and uses a simplified delivery that always leaves him in good fielding position. "He's a great glove," Craig says, "and a tough out at the plate. I think Reuschel is the best all-around pitcher of the decade."

Jim Kaat's quick move to the plate made life difficult for base stealers. Some runners claimed that his unorthodox motion was illegal, but Kaat was

In Game 3 of the 1978 NLCS, Philadelphia southpaw Steve Carlton destroyed the Dodgers almost single-handedly. Carlton pitched an eight-hitter, smashed a three-run homer off Don Sutton (above) in the second and drove in another run with a single in the sixth as the Phillies won, 9–4. It was the only game the Phillies won in the Series.

Like a lot of pitchers, the Mets' Sid Fernandez (opposite) loves to hit. And even though he hit .250 in 1988, 59 points better than opposing batters hit against him, Fernandez knows his livelihood depends on keeping his left arm safe and warm.

charged with only six balks in a quarter century. Of course, as a southpaw he had a more natural pick-off move to first base, but picking off runners was not the main point. According to Tom House, the Rangers' pitching coach and a former southpaw hurler, "A pick-off move is really a 'hold close' move." With a runner on first, House says, the pitcher should deliver the ball to home plate in less than 1.2 seconds—because it takes most catchers 2.0 seconds to receive the ball and get it to second base, and the total of 3.2 is just fast enough to nail a fast runner.

Right-handed pitchers usually check a runner at first base by tucking the chin into the left shoulder and relying on peripheral vision. The runner studies the pitcher's right heel. To pivot and throw to first, most right-handers must start by lifting that heel. If the runner sees the pitcher begin the delivery without a heel raise, he knows that the ball is going to the plate and he can begin his takeoff. Some righties, like the Mets' Ron Darling, use a counter-strategy: throwing to first base by jumping off the rubber, firing as they land on the right foot. This maneuver, Tom Seaver says, requires "quick, almost dancing feet."

Seaver did not have quick feet, and he used a high knee lift that slowed his move to the plate. But he tirelessly practiced his pick-off motion in front of a mirror, looking for the tiniest tipoff—just as a runner would. On the mound Seaver always varied his pauses before the delivery. He often threw to first just as the baserunner started to take a lead, because a runner who begins with a cross-over step is most vulnerable at that point. He also believed in harrying a runner at second base. "Keeping him close to the bag," Seaver said, "will give your outfielders a better chance of throwing him out at the plate on a single."

CALCULATING THE ERA

A pitcher's earned run average (ERA) records the average number of earned runs he allows per nine innings pitched. It remains unchallenged as the best statistical measure of pitching performance.

To calculate a pitcher's ERA, multiply the number of earned runs he has given up by nine. Divide the result by the number of innings he's pitched. The result is his ERA.

Earned runs are those for which the pitcher is held accountable—those that score without benefit of fielding errors. Unearned runs are those scored with the benefit of an error, catcher's interference, or a passed ball. If, for example, with two outs and a runner on third, a fielder commits an error that allows a runner to score, the run is scored as unearned. It is not charged against the pitcher's ERA because, had the fielder made the play, the run would not have scored and the inning would have been over. Any and all subsequent runs that score after a two-out error are also unearned.

Generally, an ERA of under 3.00 is considered excellent; 3.00 to 4.00 is good; above 4.00 needs improvement.

For Minnesota's Frank Viola, the 1987 World Series was an ERA see-saw. In Game 1, Viola pitched eight innings, allowing one earned run for a 1.13 ERA (nine times one, divided by eight). In Game 4 he allowed five earned runs in 3⅓ innings, and his totals gave him an ERA of 4.76 (nine times six, divided by 11⅓). In Game 7 Viola lowered his ERA, allowing two runs in eight innings. His ERA for the Series was 3.72 (nine times eight, divided by 19⅓).

Viola's 1987 World Series

	IP	H	R	ER	BB	SO	W	L	ERA
Total	19⅓	17	8	8	3	16	2	1	3.72

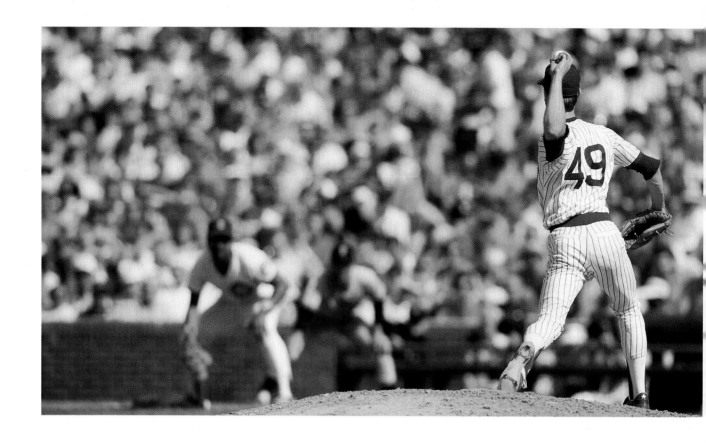

When making their pick-off move to first base, many left-handers—like the Cubs' Jamie Moyer (above, 49)—wind up with their right foot pointed halfway between first base and home plate. This ambiguous and technically illegal maneuver keeps potential base-stealers off balance.

LA's Fernando Valenzuela (opposite) is rated among the NL's best at all phases of the game. As a rookie in 1981 Valenzuela won the NL Cy Young Award, in 1983 he received the Silver Bat as the league's best hitting pitcher, and in 1985 won the Gold Glove Award for his defensive skill.

The pick-off play at second is a work of art. Using a prearranged signal with the shortstop, often relayed by the catcher, the pitcher faces the plate, counts silently to himself, then whirls and throws to the bag while the shortstop is still moving. Seaver aptly describes it as "one of the prettiest plays in the sport." Shortstop Lou Boudreau, the Indians' player-manager, engineered eight pick-offs at second base during the 1948 pennant race. In the World Series opener, at Boston against the Braves, Boudreau signaled for the play with the game on the line. Bob Feller and Johnny Sain were hooked up in a classic duel, 0–0 in the bottom of the eighth. With one out and the Braves' Phil Masi on second, Feller turned and fired to Boudreau as the startled baserunner tried to get back with a head-first slide. The play looked clear-cut; even Sain thought his teammate had been tagged out. But umpire Billy Stewart called Masi safe, amid howls of Indian protest, and moments later Tommy Holmes singled home the game's only run. "We caught two fellows napping—Masi and Stewart," Feller said. He lost a two-hitter, the closest he would ever come to winning a World Series game.

Cleveland took revenge the next day. In Game 2 the Braves had Cleveland hurler Bob Lemon on the ropes in the first inning: one run in, two men on, only one out. Suddenly Lemon wheeled and threw to Boudreau, picking Earl Torgeson off second base to kill the rally. It was the turning point of the game, a 4–1 Cleveland victory, and the turning point of the Series too, which Cleveland won, 4 games to 2. ◑

Warren Spahn

"Facing Warren was the greatest challenge I knew, because this man was a pitching scientist, an artist with imagination." —*Stan Musial*

Stan Musial and Warren Spahn faced each other across 18 seasons, 1946 through 1963, time enough for a lot of adjustments on both sides. Musial hit Spahn pretty well—.314 with 14 home runs—but pointed out that, "Most of those long balls came early in both our careers, when he could really throw hard and I had quicker reflexes and he'd try to buzz one by me."

Over the years, as Spahn began to change speeds, Musial had to avoid being drawn off-stride. "I learned I had to give in, to go to the opposite field against him, to wait on the ball a split-second longer, or I wouldn't have had a chance."

Spahn was learning too. He began with a repertoire of a fastball, curve and change-up. At about the age of 30, often a key transition time for pitchers, Spahn developed a paralyzing screwball. At 37 he mastered the slider. And he kept getting better at what he called "the cat-and-mouse game with the hitter."

Spahn's control was so good, on all his pitches, that he claimed to ignore the middle 12 inches of the 17-inch-wide plate. There were, he said, two places to throw to a hitter: "Low and outside, where he can't see the ball very well, and up close on the handle of the bat at the belt, where he can't get the bat around." One reason he could hit those spots consistently was a pitching motion that never varied in its grace or efficiency. In 1949, at the Dodgers' Vero Beach training camp, Branch Rickey installed a new pitching machine: it had a steel arm and threw overhand strikes with unfailing precision. The Dodger players dubbed the machine "The Warren Spahn."

Spahn preached and practiced the art of disrupting the hitter's timing. He had a stunning change-up and changed speeds on all of his pitches. Underlying it all was a fastball that stayed hot until very late in his career. When Spahn was 42, Branch Rickey was still talking about his "mysterious speed."

Spahn was a remarkably deceptive pitcher. His smooth delivery made the ball harder to pick up, especially with the distraction of his high leg kick. But the deception was mainly psychological. For example, Spahn often shook off his catcher simply to confuse the hitter. "He's standing up there figuring, 'Spahn's coming in with this kind of pitch and I'm going to hit it,' and then I shake my head and he stops and thinks, 'Why did he do that?' Then he figures out something else and I shake my head again, and the first thing you know, I got him thinking the way I want him to. Then I've got the confidence and he hasn't. You have to get every psychological edge you can in this game."

Spahn was not a physical intimidator. He was so good at shaving the plate that he didn't need to shave the hitter, and he hit only 41 batsmen in 5,244 career innings. In 1942 Spahn lost his first shot at a promotion to the major leagues because he refused to throw at a hitter in a spring training game. The manager who ordered Spahn to deck the hitter—and then farmed him out for disobeying—was Casey Stengel. Years later Stengel admitted, "I said 'no guts' to a kid who wound up a war hero and one of the best pitchers anybody ever saw. You can't say I don't miss 'em when I miss 'em."

After the 1942 season Spahn joined the Army Corps of Engineers, and served with the First Army in Europe. He returned as the only major leaguer to receive a battlefield commission for bravery in action. He was later awarded the Purple

In 1950, Spahn threw a lot of pitches. He won 21 games and turned in career highs in walks with 111 and strikeouts with 191.

WARREN SPAHN

Left-Handed Pitcher
Boston Braves 1942, 1946–1952
Milwaukee Braves 1953–1964
New York Mets 1965
San Francisco Giants 1965
Hall of Fame 1973

GAMES	**750**
INNINGS	
Career *(7th all time)*	5,243⅔
Season High	310⅔
WINS	
Career *(5th all time)*	363
Season High	23
LOSSES	
Career *(10th all time)*	245
Season High	19
WINNING PERCENTAGE	
Career	.597
Season High	.767
ERA	
Career	3.09
Season Low	2.10
GAMES STARTED	
Career	665
Season High	39
COMPLETE GAMES	
Career	382
Season High	26
SHUTOUTS	
Career *(6th all time)*	63
Season High	7
STRIKEOUTS	
Career	2,583
Season High	191
WALKS	
Career	1,434
Season High	111
NO-HITTERS	**1960, 1961**
WORLD SERIES	**1948, 1957**
	1958
CY YOUNG AWARD	**1957**

Though both were in their 40s, Spahn and Stan Musial (above, right) were still NL stars in 1961. Spahn won 21 games and led the league with a 3.02 ERA, while Musial hit .288 and committed just one error in 123 games.

Heart and the Bronze Star. Many years later, when a writer noted that Spahn's war service probably prevented him from becoming a 400-game winner, the pitcher shook his head. "Maybe I would never have had a 20-win season if it hadn't been for the lesson I learned in the Army. After what we went through overseas, I never could consider anything I was asked to do, or something I made myself do, in baseball, as hard work."

Spahn hit the majors to stay in 1946, had his first 20-win season the following year, and was immortalized in one of baseball's most famous rhymes: "Spahn and Sain, and pray for rain," the slogan of Boston fans who knew that after Spahn and Johnny Sain, the Braves' starting rotation was very thin. In 1948 the Braves' staff included Bill Voiselle, Vern Bickford, Red Barrett, Bobby Hogue, and Clyde Shoun, who totaled 44 regular-season wins among them. Spahn and Sain won 39.

Sain described Spahn as "one of the smartest men ever to play the game," and as the closest thing to a *complete* pitcher in modern baseball. "Spahn

was completely thorough. He hit well enough to stay in a close game late. He fielded extremely well. He ran the bases well, and his pick-off move to first base was superb. I remember that he picked off Jackie Robinson twice in one vital game during a Labor Day doubleheader at Boston in '48 when Robinson was the best base-stealer in the league."

In 1952, just before the Braves moved to Milwaukee, Lew Burdette joined the staff. He became Spahn's roommate and pitching partner, and together they combined for 421 regular-season wins in 12 seasons, and seven more in two World Series.

Spahn seemed to get better as he got older— wilier and tougher, but just as stylish as ever. In 1960, his fifth straight 20-win season, he pitched his first no-hitter at age 39. The following spring he pitched his second no-hitter, sealing it in the ninth inning with an acrobatic fielding play. In 1963, after his thirteenth 20-win season, Stengel reassessed him, this time comparing him to Carl Hubbell and Lefty Grove. "I'd have to say Spahn is the greatest left-hander I ever saw. He has the points. You have

In 1986 Spahn left his Oklahoma cattle ranch long enough to pitch in an old timer's game to benefit retired major leaguers, wearing the cap of his first major league team, the Boston Braves (left).

to go on his record. No road apple could win 350 games in this league, especially with the lively ball."

In 1965 Spahn pitched for Stengel's New York Mets on a staff of fading veterans and promising newcomers. In July, when Spahn was 4–12, Stengel decided to release him. "I'm afraid he's lost it," Stengel said, "because the pitchers are hitting him." Spahn finished the year with the Giants, went 3–4, and was released again. In 1966 and 1967 he pitched a few games in the Mexican League and the Pacific Coast League, but succeeded only in delaying his election to the Hall of Fame by two years, since to be eligible, a player must be completely retired from professional baseball for five years.

As a major league coach and now as a rancher, Spahn continues to see the world from a pitcher's perspective. He once asked, "What is life, after all, but a challenge? And what better challenge can there be than the one between the pitcher and the hitter?"

Even with the Mets in 1965—his last major league season—Spahn still started his windup with the same full arm pump he'd always used. His pitches were less effective, however, and he compiled a 7–16 mark with the Mets and Giants.

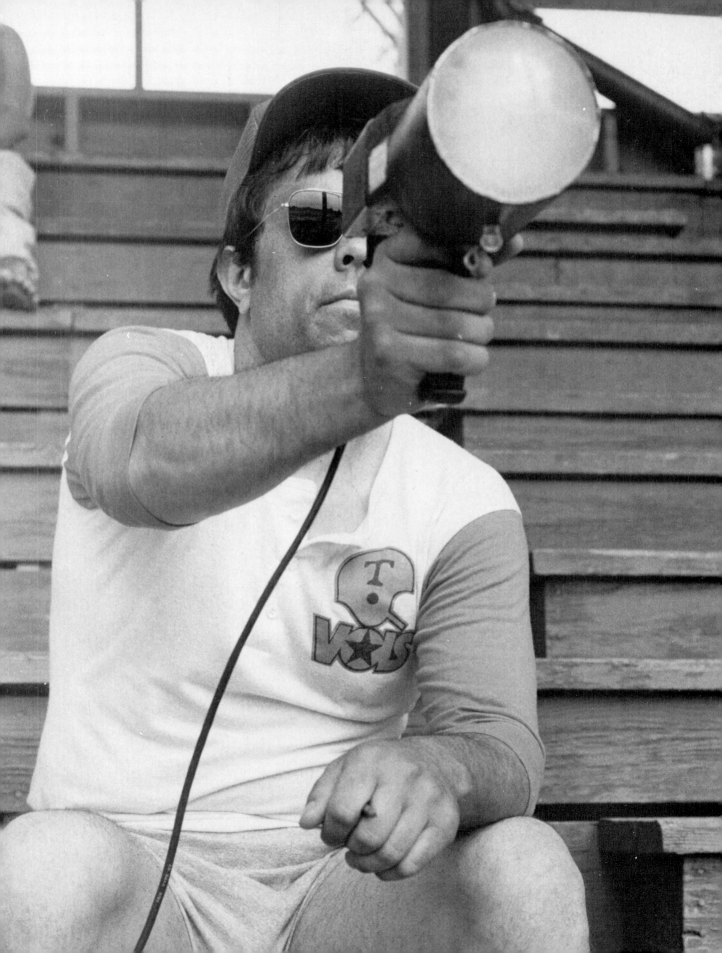

The Crystal Ball

Evaluating amateur baseball talent is a gamble with pretty long odds. Baseball scouts see thousands of talented young athletes every year, but out of every hundred players who see professional contracts, only eight will ever appear in a major league game. The reason baseball scouts are often wrong is that they try to look ahead so far. Pro basketball or football scouts study developed college-trained players and pick those they figure can help the team within a year. A baseball scout studies raw talent where he can find it, often at the high school level, and tries to project it four or five years into the future.

"Pitchers," scouts often say, "are like race horses." A young pitcher's performance may vary enormously from game to game, and he can be as liable to breakdown as a high-strung thoroughbred. But in any given game, a pitcher is easier to scout than a hitter. Jim McLaughlin, former scouting director of the Orioles and Reds, explains: "If you send a scout to look at a hitter, maybe the kid gets walked three times, or maybe he gets two good pitches to swing at the whole game. But pitchers are more consistent in *showing* their tools and makeup. There's more to see."

Consider the amateur game in Jersey City, New Jersey, on September 13, 1986. There were more scouts watching—about thirty—than fans, players, coaches and umpires put together. Brandy Davis came to watch pitcher Willie Banks, due to graduate from high school the following June. "Many scouts already see him as a first-round draft choice," he said. "Now they're starting to talk about how high in round 1 he should go."

Scouts never know where the next 95-mph fastballer will come from, so freelance scout Miles Belich (opposite) times pitchers with radar at a major league tryout camp in Waseca, Minnesota.

Scouts sometimes follow prospects so closely for so long that friendships develop. White Sox scout Ed Ford gave high school pitching sensation Willie Banks a shoulder to lean on when, after a minor injury, Banks had to pitch wearing an eye patch on May 25, 1987.

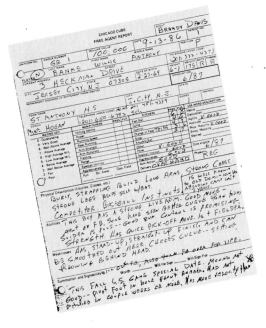

Cubs' scout Brandy Davis gave Willie Banks high marks for his fastball, slider and poise on the Cubs' player rating chart.

Davis, the Cubs' national cross-checker, evaluates blue-chip prospects before each major league draft. His report on Banks focused on four dimensions: body build, delivery, arm and demeanor—each a window into the art of pitching. A good body for a pitcher is wide through the shoulders so a young athlete can fill out in later years and still remain flexible. George Bradley, scouting director of the Yankees, looks for "long and loose shoulder and arm muscles—whippy rather than bunched for strength. Big hands are also a plus." Before Banks threw a full inning, any scout could appreciate his broad torso, long arms, and powerful legs.

Banks' delivery was tricky to judge in this game, because he was pitching off a bad mound with a big hole in front of the rubber. He had trouble balancing on his pivot foot and was inconsistent in his follow-through, sometimes straightening up to regain balance, sometimes sweeping his whole body toward the first base line like a Bob Gibson.

Brandy Davis thought the mound was to blame and the hitches were correctable in any case. He was more impressed by what he *didn't* see. Banks didn't "short-arm" the ball; he was fluid and fully extended. He didn't stiffen his front leg or land on his heel. He didn't over-stride, and the arm didn't lag behind the forward thrust of the body.

Any one of these faults would have sent up a red flag. Mechanical flaws limit pitching performance, fielding as well as throwing. More important, they can cause arm problems. And if a flaw is truly ingrained, trying to change it can cause arm problems too.

Journalist Tom Wolfe once considered himself a serious pitching prospect, and at a Giants' tryout camp he showed an impressive array of curveballs, screwballs and knucklers. "You've got a lot of cute stuff," a scout told

Wolfe. "But son, there's only one thing we're looking for, and that's a pitcher who can tear the catcher's head off with a fastball. You get one of those, come on back."

Some scouts have always talked this way, and some probably always will. But many consider speed less important than live arm action. Evaluating a fastball demands as much attention to its natural movement—its "run"—as to its location. In the "Future" column of his report, Davis projected Banks' pitches to major league average or above, with high marks to the 90 mph fastball. He saw no need to document the pitch with a radar gun.

Willie Banks lost the game, 4–2. But the scouts were impressed by Banks' performance, especially by his demeanor in defeat. "He never complained or gave up," said Billy Blitzer of the Cubs. "At the plate he hit well himself. And on the mound his attitude was: 'Gimme the ball.'"

Blitzer was thinking about Banks' "bottom half." In the language of scouting, that's not the lower body, but the inner self—mind, heart, guts— the parts the eye can't see. The term refers to "The Whole Ball Player," a chart created by former Orioles' scouting director Jim McLaughlin, many years ago. That chart, now included as a page in almost every club's staff manual, has become a familiar tool in baseball scouting. When it comes to pitchers, McLaughlin used to say, the bottom half is often the more important half.

McLaughlin insisted that his scouts learn about a prospect's character through one-on-one interviews and subtle detective work. In the 1980s, much of what passes for bottom-half scouting comes from an "Athletic Motivation Inventory," a multiple-choice test rating such traits as drive, determination, coachability, leadership, aggressiveness, and emotional control.

You can find major league scouts, armed with radar guns and clipboards, across the globe in ballparks of every shape and size. The Toronto Blue Jays, for example, employ scouts in Canada, the Dominican Republic, Puerto Rico, Panama, Australia and Guam.

Baseball scouts use two types of portable radar, the Jugs and the RA-GUN, to measure the velocity of a pitch. Both machines measure the shift in wave length of a moving object—the same principle used by police radar units. The Jugs picks up the ball as it leaves the pitcher's hand; the RA-GUN gun picks it up near home plate. A fastball generally slows about three mph on its way to the plate, so an average major league fastball may register 88 to 90 mph on the Jugs, and 85 to 87 mph on the RA-GUN.

The guns not only measure how fast a prospect throws, but allow scouts to gauge the variation in speed between a pitcher's fastball and curve, or between his speed at different stages of the game. But many scouts doubt the value of radar in evaluating young pitchers. "If you live by the gun, you die by the gun," says George Bradley, scouting director of the Yankees. "Radar doesn't tell you about the ball's movement or location. A pitch that's 94 and straight as a string and high in the zone is not as good as a pitch that's 84 and sinks and tails."

Nolan Ryan's 100.8-mph fastball was measured with elaborate equipment, not a portable gun. Red Murff, the scout who discovered Nolan Ryan in high school, didn't need radar. "I'm a hunter and I know something about ballistics," Murff says. "When I filled out my report for the Mets I said that Ryan was in the hundred-mile-per-hour range, that his ball stayed level in flight, rose as it got to the plate, and then exploded."

The Whole Ball Player

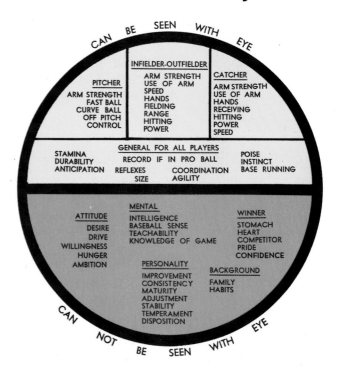

Most baseball people who have studied the AMI believe that it can be a useful tool, and there are stories of some players, like Mike Flanagan, whose high test scores led to a second look and to higher preference in the draft.

Dave Ritterpusch, an Oriole scouting director in the 1970s, began correlating player's test scores with later achievements on the field. He discovered an intriguing pattern: effective starting pitchers almost always ranked high both in aggressiveness and in emotional control. "The pitcher determines when the ball is thrown, how fast it moves, where it goes, the sequence of pitches. All the hitter can do is select." To Ritterpusch, the pitcher plays the more aggressive role, with "a tough attitude, the belief that he *owns* home plate. The starting pitcher's problem is to sustain that aggressive role, and that's where emotional control comes in. It may not be so crucial for relief pitchers—when a guy like Gossage or McGraw or Hrabosky comes into a game in the late innings, he's usually on an emotional high, really pumped up. But the starter needs *low* emotionality, because his job is more mechanistic. Guys like Carlton, Seaver, Palmer, Valenzuela—when they're on the mound, they're inside their own bubble. If you could ever program a robot to play baseball, the position you'd pick for it is starting pitcher . . . a machine that throws strike after strike to the corners of the plate—with an occasional brushback to keep those human hitters honest."

In the days before radar guns or psychological tests, a promising player's path to the majors usually meant being discovered and signed by an independent minor league team and then being sold up the ladder—if and when the minor league team was ready. A master at this system was Jack Dunn, owner of the Orioles when it was an International League franchise.

Jack Dunn (far left) had a Hall of Fame touch when it came to signing pitchers for his minor league Baltimore Orioles. Dunn signed George Herman Ruth (left) in 1914, then won seven straight International League pennants from 1919 to 1925 with the likes of Lefty Grove and George Earnshaw.

Branch Rickey (above, left) was the most innovative baseball executive of his time. Using tryout camps and painstaking techniques for evaluating talent, Rickey built a model minor league system while with the St. Louis Cardinals, then went to Brooklyn in 1942, where his talents brought Dodger manager Leo Durocher (above, right) performers like Jackie Robinson, Roy Campanella and Don Newcombe.

In 1914 Dunn signed a gangling pitcher named George Herman Ruth out of St. Mary's Industrial School in Baltimore. Dunn made Ruth a starter at the tender age of 18, which earned the big left-hander the nickname "Babe." Less than a year later, strapped for cash because of Federal League competition, Dunn let his prize pitcher go to the majors. The Boston Red Sox paid $2,900. In 1920 Dunn discovered another lefty, Robert Moses Grove, pitching .500 ball in the Blue Ridge League. He bought Grove for $3,000, kept him for five seasons and five pennants, then sold him to the Philadelphia Athletics for the record sum of $100,600.

After World War I, Branch Rickey, general manager of the Cardinals, revolutionized scouting by building the first modern farm system. Rickey's scouts had to do rigorous analyses of young players. Instead of buying a few proven minor leaguers, the Cardinals began signing droves of amateurs, training them, and winnowing quality out of quantity. Rickey revolutionized scouting again after World War II by opening major league baseball to black talent, but integration was particularly slow for black hurlers. Rickey was less successful in adapting to the other major change in postwar scouting—big bonuses. After the Phillies signed Curt Simmons for a $65,000 bonus in 1947, the floodgates opened. In 1950, Rickey, then with the Pirates, gave $100,000 bonus money for a left-hander named Paul Pettit, who went on to win one game in the major leagues. Skyrocketing bonuses so depleted Rickey's treasury that in 1954 he couldn't risk $10,000 on another left-handed pitcher named Sandy Koufax.

The bonus era came to an end in 1965, when baseball instituted a draft modeled after those in other pro sports, eliminating the open market for amateur talent. The first player chosen in the first major league draft was college

5'10" 165 lbs.   b 3/23/1886
BB TR   d 10/20/79

CY SLAPNICKA
Right-Handed Pitcher

Cyril "Cy" Slapnicka pitched in parts of two major league seasons, 1911 and 1918, appearing in only ten games. His lifetime record was 1–6. He hung on as a minor league pitcher, manager and umpire until 1923, and then began a career as one of baseball's greatest scouts.

For more than three decades with the Cleveland Indians, Slapnicka demonstrated a gift for scouting pitchers: Willis Hudlin, Mel Harder, Bob Feller and Herb Score among them. During the Depression he signed Feller for $1 and an autographed ball. In the postwar bonus boom he signed Score for $60,000.

Some of Slapnicka's contract manipulations made him a target of the Commissioner. One sportswriter said, "Slap spent so much time on Judge Landis' carpet as to be practically indistinguishable from the nap."

Slapnicka said that his peak experience as a scout came on the day in 1935 when he first saw the 16-year-old Feller. "I watched a couple of pitches from the first base line, and I got the funny feeling that this was something extra. So I moved over behind the backstop and sat down on a car bumper. It must have been a hell of an uncomfortable seat, but I never noticed. All I knew was that there was a kid I had to get. I didn't know then that he was smart and that he had the heart of a lion, but I knew I was looking at an arm the like of which you see only once in a lifetime."

The Tigers' Doyle Alexander is one good pitcher who almost went unnoticed by scouts. Alexander, who through 1988 had won 188 games in the majors, was the Dodgers' 44th round pick in 1968.

outfielder Rick Monday, who signed with the Kansas City A's. The second was high school pitcher Les Rohr, a 6'5" lefty who eventually pitched six major league games for the Mets. The Mets had much better luck with their tenth-round pick—a big right-handed teenager from Alvin, Texas, named Nolan Ryan. Among other pitchers drafted in 1965 were Ken Holtzman in the fourth round and Gene Garber in the 13th. Tom Seaver was picked by the Dodgers in round 24 but chose to complete his degree at Southern Cal.

The draft has often frustrated savvy scouting. For example, Willie Banks became eligible for the draft in 1987 and Brandy Davis thought the Cubs were ready for him. Chicago had fourth pick, but third belonged to the Twins. Minnesota scouting director Terry Ryan had followed up his staff's reports by traveling to see seven of Banks' pitching performances. "My favorite," Ryan said, "was one where, because of a minor injury, Banks was wearing a patch over one eye. For two innings you could see him concentrating so hard that it was scary. But he was kind of aiming the ball. Then in the third inning he just ripped off the patch and started pitching his game."

The Twins picked Banks in the first round. The Cubs selected college pitcher Mike Harkey from Cal State, Fullerton. Harkey was 21 and possibly closer to major league maturity. Banks was a chancier draft—the Twins described him as a "five-year project"—but the potential payoff seemed bigger.

While the draft system encumbers scouts, it still leaves room for imagination and intrigue. Enterprising detective work has sometimes led to very satisfactory late-round pitching selections—like Oil Can Boyd, in round 16; Bruce Sutter, 21; Paul Splittorff, 25; or Walt Terrell, 33. As Jim McLaughlin

ince said, "Conventional wisdom is always conventional. The real job is to find the exceptions."

Probably no wisdom in baseball is more conventional than the belief that little right-handers can't succeed as major league pitchers. Houston scout Gerry Craft says: "If you are a 5′9″ right-handed pitcher and have major-league ambitions, here is my best advice. Unless you have *extraordinary* pitching ability or enjoy abuse, try your hand at middle infield or find another ambition altogether."

In spring 1986 a 5′9″ right-hander named Tommy Gordon changed the minds of at least a few scouts. In his senior year of high school in Avon Grove, Florida, Gordon simply devastated opposing hitters. By the end of May he had set new state records with eight shutouts in a season and 16 in his high school career, six career no-hitters, and 22 consecutive strikeouts. In a five inning game Gordon struck out all 15 hitters. In his next start he blew away the first seven.

A scout who focused on dimensions, not just performances, would have seen a strong upper body, a live arm, and great command of two pitches—a 90 mph fastball with good run and a hard curve reminiscent of Bert Blyleven's. Gordon also showed all-around athletic skill: when he wasn't pitching, he looked impressive at shortstop and hit with power. And he had what some scouts call "Pete Rose desire." Gordon told one writer: "All I want is to play baseball the rest of my life."

Yet because of his size, Gordon was passed over until round six of the 1986 draft. Kansas City finally selected him at the insistence of Brian Murphy, the Royals' eastern cross-checker. What did the Royals see that other

Mike Brito (above) covers all of Mexico as a scout for the Los Angeles Dodgers, but knows where to look. In the same town—Navojoa in the province of Sonoma—Brito discovered Cy Young Award winner Fernando Valenzuela and Isidrio Marquez. Marquez went 8–4 for Class A Bakersfield in 1988.

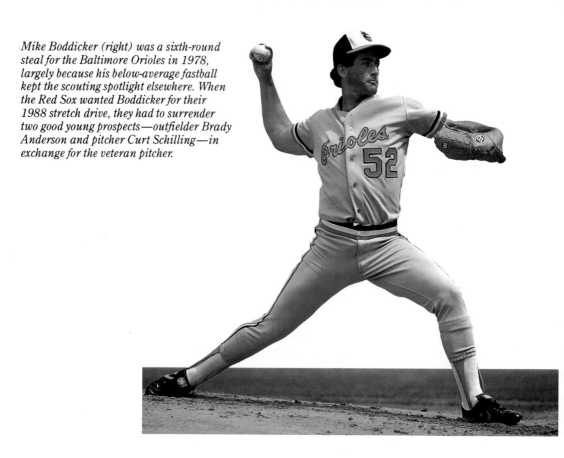

Mike Boddicker (right) was a sixth-round steal for the Baltimore Orioles in 1978, largely because his below-average fastball kept the scouting spotlight elsewhere. When the Red Sox wanted Boddicker for their 1988 stretch drive, they had to surrender two good young prospects—outfielder Brady Anderson and pitcher Curt Schilling—in exchange for the veteran pitcher.

scouting organizations missed? Besides strong performance, KC scouting director Art Stewart saw extremely long arms—"the extension of a six-footer." In 1988 Gordon pitched his way from Class A to the major leagues, striking out 281 batters in 201 innings at four levels of professional competition. Said Stewart, "We got a first-round arm on the sixth round."

"I love exceptions," Bill Werle says. Werle, a lefty for the Pirates, Cards and Red Sox from 1949 to 1954, is now a cross-checker for the Orioles. Until recently he was purely a pitching specialist, hopscotching the country every spring looking only at amateur hurlers. "After all this time," Werle says, "I believe I could see a kid pick up a *rock* and throw it, and maybe tell him that he ought to be a lawyer or something."

Werle can spot the usual red flags right away, like short-arming the ball or holding it hooked in toward the forearm, but he points out that some pitchers have been quite successful breaking the rules. "Mickey Lolich was a short-armer, and Don Drysdale and Ewell Blackwell were hookers. Actually, the only red flag I consider absolute is when a kid throws with extra arm effort, exerting himself too much. That's a sign of future arm trouble."

After surveying young American arms for 15 years, Werle believes that there are fewer overpowering fastballers than ever. "A generation ago," he says, "there were many more strong arms. There are only so many great arms in the world, and now a lot of them are probably attached to bodies playing football and basketball."

Other things happen to young pitching prospects even before scouts get near them. Some experiment early with sliders and split-finger fastballs, which can strain the arm, or train for sheer strength instead of flexibility. They also don't play as much catch as their fathers did. Terry Ryan of the

Twins laments that "long-toss used to be a standard way to pass the time. Now a lot of kids watch TV instead, and maybe that's where some of the fastballs go."

Werle thinks it's ironic that so many scouts are looking for so few great arms. He likes to scout a pitcher by focusing on the delivery for the first two or three innings, then trying to determine the prospect's "feel" for pitching, the extra sense that makes him more than a thrower. "I want to see tenacity, thinking, and presence on the mound. An ideal game for my scouting is when a boy takes a one-run lead into the last inning, and then the first hitter reaches base on an error. Does the pitcher bear down? Or does he lose his composure and then beat himself?"

Even in the very first inning of a game, a scout can evaluate a prospect's feel for pitching by measuring the performance against three of Werle's guidelines. "*First,* throw strikes. Get ahead of the batter and then make him hit your pitch. *Second,* if you do get behind in the count, change speeds. Don't give in and groove a fastball. *Third,* when you must throw the fastball, keep it low."

Of all the amateur hurlers Werle ever scouted, he thinks that Mike Boddicker may have had the best innate grasp of pitching. Werle saw him in April 1978, when Boddicker was a junior at the University of Iowa. Two months later the Orioles were able to draft Boddicker in the sixth round. "His fastball was below major-league average," Werle says. "But he showed all three bases of pitching as a craft, and I was impressed that he threw off-speed pitches when he was behind in the count. I hadn't learned that until I was in the majors, and I picked it up from listening to hitters like Stan Musial and Ted Williams. When those guys got a pitcher to a 2–0 or 3–1 count, they always

For scouts, the down side of working tryout camps is dashing the hopes of hundreds of kids who don't have major league potential. Emil Belich (above), who began his scouting career in 1955, said, "It's never easy to tell a kid he can't play. It's the hardest thing for me to do."

Kansas City's Tommy Gordon (right) is a baseball rarity—a short, right-handed pitcher who made the majors. A sixth-round Royals' draft pick in 1986, the 5'9" Gordon struck out 234 batters in 165 1/3 innings in the minors in 1988, and was promoted to the majors to start the 1989 season.

looked for the fastball. Obviously, the pitcher should think the other way, but how many amateurs are confident enough to do that? Boddicker was."

In spring 1989 Mike Boddicker, 31, began the season as Boston's number two starter, behind Roger Clemens. After the Orioles traded him to the Red Sox in mid-1988, Boddicker had posted a record of 7–3 with a 2.63 ERA, pacing the team to a divisional title. Tommy Gordon, 21, with a month of major league experience the previous September, began the 1989 season in Kansas City's bullpen. He was brimming with confidence. "When I go on the mound," Gordon said, "I tell myself I'm gonna strike out 13 guys. Every game I go out." Gordon started strong in 1989, and by the season's second week he had struck out ten batters in 6 2/3 innings. Willie Banks, 20, began the season with Minnesota's Class A Visalia Oaks. In 1988, his second year as a pro, Banks walked 169 men in 191 innings, but he also showed flashes of brilliance, including a fastball close to 100 mph.

Each of the three pitchers justified the scouts' original judgments about his character, the depth of "the bottom half." Each one believed that he owned home plate. Each one kept working on his repertoire of pitches. In his commitment to the art of pitching, each one belonged to a brotherhood of hurlers who have shared the perspective from the top of the hill. ◉

For most of the season, scouts are gypsies, traveling wherever the talent is. But during spring training they're accorded a place of their own. Opposite is the White Sox camp in Sarasota, Florida.

It was more than a happy ending. It was perfection. Cincinnati's Tom Browning took a joy ride on the shoulders of his teammates after pitching a perfect game against the Dodgers on September 16, 1988, the National League's first since 1965.

NATIONAL LEAGUE

		WINS		ERA		SO	
1901–1910	1901	W. Donovan	25	J. Tannehill	2.18	N. Hahn	239
	1902	J. Chesbro	28	J. Taylor	1.33	V. Willis	225
	1903	J. McGinnity	31	S. Leever	2.06	C. Mathewson	267
	1904	J. McGinnity	35	J. McGinnity	1.61	C. Mathewson	212
	1905	C. Mathewson	31	C. Mathewson	1.27	C. Mathewson	206
	1906	J. McGinnity	27	T. Brown	1.04	F. Beebe	171
	1907	C. Mathewson	24	J. Pfiester	1.15	C. Mathewson	178
	1908	C. Mathewson	37	C. Mathewson	1.43	C. Mathewson	259
	1909	T. Brown	27	C. Mathewson	1.14	O. Overall	205
	1910	C. Mathewson	27	G. McQuillan	1.60	E. Moore	185
1911–1920	1911	G. Alexander	28	C. Mathewson	1.99	R. Marquard	237
	1912	L. Cheney, R. Marquard	26	J. Tesreau	1.96	G. Alexander	195
	1913	T. Seaton	27	C. Mathewson	2.06	T. Seaton	168
	1914	G. Alexander, D. Rudolph	27	B. Doak	1.72	G. Alexander	214
	1915	G. Alexander	31	G. Alexander	1.22	G. Alexander	241
	1916	G. Alexander	33	G. Alexander	1.55	G. Alexander	167
	1917	G. Alexander	30	G. Alexander	1.86	G. Alexander	201
	1918	H. Vaughn	22	H. Vaughn	1.74	H. Vaughn	148
	1919	J. Branes	25	G. Alexander	1.72	H. Vaughn	141
	1920	G. Alexander	27	G. Alexander	1.91	G. Alexander	173
1921–1930	1921	W. Cooper, B. Grimes	22	B. Doak	2.59	B. Grimes	136
	1922	E. Rixey	25	R. Ryan	3.01	D. Vance	134
	1923	D. Luque	27	D. Luque	1.93	D. Vance	197
	1924	D. Vance	28	D. Vance	2.16	D. Vance	262
	1925	D. Vance	22	D. Luque	2.63	D. Vance	221
	1926	P. Donohue, R. Kremer, L. Meadows, F. Rhem	20	R. Kremer	2.61	D. Vance	140
	1927	C. Root	26	R. Kremer	2.47	D. Vance	184
	1928	L. Benton	25	D. Vance	2.09	D. Vance	200
	1929	P. Malone	22	B. Walker	3.09	P. Malone	166
	1930	R. Kremer, P. Malone	20	D. Vance	2.61	B. Hallahan	177
1931–1940	1931	J. Elliott, B. Hallahan, H. Meine	19	B. Walker	2.26	B. Hallahan	159
	1932	L. Warneke	22	L. Warneke	2.37	D. Dean	191
	1933	C. Hubbell	23	C. Hubbell	1.66	D. Dean	199
	1934	D. Dean	30	C. Hubbell	2.30	D. Dean	195
	1935	D. Dean	28	C. Blanton	2.58	D. Dean	182
	1936	C. Hubbell	26	C. Hubbell	2.31	V. Mungo	238
	1937	C. Hubbell	22	J. Turner	2.38	C. Hubbell	159
	1938	B. Lee	22	B. Lee	2.66	C. Bryant	135
	1939	B. Walters	27	B. Walters	2.29	C. Passeau, B. Walters	137
	1940	B. Walters	22	B. Walters	2.48	K. Higbe	137
1941–1950	1941	K. Higbe, W. Wyatt	22	E. Riddle	2.24	J. Vander Meer	202
	1942	M. Cooper	22	M. Cooper	1.78	J. Vander Meer	186
	1943	M. Cooper, E. Riddle, R. Sewell	21	H. Pollet	1.75	J. Vander Meer	174
	1944	B. Walters	23	E. Heusser	2.38	B. Voiselle	161
	1945	R. Barrett	23	H. Borowy	2.13	P. Roe	148
	1946	H. Pollet	21	H. Pollet	2.10	J. Schmitz	135
	1947	E. Blackwell	22	W. Spahn	2.33	E. Blackwell	193
	1948	J. Sain	24	H. Brecheen	2.24	H. Brecheen	149
	1949	W. Spahn	21	D. Koslo	2.50	W. Spahn	151
	1950	W. Spahn	21	J. Hearn	2.49	W. Spahn	191

CHARLIE ROOT
Chicago "Cubs"

		WINS		ERA		SO	
1951–1960	1951	L. Jansen, S. Maglie	23	C. Nichols	2.88	D. Newcombe, W. Spahn	164
	1952	R. Roberts	28	H. Wilhelm	2.43	W. Spahn	183
	1953	R. Roberts, W. Spahn	23	W. Spahn	2.10	R. Roberts	198
	1954	R. Roberts	23	J. Antonelli	2.30	R. Roberts	185
	1955	R. Roberts	23	B. Friend	2.83	S. Jones	198
	1956	D. Newcombe	27	L. Burdette	2.70	S. Jones	176
	1957	W. Spahn	21	J. Podres	2.66	J. Sanford	188
	1958	B. Friend, W. Spahn	22	S. Miller	2.47	S. Jones	225
	1959	L. Burdette, S. Jones, W. Spahn	21	S. Jones	2.83	D. Drysdale	242
	1960	E. Broglio, W. Spahn	21	M. McCormick	2.70	D. Drysdale	246
1961–1970	1961	J. Jay, W. Spahn	21	W. Spahn	3.02	S. Koufax	269
	1962	D. Drysdale	25	S. Koufax	2.54	D. Drysdale	232
	1963	S. Koufax, J. Marichal	25	S. Koufax	1.88	S. Koufax	306
	1964	L. Jackson	24	S. Koufax	1.74	B. Veale	250
	1965	S. Koufax	26	S. Koufax	2.04	S. Koufax	382
	1966	S. Koufax	27	S. Koufax	1.73	S. Koufax	317
	1967	M. McCormick	22	P. Niekro	1.87	J. Bunning	253
	1968	J. Marichal	26	B. Gibson	1.12	B. Gibson	268
	1969	T. Seaver	25	J. Marichal	2.10	F. Jenkins	273
	1970	B. Gibson, G. Perry	23	T. Seaver	2.81	T. Seaver	283
1971–1980	1971	F. Jenkins	24	T. Seaver	1.76	T. Seaver	289
	1972	S. Carlton	27	S. Carlton	1.97	S. Carlton	310
	1973	R. Bryant	24	T. Seaver	2.08	T. Seaver	251
	1974	A. Messersmith, P. Niekro	20	B. Capra	2.28	S. Carlton	240
	1975	T. Seaver	22	R. Jones	2.24	T. Seaver	243
	1976	R. Jones	22	J. Denny	2.52	T. Seaver	235
	1977	S. Carlton	23	J. Candelaria	2.34	P. Niekro	262
	1978	G. Perry	21	C. Swan	2.43	J. Richard	303
	1979	J. Niekro, P. Niekro	21	J. Richard	2.71	J. Richard	313
	1980	S. Carlton	24	D. Sutton	2.21	S. Carlton	286
1981–1989	1981	T. Seaver	14	N. Ryan	1.69	F. Valenzuela	180
	1982	S. Carlton	23	S. Rogers	2.40	S. Carlton	286
	1983	J. Denny	19	A. Hammaker	2.25	S. Carlton	275
	1984	J. Andujar	20	A. Pena	2.48	D. Gooden	276
	1985	D. Gooden	24	D. Gooden	1.53	D. Gooden	268
	1986	F. Valenzuela	21	M. Scott	2.22	M. Scott	306
	1987	R. Sutcliffe	18	N. Ryan	2.76	N. Ryan	270
	1988	O. Hershiser, D. Jackson	23	J. Magrane	2.18	N. Ryan	228
	1989	M. Scott	20	S. Garretts	2.28	J. DeLeon	201

BOB FRIEND
PITCHER—PITTSBURGH PIRATES

Joaquin Andujar

AMERICAN LEAGUE

		WINS		ERA		SO	
1901–1910	1901	C. Young	33	C. Young	1.62	C. Young	158
	1902	C. Young	32	E. Siever	1.91	R. Waddell	210
	1903	C. Young	28	E. Moore	1.77	R. Waddell	302
	1904	J. Chesbro	41	A. Joss	1.59	R. Waddell	349
	1905	R. Waddell	26	R. Waddell	1.48	R. Waddell	287
	1906	A. Orth	27	D. White	1.52	R. Waddell	196
	1907	A. Joss, D. White	27	E. Walsh	1.60	R. Waddell	232
	1908	E. Walsh	40	A. Joss	1.16	E. Walsh	269
	1909	G. Mullin	29	H. Krause	1.39	F. Smith	177
	1910	J. Coombs	31	E. Walsh	1.27	W. Johnson	313
1911–1920	1911	J. Coombs	28	V. Gregg	1.81	E. Walsh	255
	1912	J. Wood	34	W. Johnson	1.39	W. Johnson	303
	1913	W. Johnson	36	W. Johnson	1.09	W. Johnson	243
	1914	W. Johnson	28	D. Leonard	1.01	W. Johnson	225
	1915	W. Johnson	28	J. Wood	1.49	W. Johnson	203
	1916	W. Johnson	25	B. Ruth	1.75	W. Johnson	228
	1917	E. Cicotte	28	E. Cicotte	1.53	W. Johnson	188
	1918	W. Johnson	23	W. Johnson	1.27	W. Johnson	162
	1919	E. Cicotte	29	W. Johnson	1.49	W. Johnson	147
	1920	J. Bagby	31	B. Shawkey	2.45	S. Coveleski	133
1921–1930	1921	C. Mays, U. Shocker	27	R. Faber	2.48	W. Johnson	143
	1922	E. Rommel	27	R. Faber	2.80	U. Shocker	149
	1923	G. Uhle	26	S. Coveleski	2.76	W. Johnson	130
	1924	W. Johnson	23	W. Johnson	2.72	W. Johnson	158
	1925	T. Lyons, E. Rommel	21	S. Coveleski	2.84	L. Grove	116
	1926	G. Uhle	27	L. Grove	2.51	L. Grove	194
	1927	W. Hoyt, T. Lyons	22	W. Hoyt	2.63	L. Grove	173
	1928	L. Grove, G. Pipgras	24	G. Braxton	2.51	L. Grove	183
	1929	G. Earnshaw	24	L. Grove	2.81	L. Grove	170
	1930	L. Grove	28	L. Grove	2.54	L. Grove	209
1931–1940	1931	L. Grove	31	L. Grove	2.06	L. Grove	175
	1932	G. Crowder	26	L. Grove	2.84	R. Ruffing	190
	1933	G. Crowder, L. Grove	24	M. Pearson	2.33	L. Gomez	163
	1934	L. Gomez	26	L. Gomez	2.33	L. Gomez	158
	1935	W. Ferrell	25	L. Grove	2.70	T. Bridges	163
	1936	T. Bridges	23	L. Grove	2.81	T. Bridges	175
	1937	L. Gomez	21	L. Gomez	2.33	L. Gomez	194
	1938	R. Ruffing	21	L. Grove	3.08	B. Feller	240
	1939	B. Feller	24	L. Grove	2.54	B. Feller	246
	1940	B. Feller	27	E. Bonham	1.90	B. Feller	261
1941–1950	1941	B. Feller	25	T. Lee	2.37	B. Feller	260
	1942	T. Hughson	22	T. Lyons	2.10	T. Hughson, B. Newsom	113
	1943	S. Chandler, D. Trout	20	S. Chandler	1.64	A. Reynolds	151
	1944	H. Newhouser	29	D. Trout	2.12	H. Newhouser	187
	1945	H. Newhouser	25	H. Newhouser	1.81	H. Newhouser	212
	1946	B. Feller	26	H. Newhouser	1.94	B. Feller	348
	1947	B. Feller	20	S. Chandler	2.46	B. Feller	196
	1948	H. Newhouser	21	G. Bearden	2.43	B. Feller	164
	1949	M. Parnell	25	M. Parnell	2.77	V. Trucks	153
	1950	B. Lemon	23	E. Wynn	3.20	B. Lemon	170

JOSS, CLEVELAND

		WINS		ERA		SO	
1951–1960	1951	B. Feller	22	S. Rogovin	2.78	V. Raschi	164
	1952	B. Shantz	24	A. Reynolds	2.06	A. Reynolds	160
	1953	B. Porterfield	22	E. Lopat	2.42	B. Pierce	186
	1954	B. Lemon, E. Wynn	23	M. Garcia	2.64	B. Turley	185
	1955	W. Ford, B. Lemon, F. Sullivan	18	B. Pierce	1.97	H. Score	245
	1956	F. Lary	21	W. Ford	2.47	H. Score	263
	1957	J. Bunning, B. Pierce	20	B. Shantz	2.45	E. Wynn	184
	1958	B. Turley	21	W. Ford	2.01	E. Wynn	179
	1959	E. Wynn	22	H. Wilhelm	2.19	J. Bunning	201
	1960	C. Estrada, J. Perry	18	F. Baumann	2.67	J. Bunning	201
1961–1970	1961	W. Ford	25	D. Donovan	2.40	C. Pascual	221
	1962	R. Terry	23	H. Aguirre	2.21	C. Pascual	206
	1963	W. Ford	24	G. Peters	2.33	C. Pascual	202
	1964	D. Chance, G. Peters	20	D. Chance	1.65	A. Downing	217
	1965	M. Grant	21	S. McDowell	2.18	S. McDowell	325
	1966	J. Kaat	25	G. Peters	1.98	S. McDowell	225
	1967	J. Lonborg, E. Wilson	22	J. Horlen	2.06	J. Lonborg	246
	1968	D. McLain	31	L. Tiant	1.60	S. McDowell	283
	1969	D. McLain	24	D. Bosman	2.19	S. McDowell	279
	1970	M. Cuellar, D. McNally, J. Perry	24	D. Segui	2.56	S. McDowell	304
1971–1980	1971	M. Lolich	25	V. Blue	1.82	M. Lolich	308
	1972	G. Perry, W. Wood	24	L. Tiant	1.91	N. Ryan	329
	1973	W. Wood	24	J. Palmer	2.40	N. Ryan	383
	1974	C. Hunter, F. Jenkins	25	C. Hunter	2.49	N. Ryan	367
	1975	C. Hunter, J. Palmer	23	J. Palmer	2.09	F. Tanana	269
	1976	J. Palmer	22	M. Fidrych	2.34	N. Ryan	327
	1977	D. Goltz, D. Leonard, J. Palmer	20	F. Tanana	2.54	N. Ryan	341
	1978	R. Guidry	25	R. Guidry	1.74	N. Ryan	260
	1979	M. Flanagan	23	R. Guidry	2.78	N. Ryan	223
	1980	S. Stone	25	R. May	2.47	L. Barker	187
1981–1989	1981	D. Martinez, S. McCatty, J. Morris, P. Vuckovich	14	S. McCatty	2.32	L. Barker	127
	1982	L. Hoyt	19	R. Sutcliffe	2.96	F. Bannister	209
	1983	L. Hoyt	24	R. Honeycutt	2.42	J. Morris	232
	1984	M. Boddicker	20	M. Boddicker	2.79	M. Langston	204
	1985	R. Guidry	22	D. Stieb	2.48	B. Blyleven	206
	1986	R. Clemens	24	R. Clemens	2.48	M. Langston	245
	1987	R. Clemens, D. Stewart	20	J. Key	2.76	M. Langston	262
	1988	F. Viola	24	A. Anderson	2.45	R. Clemens	291
	1989	B. Saberhagen	23	B. Saberhagen	2.16	N. Ryan	301

Dave Stieb

All records are accurate through the 1989 baseball season.

Wins

Career		Season		
1. Cy Young	511	1. Jack Chesbro	1904	41
2. Walter Johnson	416	2. Ed Walsh	1908	40
3. Christy Mathewson	373	3. Christy Mathewson	1908	37
– Grover Alexander	373	4. Cy Young	1892	36
5. Warren Spahn	363	– Jouett Meekin	1894	36
6. Pud Galvin	361	– Amos Rusie	1894	36
7. Kid Nichols	360	– Walter Johnson	1913	36
8. Tim Keefe	344	8. Cy Young	1895	35
9. Steve Carlton	329	– Joe McGinnity	1904	35
10. Eddie Plank	327	10. Frank Killen	1893	34
		– Smoky Joe Wood	1912	34

Complete Games

Career		Season		
1. Cy Young	751	1. Amos Rusie	1893	50
2. Pud Galvin	639	2. Jack Chesbro	1904	48
3. Tim Keefe	558	3. Ted Breitenstein	1894	46
4. Kid Nichols	533	– Ted Breitenstein	1895	46
5. Walter Johnson	531	5. Amos Rusie	1894	45
6. Mickey Welch	525	– Vic Willis	1902	45
7. Old Hoss Radbourn	489	7. K. Nichols, C. Young,		
8. John Clarkson	485	P. Hawley, F. Killen,		
9. Tony Mullane	469	J. McGinnity		44
10. Jim McCormick	466			

Losses

Career		Season		
1. Cy Young	313	1. Red Donahue	1897	33
2. Pud Galvin	310	2. Ted Breitenstein	1895	30
3. Walter Johnson	279	– Jim Hughey	1899	30
4. Phil Niekro	274	4. Bill Hart	1896	29
5. Gaylord Perry	265	– Jack Taylor	1898	29
6. Nolan Ryan	263	– Vic Willis	1905	29
7. Don Sutton	256	7. Duke Esper	1893	28
8. Jack Powell	255	– Still Bill Hill	1896	28
9. Eppa Rixey	251	9. Six players tied		27
10. R. Roberts, W. Spahn	245			

Innings

Career		Season		
1. Cy Young	7356	1. Amos Rusie	1893	482
2. Pud Galvin	5941	2. Ed Walsh	1908	464
3. Walter Johnson	5924	3. Jack Chesbro	1904	455
4. Phil Niekro	5401	4. Ted Breitenstein	1894	447
5. Gaylord Perry	5351	5. Amos Rusie	1894	444
6. Don Sutton	5280	– Pink Hawley	1895	444
7. Warren Spahn	5244	7. Joe McGinnity	1903	434
8. Steve Carlton	5217	8. Frank Killen	1896	432
9. Grover Alexander	5189	9. Ted Breitenstein	1895	430
10. Kid Nichols	5084	10. Kid Nichols	1893	425

Winning Percentage

Career		Season		
1. Bob Caruthers	.692	1. Roy Face	1959	.947
2. Dave Foutz	.690	2. Johnny Allen	1937	.938
– Whitey Ford	.690	3. Ron Guidry	1978	.893
4. Lefty Grove	.680	4. Freddie Fitzsimmons	1940	.889
5. Vic Raschi	.667	5. Lefty Grove	1931	.886
6. Christy Mathewson	.665	6. Bob Stanley	1978	.882
7. Larry Corcoran	.663	7. Preacher Roe	1951	.880
8. Sal Maglie	.657	8. Tom Seaver	1981	.875
9. Sam Leever	.656	9. Smoky Joe Wood	1912	.872
10. Sandy Koufax	.655	10. David Cone	1988	.870

Strikeouts

Career		Season		
1. Nolan Ryan	5076	1. Nolan Ryan	1973	383
2. Steve Carlton	4136	2. Sandy Koufax	1965	382
3. Tom Seaver	3640	3. Nolan Ryan	1974	367
4. Don Sutton	3574	4. Rube Waddell	1904	349
5. Bert Blyleven	3562	5. Bob Feller	1946	348
6. Gaylord Perry	3534	6. Nolan Ryan	1977	341
7. Walter Johnson	3508	7. Nolan Ryan	1972	329
8. Phil Niekro	3342	8. Nolan Ryan	1976	327
9. Ferguson Jenkins	3192	9. Sam McDowell	1965	325
10. Bob Gibson	3117	10. Sandy Koufax	1966	317

ERA

Career		Season		
1. Ed Walsh	1.82	1. Dutch Leonard	1914	1.01
2. Addie Joss	1.88	2. Three Finger Brown	1906	1.04
3. Three Finger Brown	2.06	3. Walter Johnson	1913	1.09
4. Monte Ward	2.10	4. Bob Gibson	1968	1.12
5. Christy Mathewson	2.13	5. Christy Mathewson	1909	1.14
6. Rube Waddell	2.16	6. Jack Pfiester	1907	1.15
7. Walter Johnson	2.17	7. Addie Joss	1908	1.16
8. Orval Overall	2.24	8. Carl Lundgren	1907	1.17
9. Tommy Bond	2.25	9. Grover Alexander	1915	1.22
10. Will White	2.28	10. Cy Young	1908	1.26

Shutouts

Career		Season		
1. Walter Johnson	110	1. Grover Alexander	1916	16
2. Grover Alexander	90	2. Jack Coombs	1910	13
3. Christy Mathewson	80	– Bob Gibson	1968	13
4. Cy Young	76	4. Christy Mathewson	1908	12
5. Eddie Plank	69	– Grover Alexander	1915	12
6. Warren Spahn	63	6. Ed Walsh	1908	11
7. Tom Seaver	61	– Walter Johnson	1913	11
8. Bert Blyleven	60	– Sandy Koufax	1963	11
9. Don Sutton	58	– Dean Chance	1964	11
10. Four players tied	57			

Games

Career		Season		
1. Hoyt Wilhelm	1070	1. Mike Marshall	1974	106
2. Kent Tekulve	1050	2. Kent Tekulve	1979	94
3. Lindy McDaniel	987	3. Mike Marshall	1973	92
4. Rollie Fingers	944	4. Kent Tekulve	1978	91
5. Gene Garber	931	5. Wayne Granger	1969	90
6. Cy Young	906	– Mike Marshall	1979	90
7. Sparky Lyle	899	– Kent Tekulve	1987	90
8. Jim Kaat	898	8. Mark Eichhorn	1987	89
9. Don McMahon	874	9. Wilbur Wood	1968	88
10. Phil Niekro	864	10. Rob Murphy	1987	87

Saves

Career		Season		
1. Rollie Fingers	341	1. Dave Righetti	1986	46
2. Goose Gossage	302	2. Dan Quisenberry	1983	45
3. Bruce Sutter	300	– Bruce Sutter	1984	45
4. Jeff Reardon	266	– Dennis Eckersley	1988	45
5. Dan Quisenberry	244	5. Dan Quisenberry	1984	44
6. Sparky Lyle	238	– Mark Davis	1989	44
7. Lee Smith	234	7. Jeff Reardon	1988	42
8. Hoyt Wilhelm	227	8. Jeff Reardon	1985	42
9. Gene Garber	218	9. Steve Bedrosian	1987	40
10. Roy Face	193	10. John Franco	1988	39

FOR FURTHER READING

L. Robert Davids, *Great Hitting Pitchers*.
Society for American Baseball Research,
1979.

Bill James, *The Bill James Historical Baseball
Abstract*. Villard, 1988.

Martin Quigley, *The Crooked Pitch: The
Curveball in American Baseball History*.
Algonquin, 1988.

Lawrence Ritter, *The Glory of Their Times*.
Vintage, 1985.

Tom Seaver with Lee Lowenfish, *The Art of
Pitching*. Hearst, 1984.

Harold Seymour, *Baseball: The Early Years*
and *Baseball: The Golden Age* . Oxford
University Press, 1960 and 1971.

John Thorn and John Holway, *The Pitcher*.
Prentice Hall, 1987.

David Voigt, *Baseball: An Illustrated History*.
Pennsylvania State University Press, 1987.

PICTURE CREDITS

Front cover: Nolan Ryan by Fred Kaplan.

Back cover: Bob Gibson by Malcolm W. Emmons

Front and Back Matter
4-5 Keiichi Sato; 180-181 *The Cincinnati Enquirer*/Gary Landers; 182 Ron Menchine Collection/Renée Comet Photography; 183 (top) Ron Menchine Collection/Renée Comet Photography; 183 (bottom) David Walberg; 184 Ron Menchine Collection/Renée Comet Photography; 185 (top) Ron Menchine Collection/Renée Comet Photography; 185 (bottom) Bryan Yablonsky.

A Great Day on the Mound
6 *Houston Chronicle;* 7 *Houston Chronicle;* 8 *Houston Chronicle;* 9 *Houston Chronicle;* 10 *Houston Chronicle;* 11 *Houston Chronicle;* 12 *Houston Chronicle;* 13 (left) *Houston Chronicle;* 13 (right) *Houston Chronicle*; 14 David Walberg; 15 (top) Walter Iooss, Jr.; 15 (bottom) Diane Johnson/ALLSPORT USA.

Who Owns Home Plate?
16 National Baseball Library, Cooperstown, New York; 17 Scott Halleran; 18 (left) Nancy Hogue; 18 (right) UPI/Bettmann Newsphotos; 19 (left) Walter Iooss, Jr.; 19 (right) UPI/Bettmann Newsphotos; 20 National Baseball Library, Cooperstown, New York; 21 (top left) *Washington Post*, reprinted by permission of the DC Public Library; 21 (bottom left) Library of Congress; 21 (right) Ron Menchine Collection/Renée Comet Photography; 22 (left) UPI/Bettmann Newsphotos; 22 (right) National Baseball Library, Cooperstown, New York; 23 Nancy Hogue; 24 (left) Malcolm W. Emmons; 24 (right) UPI/Bettmann Newsphotos; 26 Richard Darcey; 27 Marvin E. Newman; 28 Thomas Carwile Collection; 29 UPI/Bettmann Newsphotos; 30 (left) The Bettmann Archive; 30 (right) Ron Menchine Collection/Renée Comet Photography; 31 (left) Library of Congress; 31 (right) Culver Pictures.

Good Stuff
32 Ron Vesely; 33 Ron Menchine Collection/Renée Comet Photography; 34 (left) National Baseball Library, Cooperstown, New York; 34 (right) Malcolm W. Emmons; 35 (left) Ron Vesely; 35 (right) Ron Menchine Collection/Renée Comet Photography; 36 (left) National Baseball Library, Cooperstown, New York; 36 (right) Malcolm W. Emmons; 37 AP/Wide World Photos; 38 Ron Menchine Collection/Renée Comet Photography; 39 UPI/Bettmann Newsphotos; 40 (left) UPI/Bettmann Newsphotos; 40 (right) National Baseball Library, Cooperstown, New York; 41 Malcolm W. Emmons; 44 (left) National Baseball Library, Cooperstown, New York; 44 (right) Bruce L. Schwartzman; 45 AP/Wide World Photos; 46 AP/Wide World Photos; 47 Tony Tomsic; 48 (left) National Baseball Library, Cooperstown, New York; 48 (right) National Baseball Library, Cooperstown, New York; 49 Lew Lipset Collection; 50 (left) UPI/Bettmann Newsphotos; 50 (right) 1988 Mickey Pfleger/Photo 20-20; 51 Ron Vesely; 52 Bruce L. Schwartzman; 53 (top) UPI/Bettmann Newsphotos; 53 (bottom) AP/Wide World Photos; 54 AP/Wide World Photos; 55 (left) *The Cincinnati Enquirer*/Gary Landers; 55 (right) Courtesy Nu-Card Company.

Rhythms and Forms
56-57 Ronald C. Modra; 58 (left) Ron Vesely; 58 (right) UPI/Bettmann Newsphotos; 59 (left) Ronald C. Modra; 59 (right) Nancy Hogue; 60-61 Richard Darcey; 62 (left) National Baseball Library, Cooperstown, New York; 62 (right) Fred Kaplan; 63 Walter Iooss, Jr.; 64 Heinz Kluetmeier/*Sports Illustrated*; 65 (left) Marvin E. Newman; 65 (right) AP/Wide World Photos; 66 Index/Stock International, Inc.; 67 Nancy Hogue; 69 Walter Iooss, Jr.; 70 Ron Menchine Collection/Renée Comet Photography; 71 National Baseball Library, Cooperstown, New York; 72 National Baseball Library, Cooperstown, New York; 73 (top) UPI/Bettmann Newsphotos; 73 (bottom) Ron Menchine Collection/Renée Comet Photography.

The Balancing Act
74 Ron Menchine Collection/Renée Comet Photography; 75 Ron Menchine Collection/Renée Comet Photography; 76 (left) Brown Brothers; 76 (right) Mark Rucker; 77 (top) National Baseball Library, Cooperstown, New York; 77 (bottom) Ron Menchine Collection/Renée Comet Photography; 78 Culver Pictures; 79 Ron Menchine Collection/Renée Comet Photography; 80 Ron Menchine Collection/Renée Comet Photography; 81 National Baseball Library, Cooperstown, New York; 82 (left) National Baseball Library, Cooperstown, New York; 82 (right) Library of Congress; 83 (left) Library of Congress; 83 (right) Library of Congress; 84 Ron Menchine Collection/Renée Comet Photography; 85 National Baseball Library, Cooperstown, New York; 86 © 1988 Mickey Pfleger/Photo 20-20; 87 (top row) National Baseball Library, Cooperstown, New York; 87 (left center) National Baseball Library, Cooperstown, New York; 87 (center) Rawlings Sporting Goods, St. Louis, Missouri; 87 (center right) National Baseball Library, Cooperstown, New York; 87 (bottom row) National Baseball Library, Cooperstown, New York; 88 (left) National Baseball Library, Cooperstown, New York; 88 (right) UPI/Bettmann Newsphotos; 90 (left) National Baseball Library, Cooperstown, New York; 90 (right) AP/Wide World Photos; 91 © 1989 The Gifted Line, John Grossman, Inc., from the John Grossman Collection of Antique Images; 92 Library of Congress; 93 Library of Congress; 94 (left) Boston Public Library; 94 (right) Boston Public Library; 95 (left) National Baseball Library, Cooperstown, New York; 95 (right) National Baseball Library, Cooperstown, New York.

Constellations
96-97 Jeffrey E. Blackman; 98 Ron Menchine Collection/Renée Comet Photography; 98-99 Library of Congress; 99 National Baseball Library, Cooperstown, New York; 100 National Baseball Library, Cooperstown, New York; 101 National Baseball Library, Cooperstown, New York; 102 Ron Menchine Collection/Renée Comet Photography; 103 UPI/Bettmann Newsphotos; 104 (left) Library of Congress; 104 (right) Culver Pictures; 105 The Historical Society of Pennsylvania; 106 (top) National Baseball Library, Cooperstown, New York; 106 (bottom) Cleveland Public Library; 107 (top) UPI/Bettmann Newsphotos; 107 (bottom) Ron Menchine Collection/Renée Comet Photography; 108 Ron Menchine Collection/Renée Comet Photography; 109 UPI/Bettmann Newsphotos; 110 (left) National Baseball Library, Cooperstown, New York; 110 (right) National Baseball Library, Cooperstown, New York; 111 Cranston & Elkins/Photofest; 112 UPI/Bettmann Newsphotos; 113 UPI/Bettmann Newsphotos; 114 Ron Menchine

Collection/Renée Comet Photography; 115 (top left) James Blank/West Stock; 115 (top right) *The Seattle Times*; 115 (bottom) Tim Thompson/Aperture Photobank; 116 AP/Wide World Photos; 117 AP/Wide World Photos; 118 (left) National Baseball Library, Cooperstown, New York; 118 (right) Richard Mackson/*Sports Illustrated*; 119 David Madison/Duomo; 120 Joe McNally/Wheeler Pictures; 121 Mickey Pfleger; 122 Ron Menchine Collection/Renée Comet Photography; 123 UPI/Bettmann Newsphotos; 124 UPI/Bettmann Newsphotos; 125 (left) Culver Pictures; 125 (right) Ron Menchine Collection/Renée Comet Photography.

Southpaws
126-127 David Walberg; 128 Jeffrey E. Blackman; 129 (left) Tony Tomsic; 129 (right) Bob Gomel/*LIFE* Magazine © 1963 Time Inc.; 130 UPI/Bettmann Newsphotos; 131 (left) Malcolm W. Emmons; 131 (right) David Walberg; 132 (left) National Baseball Library, Cooperstown, New York; 132 (right) UPI/Bettmann Newsphotos; 133 AP/Wide World Photos; 134 (left) Ron Menchine Collection/Renée Comet Photography; 134 (right) AP/Wide World Photos; 135 Jeffrey E. Blackman; 136 (left) National Baseball Library, Cooperstown, New York; 136 (right) Bruce L. Schwartzman; 137 Tony Tomsic; 138 Ron Menchine Collection/Renée Comet Photography; 139 Brown Brothers; 140 UPI/Bettmann Newsphotos; 141 (left) The Historical Society of Pennsylvania; 141 (right) Ron Menchine Collection/Renée Comet Photography.

The Battery
142 Bruce L. Schwartzman; 143 Smithsonian Institution; 144 (top) National Baseball Library, Cooperstown, New York; 144 (bottom) Ron Menchine Collection/Renée Comet Photography; 145 Focus On Sports; 146 (left) National Baseball Library, Cooperstown, New York; 146 (right) AP/Wide World Photos; 147 (left) Richard Mackson/*Sports Illustrated*; 147 (right) Mickey Pfleger; 148 (left) AP/Wide World Photos; 148 (right) Malcolm W. Emmons; 149 (left) Nancy Hogue; 149 (right) National Baseball Library, Cooperstown, New York; 150 Ron Menchine Collection/Renée Comet Photography; 151 (top left) David Madison/Duomo; 151 (bottom left) AP/Wide World Photos;

151 (right) National Baseball Library, Cooperstown, New York.

Helping Himself
152-153 Mickey Pfleger; 154 (left) National Baseball Library, Cooperstown, New York; 154 (right) David Walberg; 155 Mickey Pfleger; 156 Mickey Pfleger; 157 Ron Menchine Collection/Renée Comet Photography; 158 (left) National Baseball Library, Cooperstown, New York; 158 (right) Courtesy of Larry Lester; 159 (left) Bruce L. Schwartzman; 159 (right) National Baseball Library, Cooperstown, New York; 160 AP/Wide World Photos; 161 David Walberg; 162 Ron Vesely; 163 Bryan Yablonsky; 164 Ron Menchine Collection/Renée Comet Photography; 165 Cranston & Elkins/Photofest; 166 AP/Wide World Photos; 167 (left) Bruce L. Schwartzman; 167 (right) AP/Wide World Photos.

The Crystal Ball
168 Jonathan Kronstadt; 169 Scott Halleran; 170 (bottom) courtesy of Kevin Kerrane; 170 (top) Clifford Hausner/*The New York Times*; 171 Ron Vesely; 172 courtesy of Kevin Kerrane; 173 (left) National Baseball Library, Cooperstown, New York; 173 (right) AP/Wide World Photos; 174 (left) National Baseball Library, Cooperstown, New York; 174 (right) Jerry Wachter/*Sports Illustrated*; 175 ALLSPORT USA; 176 Jeffrey E. Blackman; 177 (left) Fred Kaplan; 177 (right) Jonathan Kronstadt; 178 Dave Stock/ALLSPORT USA; 179 Bruce L. Schwartzman.

ACKNOWLEDGMENTS

The editors wish to thank:

Tom Heitz, Bill Deane, Gretchen Curtis, Patricia Kelly, Peter Clark, John Blomquist, and the staffs of the National Baseball Hall of Fame and Museum and the National Baseball Library, Cooperstown, New York; the staff of the University of Delaware Library, Newark, Delaware; Lloyd Johnson, SABR, Kansas City, Missouri; Shane O'Neill, Preview Publishing, Seattle, Washington; Alan Blitzblau, Bio-Kinetics, Laguna Hills, California; Rich Ashburn, Gladwynne, Pennsylvania; George Bradley, New York, New York; Ellis Clary, Valdosta, Georgia; Jeff Cooper, Wilmington, Delaware; Gerry Craft, St. Clairsville, Ohio; Brandy Davis, Newark, Delaware; Bob Feller, Chagrin Falls, Ohio; Pat Gillick, Toronto, Ontario, Canada; Howie Haak, Palm Springs, California; Keith Handling, Newark, Delaware; Peter Heilbroner, Cambridge, Massachusetts; Len Hochberg, Falls Church, Virginia; John Holway, Alexandria, Virginia; Tom House, Arlington, Texas; Bill James, Winchester, Kansas; Barry Kerrane, Dallas, Texas; Katharine and Sean Kerrane, Newark, Delaware; Ed Lopat, Hillsdale, New Jersey; Sam McDowell, Pittsburgh, Pennsylvania; Tug McGraw, Media, Pennsylvania; Dale McReynolds, Walwerth, Wisconsin; Claude Osteen, Annville, Pennsylvania; Pete Palmer, Lexington, Massachusetts; Larry Shenk, Philadelphia, Pennsylvania; Warren Spahn, Hartshorne, Oklahoma; John Ware, New York, New York; John Weiss, Newark, Delaware; Bill Werle, San Mateo, California; Rich Wescott, Springfield, Pennsylvania; Scott Smith, Rawlings Sporting Goods, St. Louis, Missouri; Kirk Schlea, Allsport Photography USA, San Diego, California; Ron Menchine, Baltimore, Maryland; Helen Bowie Campbell and Gregory J. Schwalenberg, Babe Ruth Museum, Baltimore, Maryland; Steven P. Gietschier, *The Sporting News,* St. Louis, Missouri; Karen Carpenter, *Sports Illustrated*, New York, New York; Renée Comet, Washington, D.C.; Sy Berger, The Topps Company, Inc., New York, New York; Ellen Hughes, National Museum of American History, Smithsonian Institution, Washington, D.C.; Nat Andriani, Wide World Photos, New York, New York; Sarah Goodyear and Katherine Bang, Bettmann Newsphotos, New York, New York; Jo Ann Palmer, Focus on Sports, New York, New York; Thomas Carwile, Petersburg, Virginia; Marcy Silver, The Historical Society of Pennsylvania, Philadelphia, Pennsylvania; Mary Ternes, The Martin Luther King Library, Washington, D.C.; Mary Ison, The Library of Congress, Washington, D.C.; Lillian Clark and Mary Perencevic, Cleveland Public Library, Cleveland, Ohio; Jo Gutierrez, *The Houston Chronicle*, Houston, Texas; Joe Borras, Accokeek, Maryland.

Special research assistance by Jim Elfers, Newark, Delaware.

World of Baseball is produced and published
by Redefinition, Inc.

WORLD OF BASEBALL

Editor	Glen B. Ruh
Design Director	Robert Barkin
Production Director	Irv Garfield
Picture Research	Rebecca Hirsh
	Louis P. Plummer
	Catherine M. Chase
Senior Writer	Jonathan Kronstadt
Associate Editor	Larry Moffi
Design	Randy Cook
	Sharon M. Greenspan
	Edwina Smith
Copy Editor	Anthony K. Pordes
Editorial Research	Ed Dixon
Editorial Assistants	Elizabeth D. McLean
	Ginette Gauldfeldt
	Janet Pooley
Production Assistant	Kimberly Fornshill
Design Assistants	Collette Conconi
	Sue Pratt
	Monique Strawderman
Picture Assistant	Dana Wolf
Illustration	Dale Glasgow
Copy Preparation	Gail Cerra
Index	Lynne Hobbs

REDEFINITION

Administration	Margaret M. Higgins,
	June M. Nolan
Fulfillment Manager	Karen L. DeLisser
Marketing Director	Harry Sailer
Finance Director	Vaughn A. Meglan
PRESIDENT	Edward Brash

CONTRIBUTORS

Kevin Kerrane, author of *The Hurlers,* is also the author of *Dollar Sign on the Muscle: The World of Baseball Scouting.* He has coedited *Baseball Diamonds,* an anthology of fiction and non-fiction about the game, and is a regular contributor to *Bill Mazeroski's Baseball.* He is a professor of English and American Studies at the University of Delaware. No stranger to the mound, Kerrane has pitched and managed for semi-professional teams in Wilmington, Delaware.

Henry Staat is Series Consultant for World of Baseball. A member of the Society for American Baseball Research since 1982, he helped initiate the concept for the series. He is an editor with Wadsworth, Inc., a publisher of college textbooks.

Ron Menchine, an advisor and special sports collector, shared baseball materials he has been collecting for 40 years. A sportscaster and sports director for numerous radio stations, he announced the last three seasons played by the Senators in Washington, D.C. He currently freelances on radio and television and has had roles in two motion pictures.

Library of Congress Cataloging-in-Publication Data
The hurlers/Kevin Kerrane,
   (World of Baseball; 3)
   Includes index.
   1. Baseball—United States—History.
I. Title II. Series
GV863.A1k47   1989   89-10131
796.357 0973
ISBN 0-924588-02-0

Printed in U.S.A.
10 9 8 7 6 5 4 3 2

This book is one of a series that celebrates America's national pastime.

Redefinition also offers a World of Baseball Top Ten Stat Finder.

For subscription information and prices please write:
   Customer Service, Redefinition, Inc.,
   P.O. Box 25336, Alexandria, Virginia 22313

The text of this book is set in Century Old Style; display type is Helvetica and Gill Sans. The paper is 70 pound Warrenflo Gloss supplied by Stanford Paper Company. Typesetting by Darby Graphics, Alexandria, Virginia. Color separation by Colotone, Inc., North Branford, Connecticut. Printed and bound by W.A. Krueger Company, New Berlin, Wisconsin.